Liber Amoris

WILLIAM HAZLITT was born in Maidstone, Kent in 1778, the son of a Unitarian minister. After a short period in America, the family settled in the village of Wem, Shropshire. Hazlitt was educated at the Unitarian College in Hackney from 1793 to 1795, although he decided against the religious life, and began to move in the political and literary circles of Coleridge, Wordsworth, Lamb and Godwin. He had an early, unsuccessful, career as a painter, then wrote on philosophy and politics. In 1814 he became the *Morning Chronicle* parliamentary reporter and theatre critic, while also writing essays for journals, including the *Edinburgh Review* and Leigh Hunt's *Examiner*. His works on literature include the *Characters of Shakespeare* (1817), dedicated to Lamb and admired by Keats; *Lectures on the English Poets* (1818); *The Round Table*, in collaboration with Leigh Hunt (1818); and *Lectures on the English Comic Writers* (1819). His *Political Essays* were also published in 1819, and *Table Talk* in 1821–2. *Liber Amoris*, his controversial memoir of an unhappy love affair, came out in May 1823. In 1825 and 1826 much of his best work was collected in two volumes of essays, *The Spirit of the Age* and *The Plain Speaker*. In the last ten years of his life Hazlitt experienced emotional turmoil and poverty, although he continued to publish until his death in 1830.

GREGORY DART taught English Literature at the University of York from 1993 to 2000, and is now teaching at University College London. He also writes for the *TLS* and contributes programme notes for the Royal Opera House, Covent Garden. He is the author of *Rousseau, Robespierre and English Romanticism* (Cambridge, 1999), and has edited Hazlitt's *Metropolitan Writings* for Fyfield Books.

Fyfield*Books* aim to make available some of the great classics of British and European literature in clear, affordable formats, and to restore often neglected writers to their place in literary tradition.

Fyfield*Books* take their name from the Fyfield elm in Matthew Arnold's 'Scholar Gypsy' and 'Thyrsis'. The tree stood not far from the village where the series was originally devised in 1971.

Roam on! The light we sought is shining still.
Dost thou ask proof? Our tree yet crowns the hill,
Our Scholar travels yet the loved hill-side

from 'Thyrsis'

WILLIAM HAZLITT

Liber Amoris
and related writings

Edited with an introduction by
GREGORY DART

To Edward Aleksander

First published in Great Britain in 2008 by
Carcanet Press Limited
Alliance House
Cross Street
Manchester M2 7AQ

A CIP catalogue record for this book is available from the British Library
ISBN 978 1 85754 857 0

The publisher acknowledges financial assistance from
Arts Council England

Typeset by XL Publishing Services, Tiverton
Printed and bound in England by SRP Ltd, Exeter

Contents

Introduction

> I cannot describe the weakness of mind to which she has reduced me. This state of suspense is like hanging in the air by a single thread that exhausts all your strength to keep hold of it; and yet if that fails you, you have nothing in the world else left to trust to. (*Liber Amoris*, Part II, Letter V)

William Hazlitt's *Liber Amoris, or the New Pygmalion* (1823) is the most powerful account of unrequited love in English literature. Exasperating, embarrassing and reprehensible in many of the sentiments it expresses, it is also movingly candid and compelling, an exemplary case study of 'that madness we want'.[1] The book is a paradoxical amalgam of the artful and the abject, of literary sophistication and undigested feeling, and offers itself to us, as it were simultaneously, as a romance and a satire. Never has the sweet sickness of unreflecting passion been better captured, nor the characteristically modern spectacle of high sentiments in a low setting.

Based on real events, Hazlitt's book of love 'has all the romance of private life' (as he himself said of Thomas Dekker's Jacobean drama *The Honest Whore*). In August 1820 the writer had taken two second-floor back rooms at No. 9 Southampton Buildings, Holborn, in a house owned by a tailor called Micaiah Walker. He was forty-three at the time, and a radical journalist, critic and essayist of some renown (his *Lectures on the Dramatic Literature of the Age of Elizabeth* had been published six months earlier, and he was publishing regular *Table-Talks* in the *London Magazine*). Sarah Walker, the anti-heroine of *Liber Amoris*, was the second of his landlord's three daughters, the oldest of whom, Martha, had recently made a highly advantageous marriage to a former lodger. Part mistress, part maid, the nineteen-year-old Sarah cut an ambiguous figure in the household, both in terms of status and character. 'Her face,' wrote Hazlitt's friend B.W. Proctor, 'was round and small, and her eyes were motionless, glassy, and without any speculation (apparently) in them [...] she was silent, or uttered monosyllables only, and was very demure.'[2]

Hazlitt's private life was in a ragged state even before he arrived at Southampton Buildings. His marriage to his first wife, Sarah

Stoddart, had broken down the previous year, and his old father, William senior, had died only a few weeks previously. He had also fallen out with his closest literary friends, Leigh Hunt and Charles Lamb. Add to this the considerable damage done to his political hopes by the Queen Caroline affair and to his literary reputation by the repeated Tory attacks upon him (in *Blackwood's Edinburgh Magazine* and the *Quarterly Review* especially), and his morale, if not his literary productivity, was at a low ebb. 'My public and private hopes have been left a ruin, or remain only to mock me' he wrote in February 1822, in 'On the Fear of Death', 'I would wish them to be re-edified' (p.184). This need for 're-edification' goes some way towards explaining why a shy, suspicious man of books like Hazlitt should have become so quickly besotted with a girl half his age. When Sarah brought up his breakfast tray for the first time on that fateful August morning in 1820, turning 'full round' (as the writer himself recalled it) before leaving and fixing her eyes 'full' upon him 'as much as to say "Is he caught?"' (p.50) what he saw was not a pretty diminutive young woman with little or no conversation, but pure 'fullness', complete redemption, the lovely return of all his late departed hopes.

Sarah Walker may well have been in a hurry to secure a good match like her sister's; that is one explanation, at least, for the flirtatious attitude she seems to have adopted with the gentleman lodgers; another, and equally likely, is that, as her parents' eldest unmarried daughter and a domestic servant in all but name, she may have been *obliged* to indulge the residents, as a filial duty. But whatever the nature and motive of Sarah's behaviour (and it has been debated many times, by critics, novelists and biographers),[3] one thing is clear: William Hazlitt was thunderstruck by her, and fell deeply in love. Intoxicated by the easy intimacy she so speedily granted him, he took no heed of her early warning that they could never be lovers. Instead he became ever more obsessed by his 'Infelice', and she ever more taciturn, evasive and even fearful towards him.

In the spring of 1822 Hazlitt asked his estranged wife, Sarah Stoddart, for an Edinburgh divorce (practically the only kind available at that time). Filing for divorce in Scotland required a forty-day residence qualification, and he chose to spend it at Renton, on the Borders, working on the extra essays required to make up a second volume of *Table-Talk*. (It was in this period that he composed pieces such as 'On the Knowledge of Character', 'On the Fear of Death' and 'On the Disadvantages of Intellectual Superiority', all of which are reproduced in the current volume.) With the divorce proceedings dragging on interminably, Hazlitt returned to London in the second half of May, hoping to prepare Sarah for a proposal of marriage. But the brief meeting between them (which is described in the first letter of Part III of *Liber Amoris*) was so catastrophic that it only compounded his torment. Two months later, with the divorce finally through, Hazlitt discovered quite by chance that Sarah had been secretly involved with another lodger for much of the time they had been intimate, and that she was still continuing to see this man even now he had left. The gentleman in question was one John Tomkins, a young lawyer's clerk, with whom she was eventually to set up home after becoming pregnant in 1824.[4] It was some time before this revelation however, while *en route* to Scotland in the spring of 1822, that Hazlitt first hit upon the idea of penning a volume on his relationship with Sarah, a *Liber Amoris*, or 'book of love'.

The desire to cure (and also possibly revenge) himself in print must have been irresistible, because even before the spring of 1822 his feelings had begun to obtrude into his writings. In the manuscript draft of his celebrated boxing piece 'The Fight', which dates from late 1821, there were already a number of ardent references to Sarah, and it was only at a very late stage that he decided to remove them.[5] The entire essay, in fact, can be seen as a drastic attempt on Hazlitt's part to cure himself of effeminacy by plunging into the brutal, heroic world of Regency boxing. No such self-censorship took place in the case of another *New Monthly Magazine* essay 'On Great and Little Things', where the writer talks freely of his general weakness for 'humble beauties' and also of 'the image of some fair creature' that 'is engraven on my inmost soul' (p.145). Sarah Walker was embarrassed and alienated by this declaration, and by the underlying insinuation that she herself was nothing but a servant. But worse was still to come, for it was in some of the essays that Hazlitt wrote in Scotland in February 1822 (and published sometime later) that his frustration really boiled over. 'On the Disadvantages of Intellectual Superiority' is a fascinatingly disagreeable essay on social, sexual and intellectual difference, with a contrast set up between the naïve idealism of scholars and the native chicanery of 'chamber-maids and wenches at lodging-houses' (p.161). 'On the Knowledge of Character' is a richer, more wide-ranging piece, on the great difficulty of judging character, but once again the image of Sarah Walker is lurking in the background. 'The greatest hypocrite I ever knew,' Hazlitt insists, near the beginning, 'was a little, demure, pretty, modest-looking girl with eyes timidly cast upon the ground, and an air soft as enchantment' (p.166).

Even after Sarah's relationship with Tomkins had been discovered, Hazlitt did not achieve closure. Bewitched by an alternating vision of her as an angel or a whore, he couldn't be satisfied until he had revealed her in one guise or the other. He moved out of Southampton Buildings in September 1822, but in the March of the following year, and only a few weeks before the publication of *Liber Amoris,* he commissioned a young friend of his, F., to take up residence there and 'try her'. The unpublished diary that Hazlitt kept during this period, the so-called 'Journal of F', gives further evidence, if evidence were needed, of the darkly sexual side to Hazlitt's obsession, but it also goes to show that, even with *Liber Amoris* on the brink of going to press, he still didn't feel he had solved Sarah's mystery. Writing, during this period of Hazlitt's career, becomes the desperate search for an antidote. Whether it be the simple, stoical masculinity celebrated in 'The Fight', the social and sexual snobbery of 'On the Disadvantages of Intellectual Superiority', or the dry old-world cynicism of the *Characteristics,* all of the pieces collected here can be seen as ingenious attempts at self-therapy, as well as mordantly honest investigations of personal prejudice and class feeling.

Published anonymously on 9 May 1823, *Liber Amoris* was offered to the public as the memoir of a 'native of North Britain', now dead, it was supposed, 'of disappointment preying on a sickly frame and morbid state of mind' (p.41). Apologising for the presence of many details 'either childish or redundant' the fictional editor explained that it had been the author's last wish that the manuscript should appear without revisions; the text was thus presented to the reader as a raw record of events. Under this thin disguise Hazlitt then proceeded to offer an account of the Sarah Walker affair that was painfully minute in its detail and increasingly obsessive in its force. Part I succeeds in presenting the central relationship with a kind of dramatic impartiality, recording a series of past dialogues between a harrying, lovelorn H. and a cagey, reluctant S. But almost all sense of S.'s voice – and of her side of the story – is lost in Part II, which is based on the letters Hazlitt sent to his friend P.G. Patmore while awaiting his divorce.

A high proportion of what the essayist actually wrote to Patmore during this period was included in *Liber Amoris*; it was only those letters and parts of letters which betrayed the ferocious extent of his sexual jealousy that were omitted from the text. (These extracts which are contained in the footnotes to this edition, include a number of references to Sarah as a 'bitch' and a 'whore', and some prophetic appeals to Patmore for him to get a friend to 'try her').[6] Part III, which brings the unhappy story to an end, is also presented as a series of letters – to 'J.S.K——' (another friend of Hazlitt's, the dramatist James Sheridan Knowles). But in this case the correspondence was entirely fictional, deliberately concocted as a means of relating the dénouement. Hence *Liber Amoris* starts off by trying to maintain a degree of distance from H.'s monomania, yet slowly but surely becomes consumed by it. It moves inexorably from dialogue to monologue, and from trial to conviction:

> One more count finishes the indictment. She not only discovered the most hardened indifference to the feelings of others; she has not shown the least regard to her own character, or shame when she was detected. When found out, she seemed to say, 'Well, what if I am? I have played the game as long as I could; and if I could keep it up no longer, it was not for want of good will!' (p.107)

Two major factors undermined *Liber Amoris*'s anonymity when it first hit the bookstands in 1823. The first was that for months on end a near-crazed Hazlitt had been telling 'the whole cursed story' to anybody who would listen, as the testimonies of his friends B.R. Haydon and B.W. Proctor both confirm.[7] So by the time of publication it was already common knowledge in literary London that the author of *Table-Talk* had been 'jilted' by his landlady's daughter. The second related to the book itself. Sticking purely to the information contained in the published text, H. emerges as a London-based author with a young son called William, a man who was a former supporter of Bonaparte and who had recently gone up to Scotland to seek a divorce. With all this information freely avowed, Hazlitt might as well have put his name on the title page; the literary jigsaw puzzle was only too easy.

Sure enough, within a week of *Liber Amoris*'s publication the *Literary Register* had successfully identified all of the main *dramatis personae*, including Hazlitt and Sarah. And on 22 June the virulently Tory *John Bull* somehow got hold of an unpublished love letter from the essayist, parading it before the public as an example of Cockney mawkishness.[8] Conservative critics were appalled by the naked candour of the book; to them it summed up all that was worst about the current craze for autobiography. As one *Blackwood's* contributor had complained only a few months earlier, with Rousseau's notorious *Confessions* (1788), De Quincey's recent *Confessions of an English Opium-Eater* (1821) and Lamb's republished 'Confessions of a Drunkard' (1822) foremost in mind:

> This is confessedly the age of confession, – the era of individuality – the triumphant reign of the first person singular. Writers no longer talk in generals. All their observations are bounded in the narrow compass of self. They think only of number one.[9]

In one of the few positive reviews of *Liber Amoris,* the politically liberal *Examiner* newspaper defended the book in precisely these terms, that is, by placing it squarely within the Rousseauvian confessional tradition (11 May 1823). Hazlitt would certainly have approved. In his 1816 *Round Table* essay 'On the Character of Rousseau' the essayist had highlighted the peculiar paradox of the author of the *Confessions,* which was that a man so egotistically narrow in his sympathies should have evoked such powerfully sympathetic feelings in his readers. He even went on to argue that the two things might be connected: '[Rousseau's] interest in his own thoughts and feelings was always wound up to the highest pitch,' he wrote, 'and hence the enthusiasm which he excited in others.'

> He owed the power which he exercised over the opinions of all Europe, by which he created numberless disciples, and overturned established systems, to the tyranny which his feelings, in the first instance, exercised over himself.[10]

Represented in these terms, Rousseau emerges as a revolutionary martyr whose self-immolation at the burning stake of sensibility had helped others to discover a new democracy of feeling. The *Confessions* had undoubtedly been important to the men of 1789 – indeed Robespierre had singled it out as Rousseau's most inspirational text on becoming a French deputy. But it was indicative of Hazlitt's rather curmudgeonly post-revolutionary republicanism that for him Jacobinism was now *all* about personality. In his eyes those new 'state-doctors' the utilitarians had hijacked the French project to regenerate the human race and turned it into 'petty projects, speculative details and dreams of practical matter-of-fact improvement'[11] and so the only possibility for an old-style Jacobin like himself was to incubate idealism within the ego, remain steadfast in defence of the old values, and devote himself to being a 'good hater'.[12] *Liber Amoris* takes this attitude – which is so effective in his political writings – and directs it towards the private. It is a daring if foolhardy experiment in the pursuit of virtue through candour.

Tory reviewers disliked the confessional quality of *Liber Amoris*, but it was only in combination with the book's 'Cockney' setting that it became truly contemptible. There was something in the idea of love in a lodging-house that they found both ridiculous and reprehensible. To the *Literary Register* the story was 'unprincipled and indecent trash' and 'the ordure of a filthy mind'. *The Times* considered it 'tawdry', and the *Country Literary Chronicle* 'an insult to public decency and public morals'. Abuse was also showered on the character of S., who was pilloried as a 'pert, cunning, coming, good-for-nothing chit', and 'a tradesman's daughter – a common flirt – a common lodging-house servant – nay, a common trader in indecencies with every fellow in the house'. Tellingly, the violently reactionary *Blackwood's Magazine*, which had been directing anti-Cockney abuse at Hazlitt and Keats and Leigh Hunt for years, was (by its standards) fairly restrained. The reviewer simply quoted large chunks of the text – clearly considering that it condemned itself – and kept his own critical remarks to a minimum: 'What delicacy! What manliness! What a veil is here rent away! What abomination is disclosed! What, after this, is a COCKNEY and a LIBERAL?'[13]

Hostile critics of *Liber Amoris* returned again and again to the lodging-house setting, contrasting the grubby, cramped milieu of the story – the sheer littleness of it – with the soaring, self-important language in which it was couched. Lodging-houses, such as the one kept by the Walker family, were curiously indeterminate in status, hovering in an ambiguous, aspirational realm somewhere between the polite and the plebeian. One of the main aims of *Blackwood's* was to put such Cockney places – and their inhabitants – *in* their place, to insist upon their fundamentally vulgar character. The task was particularly urgent in the case of lodging-houses because of the challenge they seemed to pose to middle-class respectability. The product of a kind of artificial intimacy, the relationship between a lodger and his landlord might pretend to the familial but was always in fact commercial, and the same might often be said, in a more provocative sense, of that between lodgers and their landlord's daughters. It was for these reasons that lodging-houses were often seen as a challenge to domestic morals, with the threat being all the more insidious because thinly veiled by gentility.

An amphibious, anticipatory, morally elusive space, the characteristic abode of young doctors, attorneys and clerks, the London lodging-house was also seen by *Blackwood's* as the natural habitat of Cockney artists and writers. In July 1823, in an article on George Cruikshank, the magazine made a playful swipe at the painters of the day, offering a vivid caricature of Regency bohemianism:

> They live among themselves – they marry (most commonly as the modern Pygmalion would fain have married) or they are bachelors – men of the third floor and the mutton chop – cheerful over ale or gin-twist 'of an evening' – smokers of shag, frequenters of the pit, emergers into sunshine on 'clean-shirt day' – dry, yellow, absurd men with fantastic curls or picturesque baldness – the solemn smile of a recluse – the ease of an actor *off the stage* – a shuffling lounging gait – and too often green spectacles.[14]

And two months later, in an article on the 'Cockney' authors of the *London Magazine*, the lodging-house was again invoked as the emblem of all that was loose and ill-bred: 'They know little,' the reviewer insisted, 'and care less, about what is going on in the world, and keep chattering away fluently enough about various small matters, "great to little men" [...] The writers seem all to have lived in lodgings, and to be distinguished rather by the smoothness, than the variety of their wearing apparel. They sneer in an undertone at good society...'[15]

In 1816 Hazlitt's friend the radical writer and editor Leigh Hunt had preceded a short comic vignette of London washerwomen ('Now, drat that Betty!') with a long introduction defending the literary representation of homely subjects. Slight as it was, and notorious as it was to become, the essay was, in its way, a kind of prose *Preface to Lyrical Ballads*, offering a new and more democratic aesthetic for the nineteenth century:

> The fastidious habits of polished life generally incline us to reject, as incapable of interesting us, whatever does not present itself in a graceful shape of its own, and a ready-made suit of

> ornaments. But some of the plainest weeds become beautiful under the microscope. It is the benevolent provision of Nature, that in proportion as you feel the necessity of extracting interest from common things, you are enabled to do so.[16]

As with 'On Washerwomen', so too with *Liber Amoris*, it was not the coarseness of the canvas or the pretentiousness of the surrounding frame that vexed the Tory reviewers, but the embarrassing lack of fit between them. This was that subversive muddying of aesthetic and social distinctions that *Blackwood's* called 'Cockneyism'.[17]

Shortly before embarking upon the composition of *Liber Amoris*, at a time when he was already seriously infatuated with Sarah Walker, Hazlitt composed an essay 'On Great and Little Things' in which he reflected at great length on the tiny and the trivial. One of the most compelling things about this essay is that it feels as if it has been written by the unconscious, with the chain of association all the more eloquent for being implicit. The imagination has a peculiar affinity, Hazlitt says, with minor details – so much so, indeed, that it is invariably the little things in life that we become obsessed by:

> ... people have been known to pine and fall sick from holding the next number to the twenty thousand pound prize in the lottery. Now this could only arise from their being so near winning in fancy, from there seeming to be so thin a partition between them and success. (p.136)

Later in the essay, class difference between husband and wife is invoked as another 'little thing' that shouldn't in theory provide an obstacle but in practice does, and this immediately leads the essayist into thoughts of servant girls in general and Sarah Walker – his 'Infelice' – in particular:

> But shouldst thou ever, my Infelice, grace my home with thy loved presence, as thou hast cheered my hopes with thy smile, thou wilt conquer all hearts with thy prevailing gentleness, and I will show the world what Shakespeare's women were! – Some gallants set their hearts on princesses, others descend in imagination to women of quality; others are mad after opera singers ... I admire the Clementinas and Clarissas at a distance; the Pamelas and Fannys of Richardson and Fielding make my blood tingle. I have written love-letters to such in my time *d'un pathé-*

> *tique à faire fendre les rochers,* and with about as much effect as if they had been addressed to stone. (p.145)

This confession is embarrassing – and revealing – and represents a clear hostage to fortune. But laying aside, for a moment, the acute pain that it caused Sarah Walker, and the powerful ammunition that it gave to his political enemies, we can see, in this passage, the imaginative seed of *Liber Amoris*. We know from Sarah Stoddart Hazlitt's *Journal* that Hazlitt made regular use of prostitutes during this period, indeed that they sometimes came to visit him at Southampton Buildings. The essayist himself seems never to have tried to hide the fact – neither from Sarah Walker nor even from his eleven-year-old son William.[18] But we also know from his fervent reference to Raphael's St Cecilia at the beginning of *Liber Amoris* that his sexual imagination was heavily invested in both sides of the angel/whore dichotomy (p.42). The servant girl is an interesting figure for Hazlitt to fix upon in this respect not least because the status she occupied in the mind of the middle-class Regency male was somewhere between that of a domestic angel and a 'common trader'. Sometimes considered as only one step up from a prostitute because of her singleness, sexual availability and subservience, the London servant girl could also be seen in Pamela-like terms, as a gentlewoman in embryo, a veritable lady-in-waiting.

Reminding ourselves of Hazlitt's uncertain status at this time as an unsociable scholar, a precarious freelance, 'a man of the third floor and the mutton chop', we could well conclude that his focus on servant girls was a poor attempt to maintain power and superiority in the face of personal disappointment. But in the passage quoted above what seems equally striking is his conception of the servant as a figure of social possibility, a potent mix of politeness and approachability. Shakespeare's heroines, after all, are frequently paragons of womanhood disguised as servants, and here too Sarah Walker is explicitly imagined as a creature of revolutionary potential, promising a new intimacy and transparency between the sexes, a 'plain weed' that could become 'beautiful under the microscope'. The irony of this, of course, in both 'On Great and Little Things' and *Liber Amoris*, is that this promise is not fulfilled. In the essay Hazlitt describes how he has written ardent letters to servant girls in the past and 'the simpletons have only laughed at him'. And the experience is even more painful in *Liber*

Amoris where S. develops into a figure of extraordinary elusiveness and antipathy. But the book still captures both sides of that joke, functioning simultaneously as an agonised complaint from the pen of a middle-aged, middle-class idealist, and a lacerating critique of that same author's snobbery, sexism and self-delusion.

The reference to stone is interesting, given that the ironic subtitle of *Liber Amoris* is 'The New Pygmalion' and the book itself is referred to by H. in Part II as 'a record of my conversations with the statue'. The *Literary Register* had picked up on this in its review of the book, nicknaming the protagonist 'Pyg' throughout. Less well known is the fact that only three years previously, in May 1820, Hazlitt's friend Leigh Hunt had devoted half an issue of *The Indicator* to a new translation of Rousseau's one-act studio drama *Pygmalion*, supplying a brief critical preface on the various ways of interpreting the legend. Hunt criticised the way Rousseau had made Pygmalion fall in love with his own work 'almost out of vanity', wishing instead that he had represented him 'fashioning the likeness of a creature after his own heart, lying and looking at it with a yearning wish that he could have met such a living being, and at last, while indulging his imagination with talking to her, making him lay his head upon hers, and finding it warm'.[19] Clearly for Hunt the Pygmalion story should have been about a real romantic connection between two separate beings – about imagination becoming real. What he disliked about Rousseau's rendering was that it was so unapologetically solipsistic; to him it hovered uneasily between romance and satire.

Something of the same claustrophobic air surrounds Hazlitt's 'New Pygmalion', both in the tone of the piece and in its setting, and this lack of distance has sometimes made it difficult for readers to get any perspective on the drama. Rather as if one was trapped in the same small room as the participants, the urge has always been to take sides, get involved, defend or prosecute S. But what the passage from 'On Great and Little Things' suggests is that we should concentrate less on S.'s character in the book, enigmatic and intriguing though it is, and more on her social and spatial position within it. In Parts II and III especially she is a liminal, shadowy figure, a figure of tantalising proximity and maddening illegibility for H., the ultimate negation of a great critic's powers of reading.

It was perhaps natural that Hazlitt's first published mention of Sarah should be in an essay on the perplexing nature of little things because everything about Hazlitt's lodging-house affair was little.

There was S. herself, who is described at various points in *Liber Amoris* as 'a sublime little thing', 'my little all', a 'precise little puritanical person' and a 'little dissembler'. There was the room he rented and in which she served him breakfast; the presents he showered her with (including the 'little image' of Bonaparte); the space between them (she always seems to be hovering in H.'s doorway in *Liber Amoris,* taking up the servant's characteristic station). What is more, the conversations H. has with her – or overhears – do always seem to turn on little things – set phrases, half-heard innuendoes, indistinct vulgarities. There is the 'belowstairs conversation' darkly referred to in Part I's 'The Quarrel' (and fleshed out more fully in the notes to this edition).[20] There are also those little remarks of S.'s – 'I despise looks' and 'you are the same to me as ever' – that H. keeps obsessively returning to in the course of the narrative.

Littleness – the mind's capacity to linger self-tormentingly over tiny details – is central to Hazlitt's analysis of the role of the imagination in love. But so too is likeness. In the opening section of *Liber Amoris* H. shows S. a picture that he believes has a great resemblance to her, but S. cannot see it. 'No: it's much handsomer than I can pretend to be' she says, 'Besides, the complexion is fair, and mine is dark'. Tossing such inessential details aside, H. insists that the eyes in the picture are just like hers, when she looks up and says 'No, never!' (p.42). Beginning *in medias res, Liber Amoris* presents us with a situation in which Stendhalian crystallisation around the image of the beloved has already obscured the underlying object.[21] The picture in question turns out to be a small and delicate copy of some old master, whose author and subject remain unknown. 'Some say it is a Madonna', H. says, 'others call it a Magdalene' (p.42). Like the picture she resembles, S. is beautiful but indecipherable, equally convincing as an angel or a whore. She is like a proletarian version of Proust's Odette: tantalising not so much because of her positive qualities, but because of her resistance to being read.

Much of the literary allusion in *Liber Amoris* has an equally specious, insecure quality, tending to function as a 'goodly temple / That's built on vaults where carcasses lie rotting' (to quote from Middleton's *Women Beware Women*). Part II partakes of that most apparently bright and breezy of forms, the epistolary travel narrative, as H. roams through Scotland – Edinburgh, the Borders, Stirling Castle, the mountains – while waiting for his divorce. But its deep affinities are with Rousseau's *New Heloise* (1758), Goethe's *Sorrows of Young Werther* (1774) and Mary Wollstonecraft's *Letters from Sweden, Denmark and Norway* (1796), all stories of unrequited love, exile and alienation in which the threat of suicide is prominent. There are verbal reminiscences of Shakespearean tragedy everywhere, with *Othello* giving way to *Macbeth* and then to *Lear* as H.'s state of mind worsens. But the most striking allusions of all are to Jacobean drama. Stray images or quotations push us towards tales of domestic suspicion and adultery in middle-class settings: the pretended infidelity of Infelice with her footman in Thomas Dekker's *The Honest Whore*, the real adultery of Ann Frankford and Wendoll in John Ford's *A Woman Killed With Kindness* and the betraying of Leantio by Bianca in Thomas Middleton's *Women Beware Women*. Slowly but surely S.'s image becomes decorated with suspicious allusions, as the process of crystallisation becomes increasingly negative.

Culturally and geographically wide-ranging though it is, the *Liber Amoris* remains an intense, even claustrophobic reading experience, not least because even the most apparently far-flung reference always brings us back to the little lodging house in Holborn. From the moment when S. looks deliberately back at H. before closing the door on their first meeting, it is her extreme proximity that torments him, the maddeningly 'thin partition' that seems to stand between him and success. Perpetually up and down stairs and in and out of his room, she is always around and always – apparently – available. And it is this that fuels H.'s dream of domesticity – and its nightmare opposite. At the beginning of the fifth dialogue in Part I, H. displays the unstable nature of his imaginings, as he questions S. about her behaviour towards the other male lodgers:

> H. Are you angry with me?
> S. Have I not reason?
> H. I hope you have; for I would give the world to believe my suspicions unjust. But, oh! My God! After what I have thought of you and felt towards you, as little less than an angel, to have but a doubt cross my mind for an instant that you were what I dare not name – a common lodging-house decoy, a kissing convenience, that your lips were as common as the stairs –
> S. Let me go, Sir! (pp.48–9)

Like a new Rousseau, or like a Robespierre in love, H. develops a

Jacobin plot about S. in which either she loves him, and it is only difficult circumstances that prevent her from saying so, or she is actively and poisonously treacherous towards him, a monumental pillar of ill-will. To speak of *Liber Amoris* in terms of the final defeat of revolutionary idealism might seem a little far-fetched, but there are a number of threads that back up this line of analysis, and which give this very domestic disaster, this crisis of 'commonness', a wider resonance. In Part I of the narrative S. expresses a passing interest in H.'s little bust of Bonaparte, if only because it reminds her of a former beau. H. gives it to her only too willingly, but in such a manner as makes clear that all his former public hopes are being invested in it for S.'s personal safe-keeping (p.55). Later, in despair at the collapse of their relationship, and full of suspicion that S. has started seeing someone else, H. smashes the little Bonaparte on the floor, and the effect of this on the page is simultaneously both frightening and farcical:

> I then dashed the little Bonaparte on the ground, and stamped upon it, as one of her instruments of mockery. I could not stay in the room; I could not leave it; my rage, my despair were uncontrollable. I shrieked curses on her name, and on her false love; and the scream I uttered (so pitiful and so piercing was it, that the sound of it terrified me), instantly brought the whole house, father, mother, lodgers and all, into the room. They thought I was destroying her and myself. (p.90)

Can it be an accident that the two great texts on frustrated love in the period – Stendhal's *De l'Amour* and Hazlitt's *Liber Amoris* – were both written by disappointed Bonapartists, by militant liberals whose hopes rose and fell with Napoleon? Certainly, what Bonaparte represented to Hazlitt and Stendhal was not simply a body of political ideas – republicanism, equality, meritocracy, but also, more concretely, a certain model of masculinity, a model that did not celebrate aristocracy, breeding or physical stature, but genius, enthusiasm, and the individual energy of the man of destiny. The anger and frustration in the passage quoted above is not, I would suggest, solely directed towards Sarah, but also, through and beyond her, to the figure of the 'little Bonaparte', which serves as an ironic reminder of Hazlitt's own failure to rechannel disappointed public hopes into the private realm, and more painfully, of the pathetic diminution of his middle-aged masculinity. On smashing the Bonaparte to the ground, H. utters a shriek so loud and piercing that everyone in the house assumes it must have come from a woman. He has been unmanned by love and history. This is his personal Waterloo.

In the *Lyrical Ballads* (1798) and the *Poems* of 1807 Wordsworth had made much of the imagination's capacity to attach deep significance to apparently mean or trivial things; a ruined cottage, a withered thorn, leech gatherers, clouds, daffodils. So too in Rousseau's *Confessions* seemingly insignificant objects – ribbons and periwinkles – were often the prompt for the most sublime personal associations.[22] Hazlitt saw a democratic quality in all this. To him such highly individual imaginative investments were a potent antidote to more established – and establishment – images of sublimity (such as the image of Windsor Keep in Burke's *Letter to a Noble Lord*). Characteristically, in the Cockney drama of *Liber Amoris*, the fetish object is not a ribbon or a flower but a kitschy ornament, and its cultivation as a symbolic focus for H.'s hopes is all too easy to deride. But the little Bonaparte is a resonant symbol nonetheless, not merely of the diminutive general's extraordinary career as a man of talent, but also, more generally, of the revolutionary potential of 'sublime little things'.

Not that this potential is borne out by *Liber Amoris* however. Some time after the Bonaparte-smashing incident, H. and S. come to a kind of rapprochement, and S. agrees to try and see whether the little ornament can be mended. In real life there seems to have been a certain ambiguous sweetness in Sarah Walker's behaviour at this time. Fear must have had something to do with it, since as P.G. Patmore points out in the only letter of his to be included in *Liber Amoris*: '[the family] are all of them, every soul, frightened at you; they have *seen* enough of you to make them so; and they have doubtless heard ten times more than they have seen' (p.80). More concretely, however, there was also Hazlitt's stated wish to rent all the free rooms in the house, which may have led Mrs. Walker to urge Sarah to make an extra effort to be friendly. None of the social and economic pressures upon S. are foregrounded in *Liber Amoris*; and even the startling new perspective that is presented by C.P.'s Part II letter ('They are all of them [...] (and particularly she herself) frightened out of their wits, as to what might be your treatment of her if she were yours') passes largely without comment. Instead the emphasis is entirely on H.'s misguided sense of entitlement, and on the perceived cruelty of S.'s increasingly distant manner.

In the dénouement of *Liber Amoris*, H. briefly turns stalker, following S. on a trip to Somers Town, where she is supposedly going to visit her grandmother. Discovering S. walking in the street with 'a tall, rather well-looking man', H. finds himself ignored by her completely, despite the fact that he twice crosses her path. Later H. recollects him to be 'Mr. C——', one of the family's former lodgers, the man he had been most jealous of a few months before, and soon after he discovers that S. had been carrying on with this man at the same time as she had been trifling with him. Finally, in the closing pages of the book H. is self-tormentingly exultant at having torn away S.'s 'mask'.

> Such is the creature on whom I had thrown away my heart and soul – one who was incapable of feeling the commonest emotions of human nature, as they regarded herself or any one else [...] My seeing her in the street has gone a good way to satisfy me. Her manner there explains her manner in-doors to be conscious and overdone; and besides, she looks but indifferently. She is diminutive in stature, and her measured step and timid air do not suit these public airings. I am afraid she will soon grow common to my imagination, as well as worthless in herself. Her image seems fast 'going into the wastes of time', like a weed that the wave bears farther and farther from me. Alas! poor hapless weed, when I entirely lose sight of thee, and for ever, no flower will ever bloom on earth to glad my heart again! (pp.107–8)

A possible angel in the house, S. is confirmed (in H's mind at least) as a whore in the street – the change of setting and perspective helping to rectify his former error. On first reading it's difficult to get beyond the sheer misogyny of this passage, especially when one thinks of Hazlitt's own penchant for street walkers. But there are other things going on here too. One is the subtle shift, a very painful one for an old-style Jacobin to make, between the positive, rather democratic connotation of 'common' in the phrase 'commonest emotions' and the contemptuous flavour it carries later on. The phrase 'I am afraid she will soon grow common to my imagination' recalls that earlier accusation of H.'s that S. was a 'common lodging-house decoy' with 'lips as common as the stairs'. 'Commonness', it seems, is now no longer something to be celebrated, a meeting-ground, a place of shared understanding. All it evokes is vulgarity, worthless ubiquity, prostitution.

Liber Amoris is an ironic sequel to Rousseau's *Pygmalion* in that it describes a man who falls in love with a statue only for the statue to fail to come to life. The narrator H., who is as close to Hazlitt as it is possible to be, clearly thinks that it is an indictment of everything 'common' – common humanity and common people – that S. has failed to respond to him. This is the irony of the story in his eyes. But the *book* itself, and that portion of Hazlitt's mind that could see beyond his own feelings, does keep reminding us of just how solipsistic, how *un*common, H.'s love was from the beginning – in the dialogues, in the fear of the family towards him, and in that powerful sense of another, alternative history lurking just beyond his consciousness. To look at the narrative from this perspective is to step outside the studio of Pygmalion's imagination, and explore the narrowness of *his* sympathy, not hers. Far from showing the world what Shakespeare's women were, *Liber Amoris* ends up showing us what the men of Jacobean drama were: egotistical, jealous and obsessed with sexual corruption. Both perspectives – the romantic and the ironic – are present in the final scene, because by taking S. outside into the street at the end of *Liber Amoris* Hazlitt simultaneously banishes her and frees her – from H.'s love, from the Jacobean drama of the lodging-house, and from the pressure of being a statue – so that her drift into the wastes of time is also a return from the world of art to nature, and a 'fading into the light of common day'.[23]

In pragmatic terms, Hazlitt's decision to publish his feelings about Sarah was spectacularly imprudent. *Liber Amoris* played right into his Tory enemies' hands and caused lasting damage to his reputation. (To this day many Hazlitteans still feel embarrassed by it, and think of it as a stain on his otherwise heroic record).[24] The book also represented a grave slur on Sarah Walker's character, and may have effectively forced her to settle down with 'Mr C——', the former lodger John Tomkins. But however foolish and destructive we might consider Hazlitt to have been in life, in art he knew what he was doing. Far from being 'vile kitchen stuff, fit only for the midden' (as Hazlitt's Edwardian biographer Augustine Birrell once described it),[25] *Liber Amoris* is one of the first great literary texts to offer a really honest portrayal of romantic obsession, and to display it in its modern aspect, as a lurid hothouse flower fostered alike by history and social setting.

Notes

1 Roland Barthes, 'Ravishment', *A Lover's Discourse: Fragments*, trans. Richard Howard (Harmondsworth: Penguin, 1990), p. 190.
2 Bryan Waller Proctor (Barry Cornwall), *An Autobiographical Fragment and Biographical Notes*, pp. 181–2.
3 For biographical discussion of the Sarah Walker affair see especially Jon Cook, *Hazlitt in Love*; A.C. Grayling, *The Quarrel of the Age: The Life and Times of William Hazlitt*, pp. 252–92; Stanley Jones, *Hazlitt: A Life*, pp. 319–42, and P.P. Howe, *The Life of William Hazlitt*, pp. 306–33. Two recent reworkings of the *Liber Amoris* story are Jonathan Bate's highly readable *The Cure for Love* and Anne Haverty's *The Far Side of a Kiss*, which tells the story from Sarah's point of view.
4 Jones, *Hazlitt: A Life*, pp. 336–7.
5 'The Fight', notes 11, 19, 36.
6 *Liber Amoris* Part II, notes 21, 26, 42.
7 Part III, first letter, note 10.
8 Part I, 'Letters to the Same', note 40.
9 'The Confessions of an English Glutton', *Blackwood's Magazine* (January 1823), pp. 86–92.
10 William Hazlitt, *Complete Works*, IV, pp. 88–9.
11 'On the New School of Reform', *Complete Works*, III, p. 5.
12 'On the Pleasure of Hating', *Complete Works*, XII, pp. 130–5. See also Gregory Dart, 'Sour Jacobinism: William Hazlitt and the Resistance to Reform', *Rousseau, Robespierre and English Romanticism* (Cambridge: Cambridge University Press, 1999), pp. 209–46.
13 'Liber Amoris; or the New Pygmalion', *Blackwood's Magazine* (June 1823), pp. 640–5.
14 'Lectures on the Fine Arts, No. I – George Cruikshank', *Blackwood's Magazine* (July 1823), p. 19.
15 'The General Question', *Blackwood's Magazine* (September 1823), p. 337.
16 Leigh Hunt, 'On Washerwomen', in J.B. Priestley, ed., *Selected Essays*, (London: Dent Everyman, 1929), p. 51.
17 For more on Cockneyism and the Cockney School debate see Richard Cronin, 'Keats and the Politics of Cockney Style', *Studies in English Literature* (1996), pp. 787–805; Kim Wheatley, 'The *Blackwood's* attacks on Leigh Hunt', *Nineteenth-Century Literature*, 47 (1992), pp. 1–31; Gregory Dart 'Romantic Cockneyism: William Hazlitt and the Periodical Press', *Romanticism* 6, 2 (2000), pp. 143–62, and Jeffrey Cox, *Poetry and Politics in the Cockney School* (Cambridge: Cambridge University Press, 1999).
18 See Part I, 'The Quarrel', note 21 and Willard Hallam Bonner, 'The Journals of Sarah and William Hazlitt 1822–1831', *The University of Buffalo Studies*, Vol. 24, No. 3 (February 1959), pp. 196, 247.
19 'Rousseau's Pygmalion', *The Indicator*, No. 31 (Wednesday 10 May 1820), p. 241.
20 See Part I, 'The Quarrel', notes 22–6; Part II, Letter VII, note 25 and Letter X, note 42.
21 Hazlitt was almost certainly aware of Stendhal's *De l'amour* (1822), in which his famous theory of crystallisation was first presented, as it was reviewed in the very same issue of the *New Monthly Magazine* that carried 'On Great and Little Things' and 'The Fight' (February 1822).
22 'On Byron and Wordsworth', *Complete Works*, XX, p. 156.
23 Wordsworth, 'Ode on Intimations of Immortality', line 76.
24 Most recently, Tom Paulin in *The Day-Star of Liberty: William Hazlitt's Radical Style*, p. 45.
25 *William Hazlitt* (London: Macmillan, 1902), p. 167.

Note on the Text

The texts of Hazlitt's published writings are based on *The Complete Works of William Hazlitt*, ed. P.P. Howe, 21 vols (London: Dent, 1930–4).

The texts of Hazlitt's unpublished letters and the 'Journal of F.' are based on Sikes, Bonner and Lahey's edition of Hazlitt's *Letters*, but incorporating emendations proposed by Stanley Jones and Duncan Wu in works cited overleaf.

Only the endnotes in this edition have been supplied by the editor. The footnotes, which are marked throughout by asterisks, are Hazlitt's own.

Gregory Dart
University College, London

Further Reading

Biographies

Jon Cook, *Hazlitt in Love* (London: Short Books, 2007).

A.C. Grayling, *The Quarrel of the Age: The Life and Times of William Hazlitt* (London: Weidenfeld and Nicolson, 2001).

P.P. Howe, *The Life of William Hazlitt* (Harmondsworth: Penguin, 1949).

Stanley Jones, *Hazlitt: A Life* (Oxford: Oxford University Press, 1989).

Background Sources

Johann Wolfgang von Goethe, *The Sorrows of Young Werther*, trans. Michael Hulse, (Harmondsworth: Penguin Classics, 1989).

William Hazlitt, *Letters*, ed. W. Sikes, W. Bonner and G. Lahey (New York: New York University Press, 1978).

Sarah and William Hazlitt, *Journals 1822–1831*, ed. W. Bonner, *The University of Buffalo Studies* Vol. 24, No. 3 (1959), pp. 171–271.

Stanley Jones, 'Hazlitt's Journal of 1823: Some Notes and Emendations', *The Library*, Series 5, Vol. 26 (1971), pp. 325–6.

Stanley Jones, 'Review of *The Letters of William Hazlitt*', *The Library*, Series 6, Vol. 2 (1980), pp. 356–92.

P.G. Patmore, *My Friends and Acquaintances*, 3 vols (London: Saunders and Otley, 1854).

Bryan Waller Proctor (Barry Cornwall), *An Autobiographical Fragment and Biographical Notes* (London: George Bell and Sons, 1877).

Jean-Jacques Rousseau, *Confessions*, ed. P.N. Furbank, Everyman's Library Classics (London: Dent, 1992).

William Shakespeare, *Complete Works* (London: The Arden Shakespeare, 2001).

Stendhal, *Love*, ed. J. Stewart and B. Knight (Harmondsworth: Penguin, 1975).

Duncan Wu, 'Introductory Notes' to *Liber Amoris* in *William Hazlitt: Selected Writings* (London: Pickering and Chatto, 1998), VII, xii–xviii.

Scholarly Editions of Hazlitt

The Complete Works of William Hazlitt, ed. P.P. Howe, 21 vols (London: Dent, 1930–4).

The Selected Writings of William Hazlitt, ed. Duncan Wu, 9 vols (London: Pickering and Chatto, 1998).

Selected Criticism for 'Liber Amoris' and Related Writings

David Bromwich, *William Hazlitt: The Mind of a Critic* (Oxford: Oxford University Press, 1983).

Marilyn Butler, 'Satire and the Images of the Self in the Romantic Period: The Long Tradition of Hazlitt's *Liber Amoris*', in *English Satire and the Satiric Tradition*, ed. Claude Rawson (Oxford: Blackwell, 1984).

Jeffrey Cox, *Poetry and Politics in the Cockney School* (Cambridge: Cambridge University Press, 1999).

Uttara Nattarajan, *William Hazlitt and the Reach of Sense, Criticism, Morals and the Metaphysics of Power* (Oxford: Oxford University Press, 1998).

Tom Paulin, *The Day-Star of Liberty: William Hazlitt's Radical Style* (London: Faber, 1998).

Fictional Versions of 'Liber Amoris'

Jonathan Bate, *The Cure for Love* (London: Picador, 1998).

Anne Haverty, *The Far Side of a Kiss* (London: Vintage, 2001).

A Liber Amoris Chronology

16 August 1820	Hazlitt's first meeting with Sarah Walker, when she brings him his breakfast at No. 9 Southampton Buildings for the first time (see Part I, 'The Quarrel').
11 December 1821	The fight between Tom Hickman 'the Gasman' and Bill Neat takes place in Hungerford, Berkshire. Hazlitt travels back from the fight with P.G. Patmore, and composes 'The Fight' soon afterwards.
19 January 1822	Hazlitt requests proofs of his essay 'The Fight' in order to eliminate references to his inamorata Sarah Walker.
24 January	Hazlitt takes Sarah and her mother to Covent Garden to see the famous actor Macready in *Romeo and Juliet*.
27 January	Hazlitt leaves for Scotland to get a divorce from his first wife, Sarah Stoddart Hazlitt. He breaks his journey at Stamford in eastern England, where he sets down the conversations that make up the first part of *Liber Amoris*.
4 February 1822	Hazlitt arrives in Edinburgh to make arrangements for the divorce.
10 February	In order to be eligible for a Scottish divorce, Hazlitt has to fulfil a forty-day minimum residence requirement. So while staying at the Renton Inn, Berwickshire, he sets about composing a number of essays for the second volume of *Table-Talk,* including 'On the Knowledge of Character', 'On the Disadvantages of Intellectual Superiority' and 'On the Fear of Death'.
11–19 February	Hazlitt writes to Sarah Walker saying, 'I regularly do ten pages a day' (see *Liber Amoris* Part I, 'Letters to the Same').
19–25 February	Letter to Patmore: 'Here I am in Scotland … I have begun a book of our conversations' (Part

	II, Letter I).
26 February	Sarah Walker sends a curt answer to the letter of 11–19 February. Meanwhile 'The Fight' and 'On Great and Little Things' are published in the *New Monthly Magazine*.
3 March 1822	Hazlitt sends a letter to his publisher Colburn saying he has nearly finished the second volume of *Table-Talk.*
9 March	Letter to Patmore on the receipt of Sarah Walker's franked letter of 26 February, Renton (Part II, Letter II).
	Letter to Sarah Walker in which he talks of having 'done his work – a volume in less than a month'. Hazlitt edits this letter for publication in *Liber Amoris*, but the original is found and published by the *John Bull* as part of a satirical attack on Hazlitt in June 1823 (See Part I, 'To the Same').
10 March	Hazlitt returns to Edinburgh to await his wife's arrival.
16 March	Hazlitt's forty-day residence is up; still no sign of Sarah Hazlitt.
30 March	Letter to Patmore 'I have been in a sort of purgatory'. Written in Edinburgh, but dispatched from Renton (Part II, Letter III).
7 April 1822	Letter to Patmore 'this state of suspense is like hanging in the air by a single thread', Renton (Part II, Letter V).
8 or 9 April	Proofs of second volume of *Table-Talk* arrive.
21 April	Sarah Hazlitt arrives by boat in Edinburgh. Letter to Patmore, from Edinburgh, in the middle of divorce proceedings (Part II, Letter IV).
6 May	Hazlitt lectures in Glasgow, and then the following day he and Sheridan Knowles go on a walking tour of Loch Lomond.
13 May	Hazlitt gives second lecture in Glasgow.
14 May	Returns to Edinburgh.
15 May	Leaves from Newhaven for England.
16–30 May	In London. The events that took place on Hazlitt's return, which include the smashing

	of the little Bonaparte, are described in *Liber Amoris* Part III, Letter I, where they have been placed, probably for reasons of formal neatness and dramatic impact, nearer the end of the narrative.
28 May	Hazlitt leaves London to return to Edinburgh.
30 May	Letter to Patmore, 'What I have suffered since I parted from you'. Written on the boat to Scotland, posted in Scarborough (Part II, Letter VI).
31 May	Hazlitt lands in Edinburgh. Letter to Patmore – *not* in *Liber Amoris* – calling Sarah a 'regular lodging-house decoy' and urging Patmore to 'try her' (see notes to Part II, Letter VI).
9 June 1822	Letter to Patmore, 'your letter raised me for a moment from the depths of despair', Edinburgh (Part II, Letter VIII).
10 June	Letter to Patmore, 'Here I am at St Bees once more' (Part II, Letter X). The picturesque letter that appears in *Liber Amoris* replaces a much lewder and more obsessive original, which contains a transcription of the infamous kitchen conversation (see notes to Part II, Letter X).
11 June	Sarah Stoddart Hazlitt takes oath of calumny; Hazlitt hopes to get his divorce within two weeks, on 28 June (Part II, Letter XI).
13 June	Hazlitt goes back to the Renton Inn, before returning quickly to Edinburgh, having been unable to work.
17 June	Letter to Patmore, 'the important step is taken and I am virtually a free man', Edinburgh (Part II, Letter VII).
19 June	Another unpublished letter to Patmore urging him to get a friend to 'try her'.
20–28 June	'Letter to S.L.' (Part II).
27 June	Letter to Patmore, 'tomorrow the next day decides my fate'. Hazlitt expected the divorce to be granted on the 28th. It was not to be (Part II, Letter XI).
3 July 1822	Letter to Patmore, 'you have been very kind

	to me in this business' (Part II, Letter IX).
4 July	Letter from Patmore, 'I have seen M——!' (Part II, 'From C.P., Esq').
6 July	Hazlitt drives out to Dalkeith Palace.
8 July	Letter to Patmore, 'You have saved my life'. The visit to Dalkeith Palace (Part II, Letter XIII).
16 July	Letter to Patmore, 'Letter the Last'. 'Tomorrow is the decisive day that makes or mars me.'
17 July	The Hazlitts' divorce was finally granted. Sarah Stoddart records a conversation between herself and Hazlitt on the corrupt nature of the Walkers (see notes to Part I, 'The Quarrel').
20 or 21 July	Back in London, Hazlitt sees Sarah, who is 'kind and comfortable, though cold and distant'. There is a kind of rapprochement between them, which is described in Part III, Letter II, 'To J.S.K——'.
29 July	Hazlitt sees Sarah walking in Somers Town with Tomkins, whom he later confronts (Part III, Letter II). In *Liber Amoris* Part III, Letter III 'To J.S.K——' (in conclusion) Hazlitt describes how 'my seeing her in the street has gone a good way to satisfy me', but in reality his feelings about Sarah remained painfully unresolved.
Late September 1822	Moves from Southampton Buildings to Chapel Street West.
4–16 March 1823	Hazlitt enlists a young friend of his, F., to set himself up as a lodger at No. 9 Southampton Buildings and to 'try' Sarah's virtue. Hazlitt keeps a diary of F.'s period of residence (see 'Journal of F.').
9 May 1823	Publication of *Liber Amoris*.
17, 24 May	*Liber Amoris* reviewed in the *Literary Register*, which identified everyone, including Sarah, and gave very full extracts from the text.
7 June 1823	There is a judicious review of *Liber Amoris* in *The Globe*.

8, 15, 22 June	Publication of *John Bull* attacks on *Liber Amoris.*
5 July 1823	Publication of *Characteristics.*
1824	Hazlitt marries a well-to-do widow, Isabella Bridgewater, but the relationship only lasts a year. Sarah Walker bears a son to John Tomkins, with whom she lives, apparently out of wedlock, until well into the 1850s.
1830	William Hazlitt dies, at the age of fifty-two, of stomach cancer, in cheap lodgings on Frith Street, Soho. He is buried in nearby St Anne's Church.
1878	Sarah Walker dies a spinster in Newington Crescent, South London, at the age of seventy-seven.

On the Past and Future

This was first published in the first volume of *Table-Talk* (1822).

We think too much of the future and too little of the past, Hazlitt argues, at the beginning of this essay, 'as if the one was everything and the other nothing'. In youth our feelings are soft and elastic, he says, 'the artlessness and candour of our early years are open to all impressions alike, because the mind is not clogged and pre-occupied with other objects'. But as we get older a certain narrowness sets in, and we fix ever more desperately on the future. Thus it is, the essayist says, that 'all common pleasures and cheap amusements are sacrificed to the demon of ambition, avarice, or dissipation'. In the concluding section Hazlit offers a compelling portrait of this middle-aged wilfulness coming to a crisis, and in so doing unconsciously anticipates the morbid obsessions of *Liber Amoris*: 'The machine is over-wrought', he says. 'We are suspended between tormenting desires and the horror of *ennui* [...] Some idea, some fancy, takes possession of the brain; and however ridiculous, however distressing, however ruinous, haunts us by a sort of fascination through life.'

I have naturally but little imagination, and am not of a very sanguine turn of mind. I have some desire to enjoy the present good, and some fondness for the past; but I am not at all given to building castles in the air, nor to look forward with much confidence or hope to the brilliant illusions held out by the future. Hence I have perhaps been led to form a theory, which is very contrary to the common notions and feelings on the subject, and which I will here try to explain as well as I can. When Sterne in the *Sentimental Journey* told the French Minister that if the French people had a fault, it was that they were too serious, the latter replied that if that was his opinion, he must defend it with all his might, for he would have all the world against him; so I shall have enough to do to get well through the present argument.

I cannot see, then, any rational or logical ground for that mighty difference in the value which mankind generally set upon the past and future, as if the one was every thing, and the other nothing, of no consequence whatever. On the other hand, I conceive that the past is as real and substantial a part of our being, that it is as much a *bona fide*, undeniable consideration in the estimate of human life, as the future can possibly be. To say that the past is of no importance, unworthy of a moment's regard, because it has gone by, and is no longer any thing, is an argument that cannot be held to any purpose: for if the past has ceased to be, and is therefore to be accounted nothing in the scale of good or evil, the future is yet to come, and has never been any thing. Should any one choose to assert that the present only is of any value in a strict and positive sense, because that alone has a real existence, that we should seize the instant good, and give all else to the winds, I can understand what he means (though perhaps he does not himself*): but I cannot comprehend how this distinction between that which has a downright and sensible, and that which has only a remote and airy existence, can be applied to establish the preference of the future over the past; for both are in this point of view equally ideal, absolutely nothing, except as they are conceived of by the mind's eye, and are thus rendered present to the thoughts and feelings. Nay, the one is even more imaginary, a more fantastic creature of the brain than the other, and the interest we take in it more shadowy and gratuitous; for the future, on which we lay so much stress, may never come to pass at all, that is, may never be embodied into actual existence in the whole course of events, whereas the past has certainly existed once, has received the stamp of truth, and left an image of itself behind. It is so far then placed beyond the possibility of doubt, or as the poet has it,

Those joys are lodg'd beyond the reach of fate.[1]

It is not, however, attempted to be denied that though the future is nothing at present, and has no immediate interest while we are speaking, yet it is of the utmost consequence in itself; and of the utmost interest to the individual, because it *will have* a real exis-

* If we take away from *the present* the moment that is just gone by and the moment that is next to come, how much of it will be left for this plain, practical theory to rest upon? Their solid basis of sense and reality will reduce itself to a pin's point, a hair-line, on which our moral balance-masters will have some difficulty to maintain their footing without falling over on either side.

tence, and we have an idea of it as existing in time to come. Well then, the past also has no real existence; the actual sensation and the interest belonging to it are both fled; but it *has had* a real existence, and we can still call up a vivid recollection of it as having once been; and therefore, by parity of reasoning, it is not a thing perfectly insignificant in itself, nor wholly indifferent to the mind, whether it ever was or not. Oh no! Far from it! Let us not rashly quit our hold upon the past, when perhaps there may be little else left to bind us to existence. Is it nothing to have been, and to have been happy or miserable? Or is it a matter of no moment to think whether I have been one or the other? Do I delude myself, do I build upon a shadow or a dream, do I dress up in the gaudy garb of idleness and folly a pure fiction, with nothing answering to it in the universe of things and the records of truth, when I look back with fond delight or with tender regret to that which was at one time to me *my all*, when I revive the glowing image of some bright reality,

> The thoughts of which can never from my heart?[2]

Do I then muse on nothing, do I bend my eyes on nothing, when I turn back in fancy to 'those suns and skies so pure' that lighted up my early path? Is it to think of nothing, to set an idle value upon nothing, to think of all that has happened to me, and of all that can ever interest me? Or, to use the language of a fine poet (who is himself among my earliest and not least painful recollections) –

> What though the radiance which was once so bright
> Be now for ever vanish'd from my sight,
> Though nothing can bring back the hour
> Of glory in the grass, of splendour in the flow'r –[3]

yet am I mocked with a lie, when I venture to think of it? Or do I not drink in and breathe again the air of heavenly truth, when I but 'retrace its footsteps, and its skirts far off adore?' I cannot say with the same poet –

> And see how dark the backward stream,
> A little moment past so smiling –[4]

for it is the past that gives me most delight and most assurance of reality. What to me constitutes the great charm of the *Confessions* of Rousseau is their turning so much upon this feeling. He seems to gather up the past moments of his being like drops of honeydew to distil a precious liquor from them; his alternate pleasures and pains are the bead-roll that he tells over, and piously worships; he makes a rosary of the flowers of hope and fancy that strewed his earliest years. When he begins the last of the *Reveries of a Solitary Walker*, '*Il y a aujourd'hui, jour des Pâques Fleures, cinquante ans depuis que j'ai premier vu Madame Warens*', what a yearning of the soul is implied in that short sentence![5] Was all that had happened to him, all that he had thought and felt in that sad interval of time, to be accounted nothing? Was that long, dim, faded retrospect of years happy or miserable, a blank that was not to make his eyes fail and his heart faint within him in trying to grasp all that had once filled it and that had since vanished, because it was not a prospect into futurity? Was he wrong in finding more to interest him in it than in the next fifty years – which he did not live to see; or if he had, what then? Would they have been worth thinking of, compared with the times of his youth, of his first meeting with Madame Warens, with those times which he has traced with such truth and pure delight 'in our heart's tables?' When 'all the life of life was flown', was he not to live the first and best part of it over again, and once more be all that he then was? – Ye woods that crown the clear lone brow of Norman Court,[6] why do I revisit ye so oft, and feel a soothing consciousness of your presence, but that your high tops waving in the wind recall to me the hours and years that are for ever fled, that ye renew in ceaseless murmurs the story of long-cherished hopes and bitter disappointment, that in your solitudes and tangled wilds I can wander and lose myself, as I wander on and am lost in the solitude of my own heart; and that as your rustling branches give the loud blast to the waste below – borne on the thoughts of other years, I can look down with patient anguish at the cheerless desolation which I feel within! Without that face pale as the primrose with hyacinthine locks, forever shunning and forever haunting me, mocking my waking thoughts as in a dream, without that smile which my heart could never turn to scorn, without those eyes dark with their own lustre, still bent on mine, and drawing the soul into their liquid mazes like a sea of love, without that name trembling in fancy's ear, without that form gliding before me like Oread or Dryad in fabled groves, what should I do, how pass away the listless leaden-footed hours? Then wave, wave on, ye woods of Tuderley, and lift your high tops in the air; my sighs and vows uttered by your mystic voice breathe into me my former being, and enable me to bear the thing I am!

The objects that we have known in better days are the main props that sustain the weight of our affections, and give us strength to await our future lot. The future is like a dead wall or a thick mist hiding all objects from our view: the past is alive and stirring with objects, bright or solemn, and of unfading interest. What is it in fact that we recur to oftenest? What subjects do we think or talk of? Not the ignorant future, but the well-stored past. Othello, the Moor of Venice, amused himself and his hearers at the house of Signor Brabantio by 'running through the story of his life even from his boyish days'; and oft 'beguiled them of their tears, when he did speak of some disastrous stroke which his youth suffered'. This plan of ingratiating himself would not have answered, if the past had been, like the contents of an old almanac, of no use but to be thrown aside and forgotten. What a blank, for instance, does the history of the world for the next six thousand years present to the mind, compared with that of the last! All that strikes the imagination or excites any interest in the mighty scene is *what has been*!*

Neither in itself then, nor as a subject of general contemplation, has the future any advantage over the past. But with respect to our grosser passions and pursuits it has. As far as regards the appeal to the understanding or the imagination, the past is just as good, as real, of as much intrinsic and ostensible value as the future: but there is another principle in the human mind, the principle of action or will; and of this the past has no hold, the future engrosses it entirely to itself. It is this strong lever of the affections that gives so powerful a bias to our sentiments on this subject, and violently transposes the natural order of our associations. We regret the pleasures we have lost, and eagerly anticipate those which are to come: we dwell with satisfaction on the evils from which we have escaped (*Posthæc meminisse juvabit*)[7] and dread future pain. The good that is past is in this sense like money that is spent, which is of no further use, and about which we give ourselves little concern. The good we expect is like a store yet untouched, and in the enjoy-

* A treatise on the Millennium is dull; but who was ever weary of reading the fables of the Golden Age? On my once observing I should like to have been Claude, a person said, 'they should not, for that then by this time it would have been all over with them.' As if it could possibly signify when we live (save and excepting the present minute), or as if the value of human life decreased or increased with successive centuries. At that rate, we had better have our life still to come at some future period, and so postpone our existence century after century *ad infinitum*.

ment of which we promise ourselves infinite gratification. What has happened to us we think of no consequence: what is to happen to us, of the greatest. Why so? Simply because the one is still in our power, and the other not – because the efforts of the will to bring any object to pass or to prevent it strengthen our attachment or aversion to that object – because the pains and attention bestowed upon any thing add to our interest in it, and because the habitual and earnest pursuit of any end redoubles the ardour of our expectations, and converts the speculative and indolent satisfaction we might otherwise feel in it into real passion. Our regrets, anxiety, and wishes are thrown away upon the past: but the insisting on the importance of the future is of the utmost use in aiding our resolutions, and stimulating our exertions. If the future were no more amenable to our wills than the past; if our precautions, our sanguine schemes, our hopes and fears were of as little avail in the one case as the other; if we could neither soften our minds to pleasure, nor steel our fortitude to the resistance of pain beforehand; if all objects drifted along by us like straws or pieces of wood in a river, the will being purely passive, and as little able to obviate the future as to arrest the past, we should in that case be equally indifferent to both; that is, we should consider each as they affected the thoughts and imagination with certain sentiments of approbation or regret, but without the importunity of desire, the irritation of the will, throwing the whole weight of passion and prejudice into one scale, and leaving the other quite empty. While the blow is coming, we prepare to meet it, we think to ward off or break its force, we arm ourselves with patience to endure what cannot be avoided, we agitate ourselves with fifty needless alarms about it; but when the blow is struck, the pang is over, the struggle is no longer necessary, and we cease to harass or torment ourselves about it more than we can help. It is not that the one belongs to the future and the other to time past; but that the one is a subject of action, of uneasy apprehension, of strong passion, and that the other has passed wholly out of the sphere of action into the region of reflection –

> Calm pleasures there abide, majestic pains.*[8]

* In like manner, though we know that an event must have taken place at a distance, long before we can hear the result, yet as long as we remain in ignorance of it, we irritate ourselves about it, and suffer all the agonies of suspense, as if it was still to come; but as soon as our uncertainty is removed, our fretful

It would not give a man more concern to know that he should be put to the rack a year hence, than to recollect that he had been put to it a year ago, but that he hopes to avoid the one, whereas he must sit down patiently under the consciousness of the other. In this hope he wears himself out in vain struggles with fate, and puts himself to the rack of his imagination every day he has to live in the mean while. When the event is so remote or so independent of the will as to set aside the necessity of immediate action, or to baffle all attempts to defeat it, it gives us little more disturbance or emotion than if it had already taken place, or were something to happen in another state of being, or to an indifferent person. Criminals are observed to grow more anxious as their trial approaches; but after their sentence is passed, they become tolerably resigned, and generally sleep sound the night before its execution.

It in some measure confirms this theory, that men attach more or less importance to past and future events, according as they are more or less engaged in action and the busy scenes of life. Those who have a fortune to make or are in pursuit of rank and power, think little of the past, for it does not contribute greatly to their views: those who have nothing to do but to think, take nearly the same interest in the past as in the future. The contemplation of the one is as delightful and real as that of the other. The season of hope has an end; but the remembrance of it is left. The past still lives in the memory of those who have leisure to look back upon the way that they have trod, and can from it 'catch glimpses that may make them less forlorn'.[9] The turbulence of action, and uneasiness of desire, must point to the future: it is only in the quiet innocence of shepherds, in the simplicity of pastoral ages, that a tomb was found with this inscription – 'I ALSO WAS AN ARCADIAN!'[10]

Though I by no means think that our habitual attachment to life is in exact proportion to the value of the gift, yet I am not one of those splenetic persons who affect to think it of no value at all. *Que peu de chose est la vie humaine* – is an exclamation in the mouths of moralists and philosophers, to which I cannot agree. It is little, it is short, it is not worth having, if we take the last hour, and leave out all that has gone before, which has been one way of looking at the subject. Such calculators seem to say that life is nothing when it is over, and that may in their sense be true. If the old rule – *Respice*

impatience vanishes, we resign ourselves to fate, and make up our minds to what has happened as well as we can.

finem[11] – were to be made absolute, and no one could be pronounced fortunate till the day of his death, there are few among us whose existence would, upon those conditions, be much to be envied. But this is not a fair view of the case. A man's life is his whole life, not the last glimmering snuff of the candle; and this, I say, is considerable, and not *a little matter*, whether we regard its pleasures or its pains. To draw a peevish conclusion to the contrary from our own superannuated desires or forgetful indifference is about as reasonable as to say, a man never was young because he is grown old, or never lived because he is now dead. The length or agreeableness of a journey does not depend on the few last steps of it; nor is the size of a building to be judged of from the last stone that is added to it. It is neither the first nor last hour of our existence, but the space that parts these two – not our exit nor our entrance upon the stage, but what we do, feel, and think while there – that we are to attend to in pronouncing sentence upon it. Indeed it would be easy to show that it is the very extent of human life, the infinite number of things contained in it, its contradictory and fluctuating interests, the transition from one situation to another, the hours, months, years spent in one fond pursuit after another; that it is, in a word, the length of our common journey and the quantity of events crowded into it, that, baffling the grasp of our actual perception, make it slide from our memory, and dwindle into nothing in its own perspective. It is too mighty for us, and we say it is nothing! It is a speck in our fancy, and yet what canvas would be big enough to hold its striking groups, its endless subjects! It is light as vanity, and yet if all its weary moments, if all its head and heart aches were compressed into one, what fortitude would not be overwhelmed with the blow! What a huge heap, a 'huge, dumb heap', of wishes, thoughts, feelings, anxious cares, soothing hopes, loves, joys, friendships, is it composed of! How many ideas and trains of sentiment, long and deep and intense, often pass through the mind in only one day's thinking or reading, for instance! How many such days are there in a year, how many years in a long life, still occupied with something interesting, still recalling some old impression, still recurring to some difficult question and making progress in it, every step accompanied with a sense of power, and every moment conscious of 'the high endeavour or the glad success'; for the mind fixes chiefly on that which keeps it employed, and is wound up to a certain pitch of pleasurable excitement or lively solicitude by the necessity of its own nature. The division of the map of life into its component parts is beautifully made by King Henry VI.

Oh God! methinks it were a happy life
To be no better than a homely swain,
To sit upon a hill as I do now,
To carve out dials quaintly, point by point,
Thereby to see the minutes how they run;
How many make the hour full complete,
How many hours bring about the day,
How many days will finish up the year,
How many years a mortal man may live:
When this is known, then to divide the times;
So many hours must I tend my flock,
So many hours must I take my rest,
So many hours must I contemplate,
So many hours must I sport myself;
So many days my ewes have been with young,
So many weeks ere the poor fools will yean,
So many months ere I shall shear the fleece;
So many minutes, hours, weeks, months, and years
Past over to the end they were created,
Would bring grey hairs unto a quiet grave.[12]

I myself am neither a king nor a shepherd: books have been my fleecy charge, and my thoughts have been my subjects. But these have found me sufficient employment at the time, and enough to muse on for the time to come.

The passions intercept and warp the natural progress of life. They paralyse all of it that is not devoted to their tyranny and caprice. This makes the difference between the laughing innocence of childhood, the pleasantness of youth, and the crabbedness of age. A load of cares lies like a weight of guilt upon the mind: so that a man of business often has all the air, the distraction and restlessness and hurry of feeling of a criminal. A knowledge of the world takes away the freedom and simplicity of thought as effectually as the contagion of its example. The artlessness and candour of our early years are open to all impressions alike, because the mind is not clogged and preoccupied with other objects. Our pleasures and our pains come single, make room for one another, and the spring of the mind is fresh and unbroken, its aspect clear and unsullied. Hence 'the tear forgot as soon as shed, the sunshine of the breast'.[13] But as we advance farther, the will gets greater head. We form violent antipathies, and indulge exclusive preferences. We make up our minds to some one thing, and if we cannot have that, will have nothing. We are wedded to opinion, to fancy, to prejudice; which destroys the soundness of our judgments, and the serenity and buoyancy of our feelings. The chain of habit coils itself round the heart, like a serpent, to gnaw and stifle it. It grows rigid and callous; and for the softness and elasticity of childhood, full of proud flesh and obstinate tumours. The violence and perversity of our passions comes in more and more to overlay our natural sensibility and well-grounded affections; and we screw ourselves up to aim only at those things which are neither desirable nor practicable. Thus life passes away in the feverish irritation of pursuit and the certainty of disappointment. By degrees, nothing but this morbid state of feeling satisfies us: and all common pleasures and cheap amusements are sacrificed to the demon of ambition, avarice, or dissipation. The machine is over-wrought: the parching heat of the veins dries up and withers the flowers of Love, Hope, and Joy; and any pause, any release from the rack of ecstasy on which we are stretched, seems more insupportable than the pangs which we endure. We are suspended between tormenting desires and the horror of *ennui*. The impulse of the will, like the wheels of a carriage going down hill, becomes too strong for the driver, Reason, and cannot be stopped nor kept within bounds. Some idea, some fancy, takes possession of the brain; and however ridiculous, however distressing, however ruinous, haunts us by a sort of fascination through life.

Not only is the principle here pointed out to be seen at work in our more turbulent passions and pursuits; but even in the formal study of arts and sciences the same thing takes place, and undermines the repose and happiness of life. The eagerness of pursuit overcomes the satisfaction to result from the accomplishment. The mind is overstrained to attain its purpose; and when it is attained, the ease and alacrity necessary to enjoy it are gone. The irritation of action does not cease and go down with the occasion for it; but we are first uneasy to get to the end of our work, and then uneasy for want of something to do. The ferment of the brain does not of itself subside into pleasure and soft repose. Hence the disposition to strong stimuli observable in persons of much intellectual exertion, to allay and carry off the over-excitement. The *improvisatori* poets (it is recorded by Spence in his *Anecdotes of Pope*) cannot sleep after an evening's continued display of their singular and difficult art.[14] The rhymes keep running in their head in spite of themselves, and will not let them rest. Mechanics and labouring people never know what to do with themselves on a Sunday; though they return to their work with greater spirit for the relief, and look forward to it with pleasure all the week. Sir Joshua Reynolds[15] was never comfortable out of his painting-room, and died of chagrin and regret, because he could not paint on to the last moment of his life. He used to say that he could go on retouching a picture for ever, as long as it stood on his easel but as soon as it was once fairly out of the house, he never wished to see it again. An ingenious artist of our own time has been heard to declare, that if ever the Devil got him into his clutches, he would set him to copy his own pictures. Thus the secure self-complacent retrospect to what is done is nothing; while the anxious, uneasy looking forward to what is to come is everything. We are afraid to dwell upon the past, lest it should retard our future progress; the indulgence of ease is fatal to excellence; and to succeed in life, we lose the ends of being!

Vignette from the title page of the 1823 edition of *Liber Amoris*.
Reproduced by courtesy of the Director and Librarian,
The John Rylands University Library of Manchester.

Liber Amoris
or
The New Pygmalion

This book was published anonymously in May 1823 in a duodecimo volume with the following title page: 'Liber Amoris; Or the New Pygmalion. London, Printed for John Hunt, 22 Old Bond Street, by C. H. Reynell 45 Broad Street, Golden Square 1823'. On the title page was a vignette of the picture referred to in Part I, reproduced on the facing page.

In early February 1822 the 44-year-old William Hazlitt set off for Scotland to secure a divorce from his first wife in order that he could marry his landlady's daughter, Sarah Walker. On his way north, he broke his journey at Stamford in eastern England, where he wrote up the conversations with Sarah that form the first part of *Liber Amoris*.

Part II of the book is culled from letters that Hazlitt sent to his friend P.G. Patmore between February and July 1822 while undergoing divorce proceedings in Scotland. Most of the changes made in preparing these letters for publication were very minor: names were blanked out, the odd word or phrase was cut, and there were slight adjustments to chronology. The most significant decision was to cut three of the most sexually obsessive letters entirely. But even this can be thought of as a form of aesthetic re-ordering on Hazlitt's part rather than outright self-censorship, since much of the material contained in them does resurface later, albeit in more palatable form, in the artificial letters that make up Part III.

In the case of Part III no known originals exist, and it is probable that these letters, which are all addressed 'To J.S.K——' (James Sheridan Knowles, a literary friend of Hazlitt's), were composed specifically in order to complete the narrative of *Liber Amoris*, and never actually sent.

A Key to the Dramatis Personae of Liber Amoris

H.	William Hazlitt
S. or S.L.	Sarah Walker
Mr and Mrs L.	Sarah's parents, Micaiah and Martha Walker
Martha (Mrs M——), Betsey, Cajah	Sarah's three siblings
Maria	the Walkers' servant
Mr M——	Robert Roscoe, husband of Sarah's elder sister Martha
C—— or Mr C——	John Tomkins, a young lawyer's clerk, also a lodger
Mrs E——	Mrs Follett, who had rooms at Southampton Buildings with her husband
Mrs ——	Mrs Sarah Stoddart Hazlitt, Hazlitt's first wife
William	Hazlitt's eleven-year-old son William Hazlitt junior
Mr P——, P or C.P——	P.G. Patmore, Hazlitt's friend and confidant during the *Liber Amoris* affair, and also one of his travelling companions ('Pigott') in 'The Fight'
Mr T—— or T——	Thomas Noon Talfourd, a friend of Hazlitt's
K—— or J.S.K——	James Sheridan Knowles, poet and dramatist, a companion of Hazlitt's in Scotland, and the named recipient of the (probably entirely fictional) letters that make up Part III
Mr F. or F.	An actor friend of Hazlitt's, possibly William Farren, who was enlisted to 'try' Sarah Walker's virtue in March 1823, and whose inconclusive campaign was recorded in Hazlitt's 'Journal of F.'

Liber Amoris
or
The New Pygmalion

Advertisement

The circumstances, an outline of which is given in these pages, happened a very short time ago to a native of North Britain, who left his own country early in life, in consequence of political animosities and an ill-advised connection in marriage. It was some years after that he formed the fatal attachment which is the subject of the following narrative. The whole was transcribed very carefully with his own hands a little before he set out for the Continent in hopes of benefiting by a change of scene, but he died soon after in the Netherlands – it is supposed, of disappointment preying on a sickly frame and morbid state of mind. It was his wish that what had been his strongest feeling while living, should be preserved in this shape when he was no more. It has been suggested to the friend, into whose hands the manuscript was entrusted, that many things (particularly in the *Conversations* in the First Part) either childish or redundant, might have been omitted; but a promise was given that not a word should be altered, and the pledge was held sacred. The names and circumstances are so far disguised, it is presumed, as to prevent any consequences resulting from the publication, farther than the amusement or sympathy of the reader.[1]

Part I

The Picture

H. Oh! is it you? I had something to show you – I have got a picture here.[2] Do you know any one it's like?

S. No, Sir.

H. Don't you think it like yourself?

S. No: it's much handsomer than I can pretend to be.

H. That's because you don't see yourself with the same eyes that others do. *I* don't think it handsomer, and the expression is hardly so fine as yours sometimes is.

S. Now you flatter me. Besides, the complexion is fair, and mine is dark.

H. Thine is pale and beautiful, my love, not dark! But if your colour were a little heightened, and you wore the same dress, and your hair were let down over your shoulders, as it is here, it might be taken for a picture of you. Look here, only see how like it is. The forehead is like, with that little obstinate protrusion in the middle; the eyebrows are like, and the eyes are just like yours, when you look up and say – 'No – never!'

S. What then, do I always say – 'No – never!' when I look up?

H. I don't know about that – I never heard you say so but once; but that was once too often for my peace. It was when you told me, 'you could never be mine'. Ah! if you are never to be mine, I shall not long be myself. I cannot go on as I am. My faculties leave me: I think of nothing, I have no feeling about any thing but thee: thy sweet image has taken possession of me, haunts me, and will drive me to distraction. Yet I could almost wish to go mad for thy sake: for then I might fancy that I had thy love in return, which I cannot live without!

S. Do not, I beg, talk in that manner, but tell me what this is a picture of.

H. I hardly know; but it is a very small and delicate copy (painted in oil on a gold ground) of some fine old Italian picture, Guido's or Raphael's, but I think Raphael's. Some say it is a Madonna; others call it a Magdalene, and say you may distinguish the tear upon the cheek, though no tear is there. But it seems to me more like Raphael's St Cecilia, 'with looks commercing with the skies',[3] than anything else. – See, Sarah, how beautiful it is! Ah! dear girl, these are the ideas I have cherished in my heart, and in my brain; and I never found any thing to realise them on earth till I met with thee, my love! While thou didst seem sensible of my kindness, I was but too happy: but now thou hast cruelly cast me off.

S. You have no reason to say so: you are the same to me as ever.

H. That is, nothing. You are to me everything, and I am nothing to you. Is it not too true?

S. No.

H. Then kiss me, my sweetest. Oh! could you see your face now – your mouth full of suppressed sensibility, your downcast eyes, the soft blush upon that cheek, you would not say the picture is not like because it is too handsome, or because you want complexion. Thou art heavenly-fair, my love – like her from whom the picture was taken – the idol of the painter's heart, as thou art of mine! Shall I make a drawing of it, altering the dress a little, to show you how like it is?

S. As you please. –

The Invitation

H. But I am afraid I tire you with this prosing description of the French character and abuse of the English?[4] You know, there is but one subject on which I should ever wish to talk, if you would let me.

S. I must say, you don't seem to have a very high opinion of this country.

H. Yes, it is the place that gave you birth.

S. Do you like the French women better than the English?

H. No: though they have finer eyes, talk better, and are better made. But they none of them look like you. I like the Italian women I have seen, much better than the French: they have darker eyes, darker hair, and the accents of their native tongue are much richer and more melodious. But I will give you a better account of them when I come back from Italy,[5] if you would like to hear it.

S. I should much. It is for that I have sometimes had a wish for travelling abroad, to understand something of the manners and characters of different people.

H. My sweet girl! I will give you the best account I can unless you would rather go and judge for yourself.

S. I cannot.

H. Yes, you shall go with me, and you shall go *with honour* – you know what I mean.

S. You know it is not in your power to take me so.[6]

H. But it soon may: and if you would consent to bear me company, I would swear never to think of an Italian woman while I am abroad, nor of an English one after I return home. Thou art to me more than thy whole sex.

S. I require no such sacrifices.

H. Is that what you thought I meant by *sacrifices* last night? But sacrifices are no sacrifices when they are repaid a thousandfold.

S. I have no way of doing it.

H. You have not the will. –

S. I must go now.

H. Stay, and hear me a little. I shall soon be where I can no more hear thy voice, far distant from her I love, to see what change of climate and bright skies will do for a sad heart. I shall perhaps see thee no more, but I shall still think of thee the same as ever – I shall say to myself, 'Where is she now? – what is she doing?' But I shall hardly wish you to think of me, unless you could do so more favourably than I am afraid you will. Ah! dearest creature, I shall be 'far distant from you', as you once said of another, but you will not think of me as of him, 'with the sincerest affection'. The smallest share of thy tenderness would make me blest; but couldst thou ever love me as thou didst him, I should feel like a God! My face would change to a different expression: my whole form would undergo alteration. I was getting well, I was growing young in the sweet proofs of your friendship: you see how I droop and wither under your displeasure! Thou art divine, my love, and canst make me either more or less than mortal. Indeed I am thy creature, thy slave[7] – I only wish to live for your sake – I would gladly die for you –

S. That would give me no pleasure. But indeed you greatly overrate my power.

H. Your power over me is that of sovereign grace and beauty. When I am near thee, nothing can harm me. Thou art an angel of light, shadowing me with thy softness. But when I let go thy hand, I stagger on a precipice: out of thy sight the world is dark to me and comfortless. There is no breathing out of this house: the air of Italy will stifle me. Go with me and lighten it. I can know no pleasure away from thee –

But I will come again, my love,
An' it were ten thousand mile![8]

The Message

S. Mrs E—— has called for the book, Sir.[9]

H. Oh! it is there. Let her wait a minute or two. I see this is a busy day with you. How beautiful your arms look in those short sleeves!

S. I do not like to wear them.

H. Then that is because you are merciful, and would spare frail mortals who might die with gazing.

S. I have no power to kill.

H. You have, you have – Your charms are irresistible as your will is inexorable. I wish I could see you always thus. But I would have no one else see you so. I am jealous of all eyes but my own. I should almost like you to wear a veil, and to be muffled up from head to foot; but even if you were, and not a glimpse of you could be seen, it would be to no purpose – you would only have to move, and you would be admired as the most graceful creature in the world. You smile – Well, if you were to be won by fine speeches –

S. You could supply them!

H. It is however no laughing matter with me; thy beauty kills me daily, and I shall think of nothing but thy charms, till the last word trembles on my tongue, and that will be thy name, my love – the name of my Infelice![10] You will live by that name, you rogue, fifty years after you are dead. Don't you thank me for that?

S. I have no such ambition, Sir. But Mrs E—— is waiting.

H. She is not in love, like me. You look so handsome today, I cannot let you go. You have got a colour.

S. But you say I look best when I am pale.

H. When you are pale, I think so; but when you have a colour, I then think you still more beautiful. It is you that I admire; and whatever you are, I like best. I like you as Miss L——, I should like you still more as Mrs ——. I once thought you were half inclined to be a prude, and I admired you as a 'pensive nun, devout and pure'.[11] I now think you are more than half a coquet, and I like you for your roguery. The truth is, I am in love with you, my angel; and whatever you are, is to me the perfection of thy sex. I care not what thou art, while thou art still thyself. Smile but so, and turn my heart to what shape you please!

S. I am afraid, Sir, Mrs E—— will think you have forgotten her.

H. I had, my charmer. But go, and make her a sweet apology, all graceful as thou art. One kiss! Ah! ought I not to think myself the happiest of men?

The Flageolet

H. Where have you been, my love?

S. I have been down to see my aunt, Sir.

H. And I hope she has been giving you good advice.

S. I did not go to ask her opinion about any thing.

H. And yet you seem anxious and agitated. You appear pale and dejected, as if your refusal of me had touched your own breast with pity. Cruel girl! you look at this moment heavenly-soft, saint-like, or resemble some graceful marble statue, in the moon's pale ray! Sadness only heightens the elegance of your features. How can I escape from you, when every new occasion, even your cruelty and scorn, brings out some new charm. Nay, your rejection of me, by the way in which you do it, is only a new link added to my chain. Raise those down-cast eyes, bend as if an angel stooped, and kiss me ... Ah! enchanting little trembler! if such is thy sweetness where thou dost not love, what must thy love have been? I cannot think how any man, having the heart of one, could go and leave it.

S. No one did, that I know of.

H. Yes, you told me yourself he left you (though he liked you, and though he knew – Oh! gracious God! – that you loved him) he left you because 'the pride of birth would not permit a union'. – For myself, I would leave a throne to ascend to the heaven of thy charms. I live but for thee, here – I only wish to live again to pass all eternity with thee. But even in another world, I suppose you would turn from me to seek him out who scorned you here.

S. If the proud scorn us here, in that place we shall all be equal.

H. Do not look so – do not talk so – unless you would drive me mad. I could worship you at this moment. Can I witness such perfection, and bear to think I have lost you for ever? Oh! let me hope! You see you can mould me as you like. You can lead me by the hand, like a little child; and with you my way would be like a little child's: – you could strew flowers in my path, and pour new life and hope into me. I should then indeed hail the return of spring with joy, could I indulge the faintest hope – would you but let me try to please you!

S. Nothing can alter my resolution, Sir.

H. Will you go and leave me so?

S. It is late, and my father will be getting impatient at my stopping so long.

H. You know he has nothing to fear for you – it is poor I that am alone in danger. But I wanted to ask about buying you a flageolet. Could I see that which you have? If it is a pretty one, it would hardly be worth while; but if it isn't, I thought of bespeaking an ivory one for you. Can't you bring up your own to show me?

S. Not tonight, Sir.

H. I wish you could.

S. I cannot – but I will in the morning.

H. Whatever you determine, I must submit to. Good night, and bless thee!

(*The next morning, S. brought up the tea-kettle as usual; and looking towards the tea-tray, she said, 'Oh! I see my sister has forgot the tea-pot.' It was not there, sure enough; and tripping down stairs, she came up in a minute, with the tea-pot in one hand, and the flageolet in the other, balanced so sweetly and gracefully. It would have been awkward to have brought up the flageolet in the tea-tray, and she could not have well gone down again on purpose to fetch it. Something, therefore, was to be omitted as an excuse. Exquisite witch! But do I love her the less dearly for it? I cannot.*)

The Confession[12]

H. You say you cannot love! Is there not a prior attachment in the case? Was there any one else that you *did* like?

S. Yes, there was another.

H. Ah! I thought as much. Is it long ago then?

S. It is two years, Sir.

H. And has time made no alteration? Or do you still see him sometimes?

S. No, Sir! But he is one to whom I feel the sincerest affection, and ever shall, though he is far distant.

H. And did he return your regard?

S. I had every reason to think so.

H. What then broke off your intimacy?

S. It was the pride of birth, Sir, that would not permit him to think of a union.

H. Was he a young man of rank, then?

S. His connections were high.

H. And did he never attempt to persuade you to any other step?

S. No – he had too great a regard for me.

H. Tell me, my angel, how was it? Was he so very handsome?

Or was it the fineness of his manners?

S. It was more his manner: but I can't tell how it was. It was chiefly my own fault. I was foolish to suppose he could ever think seriously of me. But he used to make me read with him – and I used to be with him a good deal, though not much neither – and I found my affections entangled before I was aware of it.

H. And did your mother and family know of it?

S. No – I have never told any one but you; nor I should not have mentioned it now, but I thought it might give you some satisfaction.

H. Why did he go at last?

S. We thought it better to part.

H. And do you correspond?

S. No, Sir. But perhaps I may see him again some time or other, though it will be only in the way of friendship.

H. My God! what a heart is thine, to live for years upon that bare hope!

S. I did not wish to live always, Sir – I wished to die for a long time after, till I thought it not right; and since then I have endeavoured to be as resigned as I can.

H. And do you think the impression will never wear out?

S. Not if I can judge from my feelings hitherto. It is now sometime since, – and I find no difference.

H. May God for ever bless you! How can I thank you for your condescension in letting me know your sweet sentiments? You have changed my esteem into adoration. Never can I harbour a thought of ill in thee again.

S. Indeed, Sir, I wish for your good opinion and your friendship.

H. And can you return them?

S. Yes.

H. And nothing more?

S. No, Sir.

H. You are an angel, and I will spend my life, if you will let me, in paying you the homage that my heart feels towards you.

The Quarrel

H. You are angry with me?

S. Have I not reason?

H. I hope you have; for I would give the world to believe my suspicions unjust. But, oh! my God! after what I have thought of you and felt towards you, as little less than an angel, to have but a doubt cross my mind for an instant that you were what I dare not name – a common lodging-house decoy,[13] a kissing convenience, that your lips were as common as the stairs[14] –

S. Let me go, Sir!

H. Nay – prove to me that you are not so, and I will fall down and worship you. You were the only creature that ever seemed to love me; and to have my hopes, and all my fondness for you, thus turned to a mockery – it is too much! Tell me why you have deceived me, and singled me out as your victim?

S. I never have, Sir. I always said I could not love.

H. There is a difference between love and making me a laughing-stock. Yet what else could be the meaning of your little sister's[15] running out to you, and saying 'He thought I did not see him!' when I had followed you into the other room? Is it a joke upon me that I make free with you? Or is not the joke rather against *her* sister, unless you make my courtship of you a jest to the whole house? Indeed I do not well see how you can come and stay with me as you do, by the hour together, and day after day, as openly as you do, unless you give it some such turn with your family. Or do you deceive them as well as me?

S. I deceive no one, Sir. But my sister Betsey was always watching and listening when Mr M——[16] was courting my eldest sister, till he was obliged to complain of it.

H. That I can understand, but not the other. You may remember, when your servant Maria looked in and found you sitting in my lap one day, and I was afraid she might tell your mother, you said 'You did not care, for you had no secrets from your mother.' This seemed to me odd at the time, but I thought no more of it, till other things brought it to my mind. Am I to suppose, then, that you are acting a part, a vile part, all this time, and that you come up here, and stay as long as I like, that you sit on my knee and put your arms round my neck, and feed me with kisses, and let me take other liberties with you, and that for a year together; and that you do all this not out of love, or liking, or regard, but go through your regular task, like some young witch, without one natural feeling, to show your cleverness, and get a few presents out of me, and go down into the kitchen to make a fine laugh of it? There is something monstrous in it, that I cannot believe of you.

S. Sir, you have no right to harass my feelings in the manner you do. I have never made a jest of you to anyone, but always felt and expressed the greatest esteem for you. You have no ground for complaint in my conduct; and I cannot help what Betsey or others do. I have always been consistent from the first. I told you my regard could amount to no more than friendship.

H. Nay, Sarah, it was more than half a year before I knew that there was an insurmountable obstacle in the way. You say your regard is merely friendship, and that you are sorry I have ever felt anything more for you. Yet the first time I ever asked you, you let me kiss you; the first time I ever saw you, as you went out of the room, you turned full round at the door, with that inimitable grace with which you do everything, and fixed your eyes full upon me, as much as to say, 'Is he caught?'[17] – that very week you sat upon my knee, twined your arms round me, caressed me with every mark of tenderness consistent with modesty; and I have not got much farther since. Now if you did all this with me, a perfect stranger to you, and without any particular liking to me, must I not conclude you do so as a matter of course with everyone? – Or, if you do not do so with others, it was because you took a liking to me for some reason or other.

S. It was gratitude, Sir, for different obligations.

H. If you mean by obligations the presents[18] I made you, I had given you none the first day I came. You do not consider yourself *obliged* to everyone who asks you for a kiss?

S. No, Sir.

H. I should not have thought anything of it in anyone but you. But you seemed so reserved and modest, so soft, so timid, you spoke so low, you looked so innocent – I thought it impossible you could deceive me. Whatever favours you granted must proceed from pure regard. No betrothed virgin ever gave the object of her choice kisses, caresses more modest or more bewitching than those you have given me a thousand and a thousand times. Could I have thought I should ever live to believe them an inhuman mockery of one who had the sincerest regard for you? Do you think they will not now turn to rank poison in my veins, and kill me, soul and body? You say it is friendship – but if this is friendship, I'll forswear love. Ah! Sarah! it must be something more or less than friendship. If your caresses are sincere, they show fondness – if they are not, I must be more than indifferent to you. Indeed you once let some words drop, as if I were out of the question in such matters, and you could trifle with me with impunity.[19] Yet you complain at other times that no one ever took such liberties with you as I have done.

I remember once in particular your saying, as you went out at the door in anger – 'I had an attachment before, but that person never attempted anything of the kind.' Good God! How did I dwell on that word *before*, thinking it implied an attachment to me also; but you have since disclaimed any such meaning. You say you have never professed more than esteem. Yet once, when you were sitting in your old place, on my knee, embracing and fondly embraced, and I asked you if you could not love, you made answer, 'I could easily say so, whether I did or not – YOU SHOULD JUDGE BY MY ACTIONS!' And another time, when you were in the same posture, and I reproached you with indifference, you replied in these words, 'DO I SEEM INDIFFERENT?' Was I to blame after this to indulge my passion for the loveliest of her sex? Or what can I think?[20]

S. I am no prude, Sir.[21]

H. Yet you might be taken for one. So your mother said, 'It was hard if you might not indulge in a little levity.' She has strange notions of levity. But levity, my dear, is quite out of character in you. Your ordinary walk is as if you were performing some religious ceremony: you come up to my table of a morning, when you merely bring in the tea-things, as if you were advancing to the altar. You move in minuet-time: you measure every step, as if you were afraid of offending in the smallest things. I never hear your approach on the stairs, but by a sort of hushed silence. When you enter the room, the Graces wait on you, and Love waves round your person in gentle undulations, breathing balm into the soul! By Heaven, you are an angel! You look like one at this instant! Do I not adore you – and have I merited this return?

S. I have repeatedly answered that question. You sit and fancy things out of your own head, and then lay them to my charge. There is not a word of truth in your suspicions.

H. Did I not overhear the conversation down-stairs last night, to which you were a party? Shall I repeat it?[22]

S. I had rather not hear it!

H. Or what am I to think of this story of the footman?[23]

S. It is false, Sir, I never did anything of the sort.

H. Nay, when I told your mother I wished she wouldn't * * * * * * * * * (as I heard she did) she said 'Oh, there's nothing in that, for Sarah very often * * * * * * *', and your doing so before company, is only a trifling addition to the sport.[24]

S. I'll call my mother, Sir, and she shall contradict you.

H. Then she'll contradict herself. But did not you boast you were 'very persevering in your resistance to gay young men', and had been 'several times obliged to ring the bell'?[25] Did you always ring it? Or did you get into these dilemmas that made it necessary, merely by the demureness of your looks and ways? Or had nothing else passed? Or have you two characters, one that you palm off upon me, and another, your natural one, that you resume when you get out of the room, like an actress who throws aside her artificial part behind the scenes? Did you not, when I was courting you on the staircase the first night Mr C——[26] came, beg me to desist, for if the new lodger heard us, he'd take you for a light character? Was that all? Were you only afraid of being *taken* for a light character? Oh! Sarah!

S. I'll stay and hear this no longer.

H. Yes, one word more. Did you not love another?

S. Yes, and ever shall most sincerely.

H. Then, *that* is my only hope. If you could feel this sentiment for him, you cannot be what you seem to me of late. But there is another thing I had to say – be what you will, I love you to distraction! You are the only woman that ever made me think she loved me, and that feeling was so new to me, and so delicious, that it 'will never from my heart'.[27] Thou wert to me a little tender flower, blooming in the wilderness of my life; and though thou should'st turn out a weed, I'll not fling thee from me, while I can help it.[28] Wert thou all that I dread to think – wert thou a wretched wanderer in the street, covered with rags, disease, and infamy, I'd clasp thee to my bosom, and live and die with thee, my love. Kiss me, thou little sorceress!

S. NEVER!

H. Then go: but remember – I cannot live without you – nor I will not.

The Reconciliation

H. I have then lost your friendship?

S. Nothing tends more to alienate friendship than insult.

H. The words I uttered hurt me more than they did you.

S. It was not words merely, but actions as well.

H. Nothing I can say or do can ever alter my fondness for you – Ah, Sarah! I am unworthy of your love: I hardly dare ask for your pity; but oh! save me – save me from your scorn: I cannot bear it – it withers me like lightning.

S. I bear no malice, Sir; but my brother, who would scorn to tell a lie for his sister, can bear witness for me that there was no truth in what you were told.

H. I believe it; or there is no truth in woman. It is enough for me to know that you do not return my regard; it would be too much for me to think that you did not deserve it. But cannot you forgive the agony of the moment?

S. I can forgive; but it is not easy to forget some things!

H. Nay, my sweet Sarah (frown if you will, I can bear your resentment for my ill behaviour, it is only your scorn and indifference that harrow up my soul) – but I was going to ask, if you had been engaged to be married to any one, and the day was fixed, and he had heard what I did, whether he could have felt any true regard for the character of his bride, his wife, if he had not been hurt and alarmed as I was?

S. I believe, actual contracts of marriage have sometimes been broken off by unjust suspicions.

H. Or had it been your old friend, what do you think he would have said in my case?

S. He would never have listened to anything of the sort.

H. He had greater reasons for confidence than I have. But it is your repeated cruel rejection of me that drives me almost to madness. Tell me, love, is there not, besides your attachment to him, a repugnance to me?

S. No, none whatever.

H. I fear there is an original dislike, which no efforts of mine can overcome.

S. It is not *you* – it is my feelings with respect to another, which are unalterable.

H. And yet you have no hope of ever being his? And yet you accuse me of being romantic in my sentiments.

S. I have indeed long ceased to hope; but yet I sometimes hope against hope.

H. My love! were it in my, power, thy hopes should be fulfilled tomorrow. Next to my own, there is nothing that could give me so much satisfaction as to see thine realised! Do I not love thee, when I can feel such an interest in thy love, for another? It was that which first wedded my very soul to you. I would give worlds for a share in a heart so rich in pure affection!

S. And yet I did not tell you of the circumstance to raise myself in your opinion.

H. You are a sublime little thing! And yet, as you have no prospects there, I cannot help thinking, the best thing would be to do as I have said.

S. I would never marry a man I did not love beyond all the world.

H. I should be satisfied with less than that – with the love, or regard, or whatever you call it, you have shown me before marriage, if that has only been sincere. You would hardly like me less afterwards.

S. Endearments would, I should think, increase regard, where there was love beforehand; but that is not exactly my case.

H. But I think you would be happier than you are at present. You take pleasure in my conversation, and you say you have an esteem for me; and it is upon this, after the honeymoon, that marriage chiefly turns.

S. Do you think there is no pleasure in a single life?

H. Do you mean on account of its liberty?

S. No, but I feel that forced duty is no duty. I have high ideas of the married state!

H. Higher than of the maiden state?

S. I understand you, Sir.

H. I meant nothing; but you have sometimes spoken of any serious attachment as a tie upon you. It is not that you prefer flirting with 'gay young men' to becoming a mere dull domestic wife?

S. You have no right to throw out such insinuations: for though I am but a tradesman's daughter, I have as nice a sense of honour as anyone can have.[29]

H. Talk of a tradesman's daughter! You would ennoble any family, thou glorious girl, by true nobility of mind.

S. Oh! Sir, you flatter me. I know my own inferiority to most.

H. To none; there is no one above thee, man nor woman either. You are above your situation, which is not fit for you.

S. I am contented with my lot, and do my duty as cheerfully as I can.

H. Have you not told me your spirits grow worse every year?

S. Not on that account: but some disappointments are hard to bear up against.

H. If you talk about that, you'll unman me. But tell me, my love, – I have thought of it as something that might account for some circumstances; that is, as a mere possibility. But tell me, there was not a likeness between me and your old lover that struck you at first sight? Was there?

S. No, Sir, none.

H. Well, I didn't think it likely there should.

S. But there was a likeness.

H. To whom?

S. To that little image! (*looking intently on a small bronze figure of Bonaparte on the mantlepiece*).[30]

H. What, do you mean to Bonaparte?

S. Yes, all but the nose was just like.

H. And was his figure the same?

S. He was taller!

(*I got up and gave her the image, and told her it was hers by every right that was sacred. She refused at first to take so valuable a curiosity, and said she would keep it for me. But I pressed it eagerly, and she took it. She immediately came and sat down, and put her arm round my neck, and kissed me, and I said, 'Is it not plain we are the best friends in the world, since we are always so glad to make it up?' And then I added 'How odd it was that the God of my idolatry should turn out to be like her Idol, and said it was no wonder that the same face which awed the world should conquer the sweetest creature in it!' How I loved her at that moment! Is it possible that the wretch who writes this could ever have been so blest! Heavenly delicious creature! Can I live without her? Oh! no – never – never.*

What is this world? What asken men to have,
Now with his love, now in the cold grave,
        Alone, withouten any compagnie![31]

Let me but see her again! She cannot hate the man who loves her as I do.)

Letters to the Same[32]

Feb., 1822

You will scold me for this and ask me if this is keeping my promise to mind my work. One half of it was to think of Sarah: and besides, I do not neglect my work either, I assure you. I regularly do ten pages a day, which mounts up to thirty guineas' worth a week,[33] so that you see I should grow rich at this rate, if I could keep on so; *and I could keep on so*, if I had you with me to encourage me with your sweet smiles, and share my lot. The Berwick smacks[34] sail twice a week, and the wind sits fair. When I think of the thousand endearing caresses that have passed between us, I do not wonder at the strong attachment that draws me to you; but I am sorry for my own want of power to please. I hear the wind sigh through the lattice, and keep repeating over and over to myself two lines of Lord Byron's Tragedy –

> So shalt thou find me ever at thy side
> Here and hereafter, if the last may be.[35]

applying them to thee, my love, and thinking whether I shall ever see thee again. Perhaps not – for some years at least – till both thou and I are old – and then, when all else have forsaken thee, I will creep to thee, and die in thine arms. You once made me believe I was not hated by her I loved; and for that sensation, so delicious was it, though but a mockery and a dream, I owe you more than I can ever pay.[36] I thought to have dried up my tears for ever, the day I left you; but as I write this, they stream again. If they did not, I think my heart would burst. I walk out here of an afternoon, and hear the notes of the thrush, that come up from a sheltered valley below, welcome in the spring; but they do not melt my heart as they used: it is grown cold and dead. As you say, it will one day be colder. – Forgive what I have written above; I did not intend it: but you were once my little all, and I cannot bear the thought of having lost you for ever, I fear through my own fault. Has any one called? Do not send any letters that come. I should like you and your mother (if agreeable) to go and see Mr Kean in *Othello*, and Miss Stephens in *Love in a Village*. If you will, I will write to Mr T——[37] to send you tickets. Has Mr P——[38] called? I think I must send to him for the picture to kiss and talk to. Kiss me, my best beloved. Ah! if you can never be mine, still let me be your proud and happy slave.[39]

H.

To the Same[40]

March, 1822

You will be glad to learn I have done my work – a volume in less than a month. This is one reason why I am better than when I came, and another is, I have had two letters from Sarah. I am pleased I have got through this job, as I was afraid I might lose reputation by it (which I can little afford to lose) – and besides, I am more anxious to do well now, as I wish you to hear me well spoken of. I walk out of an afternoon, and hear the birds sing as I told you, and think, if I had you hanging on my arm, *and that for life*, how happy I should be – happier than I ever hoped to be, or had any conception of till I knew you. '*But that can never be*' – I hear you answer in a soft, low murmur. Well, let me dream of it sometimes – I am not happy too often, except when that favourite note, the harbinger of spring, recalling the hopes of my youth, whispers thy name and peace together in my ear. I was reading something about Mr Macready today, and this put me in mind of that delicious night, when I went with your mother and you to see *Romeo and Juliet*.[41] Can I forget it for a moment – your sweet modest looks, your infinite propriety of behaviour, all your sweet winning ways – your hesitating about taking my arm as we came out till your mother did – your laughing about nearly losing your cloak – your stepping into the coach without my being able to make the slightest discovery – and oh! my sitting down beside you there, you whom I had loved so long, so well, and your assuring me I had not lessened your pleasure at the play by being with you, and giving me your dear hand to press in mine! I thought I was in heaven – that slender exquisitely turned form contained my all of heaven upon earth; and as I folded you – yes, you, my own best Sarah, to my bosom, there was, as you say, *a tie between us* – you did seem to me, for those few short moments, to be mine in all truth and honour and sacredness – Oh! that we could be always so – Do not mock me, for I am a very child in love. I ought to beg pardon for behaving so ill afterwards, but I hope the *little image* made it up between us, etc.

(*To this letter I have received no answer, not a line. The rolling years of eternity will never fill up that blank. Where shall I be? What am I? Or where have I been?*)

Written in a Blank Leaf of Endymion[42]

I want a hand to guide me, an eye to cheer me, a bosom to repose on; all which I shall never have, but shall stagger into my grave, old before my time, unloved and unlovely, unless S. L. keeps her faith with me.

* * * * * * * *

* * * *

But by her dove's eyes and serpent-shape, I think she does not hate me; by her smooth forehead and her crested hair, I own I love her; by her soft looks and queen-like grace (which men might fall down and worship) I swear to live and die for her!

A Proposal of Love

(Given to her in our early acquaintance)

Oh! if I thought it could be in a woman
(As, if it can, I will presume in you)
To feed for aye her lamp and flames of love,
To keep her constancy in plight and youth,
Outliving beauties outward with a mind
That doth renew swifter than blood decays:
Or that persuasion could but thus convince me,
That my integrity and truth to you
Might be confronted with the match and weight
Of such a winnowed purity in love –
How were I then uplifted! But, alas,
I am as true as truth's simplicity,
And simpler than the infancy of truth.

Troilus and Cressida[43]

Part II

Letters to C. P——, Esq.[1]

Bees-Inn[2]

My good Friend, Here I am in Scotland (and shall have been here three weeks, next Monday) as I may say, *on my probation.* This is a lone inn, but on a great scale, thirty miles from Edinburgh. It is situated on a rising ground (a mark for all the winds, which blow here incessantly) – there is a woody hill opposite, with a winding valley below, and the London road stretches out on either side. You may guess which way I oftenest walk. I have written two letters to S. L. and got one cold, prudish answer, beginning *Sir,* and ending *From yours truly,* with *Best respects from herself and relations.* I was going to give in, but have returned an answer, which I think is a touchstone. I send it you on the other side to keep as a curiosity, in case she kills me by her exquisite rejoinder. I am convinced from the profound contemplations I have had on the subject here and coming along, that I am on a wrong scent. We had a famous parting-scene, a complete quarrel and then a reconciliation, in which she did beguile me of my tears, but the deuce a one did she shed. What do you think? She cajoled me out of my little Bonaparte as cleverly as possible, in manner and form following. She was shy the Saturday and Sunday (the day of my departure) so I got in dudgeon, and began to rip up grievances. I asked her how she came to admit me to such extreme familiarities, the first week I entered the house. 'If she had no particular regard for me, she must do so (or more) with everyone: if she had a liking to me from the first, why refuse me with scorn and wilfulness?' If you had seen how she flounced, and looked, and went to the door, saying 'She was obliged to me for letting her know the opinion I had always entertained of her' – then I said, 'Sarah!' and she came back and took my hand, and fixed her eyes on the mantlepiece – (she must have been invoking her idol then – if I thought so, I could devour her, the darling – but I doubt her) – So I said 'There is one thing that has occurred to me sometimes as possible, to account for your conduct to me at first – there wasn't a likeness, was there, to your old friend?' She answered 'No, none – but there was a likeness' – I asked, to what? She said 'to that little image!' I said, 'Do you mean

Bonaparte?' – She said, 'Yes, all but the nose'. – 'And the figure?' – 'He was taller'. – I could not stand this. So I got up and took it, and gave it her, and after some reluctance, she consented to 'keep it for me'. What will you bet me that it wasn't all a trick? I'll tell you why I suspect it, besides being fairly out of my wits about her. I had told her mother half an hour before, that I should take this image and leave it at Mrs B.'s, for that I didn't wish to leave anything behind me that must bring me back again. Then up she comes and starts a likeness to her lover: she knew I should give it her on the spot – 'No, she would keep it for me!' So I must come back for it. Whether art or nature, it is sublime. I told her I should write and tell you so, and that I parted from her, confiding, adoring! She is beyond me, that's certain. Do go and see her, and desire her not to give my present address to a single soul, and learn if the lodging is let, and to whom. My letter to her is as follows. If she shews the least remorse at it, I'll be hanged, though it might move a stone, I modestly think. (*See above*, pp. 55–6.)

N.B. I have begun a book of our conversations (I mean mine and the statue's) which I call *Liber Amoris*. I was detained at Stamford and found myself dull, and could hit upon no other way of employing my time so agreeably.

Letter II

Dear P——, Here, without loss of time, in order that I may have your opinion upon it, is little Yes and No's answer to my last.

> Sir, I should not have disregarded your injunction not to send you any more letters that might come to you, had I not promised the Gentleman who left the enclosed to forward it the earliest opportunity, as he said it was *of consequence*. Mr P—— called the day after you left town. My mother and myself are much obliged by your kind offer of tickets to the play, but must decline accepting it. My family send their best respects, in which they are joined by
>
> Yours, truly,
S. L.

The deuce a bit more is there of it. If you can make anything out of it (or any body else) I'll be hanged. You are to understand, this comes in a frank,[3] the second I have received from her, with a name I can't make out, and she won't tell me, though I asked her, where she got franks, as also whether the lodgings were let, to neither of which a word of answer. * * * * is the name on the frank: see if you can decypher it by a *Red-Book*.[4] I suspect her grievously of being an arrant jilt, to say no more – yet I love her dearly. Do you know I'm going to write to that sweet rogue presently, having a whole evening to myself in advance of my work? Now mark, before you set about your exposition of the new Apocalypse of the new Calypso,[5] the only thing to be endured in the above letter is the date. It was written the very day after she received mine. By this she seems willing to lose no time in receiving these letters 'of such sweet breath composed'. If I thought so – but I wait for your reply. After all, what is there in her but a pretty figure, and that you can't get a word out of her? Hers is the Fabian method[6] of making love and conquests. What do you suppose she said the night before I left her?

'H. Could you not come and live with me as a friend?

S. I don't know: and yet it would be of no use if I did, you would always be hankering after what could never be!'

I asked her if she would do so at once – the very next day? And what do you guess was her answer – 'Do you think it would be prudent?' As I didn't proceed to extremities on the spot, she began to look grave, and declare off. 'Would she live with me in her own house – to be with me all day as dear friends, if nothing more, to sit and read and talk with me?' – 'She would make no promises, but I should find her the same.' – 'Would she go to the play with me sometimes, and let it be understood that I was paying my addresses to her?' – 'She could not, as a habit – her father was rather strict, and would object.' – Now what am I to think of all this? Am I mad or a fool? Answer me to that, Master Brook![7] You are a philosopher.

Letter III

Dear Friend, I ought to have written to you before; but since I received your letter, I have been in a sort of purgatory, and what is worse, I see no prospect of getting out of it. I would put an end to my torments at once; but I am as great a coward as I have been a dupe. Do you know I have not had a word of answer from her since! What can be the reason? Is she offended at my letting you know she wrote to me, or is it some new affair? I wrote to her in the tenderest, most respectful manner, poured my soul at her feet, and this is the return she makes me! Can you account for it, except on the admission of my worst doubts concerning her? Oh God! can I bear after all to think of her so, or that I am scorned and made a sport of by the creature to whom I had given my whole heart? Thus has it been with me all my life; and so will it be to the end of it! If you should learn anything, good or bad, tell me, I conjure you: I can bear anything but this cruel suspense. If I knew she was a mere abandoned creature, I should try to forget her; but till I do know this, nothing can tear me from her, I have drank in poison from her lips too long – alas! mine do not poison again. I sit and indulge my grief by the hour together; my weakness grows upon me; and I have no hope left, unless I could lose my senses quite. Do you know I think I should like this? To forget, ah! to forget – there would be something in that – to change to an idiot for some few years, and then to wake up a poor wretched old man, to recollect my misery as past, and die! Yet, oh! with her, only a little while ago, I had different hopes, forfeited for nothing that I know of! * * * * *[8] If you can give me any consolation on the subject of my tormentor, pray do. The pain I suffer wears me out daily. I write this on the supposition that Mrs ——[9] may still come here, and that I may be detained some weeks longer. Direct to me at the Post-office; and if I return to town directly as I fear, I will leave word for them to forward the letter to me in London – not at my old lodgings. I will not go back there: yet how can I breathe away from her? Her hatred of me must be great, since my love of her could not overcome it! I have finished the book of my conversations with her, which I told you of: if I am not mistaken, you will think it very nice reading.

Yours ever.

Have you read *Sardanapalus*? How like the little Greek slave, Myrrha, is to *her*![10]

Letter IV

(Written in the Winter)

My good Friend, I received your letter this morning, and I kiss the rod not only with submission, but gratitude. Your reproofs of me and your defences of her are the only things that save my soul from perdition. She is my heart's idol; and believe me those words of yours applied to the dear saint – 'To lip a chaste one and suppose her wanton' – were balm and rapture to me.[11] I have *lipped her*, God knows how often, and oh! is it even possible that she is chaste, and that she has bestowed her loved 'endearments' on me (her own sweet word) out of true regard? That thought, out of the lowest depths of despair, would at any time make me strike my forehead against the stars. Could I but think the love 'honest',[12] I am proof against all hazards. She by her silence makes my *dark hour*[13] and you by your encouragements dissipate it for twenty-four hours. Another thing has brought me to life. Mrs —— is actually on her way here about the divorce. Should this unpleasant business[14] (which has been so long talked of) succeed, and I should become free, do you think S. L. will agree to change her name to ——? If she will, she *shall*; and to call her so to you, or to hear her called so by others, would be music to my ears, such as they never drank in. Do you think if she knew how I love her, my depressions and my altitudes, my wanderings and my constancy, it would not move her? She knows it all; and if she is not an *incorrigible*, she loves me, or regards me with a feeling next to love. I don't believe that any woman was ever courted more passionately than she has been by me. As Rousseau said of Madame d'Houptot (forgive the allusion) my heart has found a tongue in speaking to her, and I have talked to her the divine language of love.[15] Yet she says, she is insensible to it. Am I to believe her or you? You – for I wish it and wish it to madness, now that I am like to be free, and to have it in my power to say to her without a possibility of suspicion, 'Sarah, will you be mine?' When I sometimes think of the time I first saw the sweet apparition, August 16, 1820, and that possibly she may be my bride before that day two years, it makes me dizzy with incredible joy and love of her. Write soon.

Letter V

My dear Friend, I read your answer this morning with gratitude. I have felt somewhat easier since. It showed your interest in my vexations, and also that you know nothing worse than I do. I cannot describe the weakness of mind to which she has reduced me. This state of suspense is like hanging in the air by a single thread that exhausts all your strength to keep hold of it; and yet if that fails you, you have nothing in the world else left to trust to. I am come back to Edinburgh about this cursed business, and Mrs —— is coming from Montrose next week.[16] How it will end, I can't say; and don't care, except as it regards the other affair. I should, I confess, like to have it in my power to make her the offer direct and unequivocal, to see how she'd receive it. It would be worth something at any rate to see her superfine airs upon the occasion; and if she should take it into her head to turn round her sweet neck, drop her eye-lids, and say – 'Yes, I will be yours!' – why then, 'treason domestic, foreign levy, nothing could touch me further'.[17] By Heaven! I dote on her. The truth is, I never had any pleasure, like love, with any one but her. Then how can I bear to part with her? Do you know I like to think of her best in her morning-gown and mob-cap – it is so she has oftenest come into my room and enchanted me![18] She was once ill, pale, and had lost all her freshness. I only adored her the more for it, and fell in love with the decay of her beauty. I could devour the little witch. If she had a plague-spot on her, I could touch the infection: if she was in a burning fever, I could kiss her, and drink death as I have drank life from her lips. When I press her hand, I enjoy perfect happiness and contentment of soul. It is not what she says or what she does – it is herself that I love. To be with her is to be at peace. I have no other wish or desire. The air about her is serene, blissful; and he who breathes it is like one of the Gods! So that I can but have her with me always, I care for nothing more. I never could tire of her sweetness; I feel that I could grow to her, body and soul. My heart, my heart is hers.

Letter VI

(Written in May)

Dear P——, What have I suffered since I parted with you![19] A raging fire is in my heart and in my brain, that never quits me. The steam-boat (which I foolishly ventured on board) seems a prison-house, a sort of spectre-ship, moving on through an infernal lake, without wind or tide, by some necromantic power – the splashing of the waves, the noise of the engine gives me no rest, night or day – no tree, no natural object varies the scene – but the abyss is before me, and all my peace lies weltering in it! I feel the eternity of punishment in this life; for I see no end of my woes. The people about me are ill, uncomfortable, wretched enough, many of them – but tomorrow or next day, they reach the place of their destination, and all will be new and delightful. To me it will be the same. I can neither escape from her, nor from myself. All is endurable where there is a limit: but I have nothing but the blackness and the fiendishness of scorn around me – mocked by her (the false one) in whom I placed my hope, and who hardens herself against me! – I believe you thought me quite gay, vain, insolent, half mad, the night I left the house – no tongue can tell the heaviness of heart I felt at that moment. No footsteps ever fell more slow, more sad than mine; for every step bore me farther from her, with whom my soul and every thought lingered. I had parted with her in anger, and each had spoken words of high disdain, not soon to be forgiven. Should I ever behold her again? Where go to live and die far from her? In her sight there was Elysium; her smile was heaven; her voice was enchantment; the air of love waved round her, breathing balm into my heart: for a little while I had sat with the Gods at their golden tables, I had tasted of all earth's bliss, 'both living and loving'! But now Paradise barred its doors against me; I was driven from her presence, where rosy blushes and delicious sighs and all soft wishes dwelt, the outcast of nature and the scoff of love! I thought of the time when I was a little happy careless child, of my father's house, of my early lessons, of my brother's picture of me when a boy, of all that had since happened to me, and of the waste of years to come – I stopped, faltered, and was going to turn back once more to make a longer truce with wretchedness and patch up a hollow league with love,[20] when the recollection of her words – 'I always told you I had no affection for you' – steeled my resolution, and I determined to proceed. You see by this she always hated me, and only played with my credulity till she could find some one to supply the place of her unalterable attachment to *the little image.* ***** I am a little, a very little better today. Would it were quietly over; and that this misshapen form (made to be mocked) were hid out of the sight of cold, sullen eyes! The people about me even take notice of my dumb despair, and pity me. What is to be done? I cannot forget *her,* and I can find no other like what *she seemed.* I should wish you to call, if you can make an excuse, and see whether or no she is quite marble – whether I may go back again at my return, and whether she will see me and talk to me sometimes as an old friend. Suppose you were to call on M—— from me, and ask him what his impression is that I ought to do. But do as you think best. Pardon, pardon.

P.S. I send this from Scarborough, where the vessel stops for a few minutes. I scarcely know what I should have done, but for this relief to my feelings.[21]

Letter VII

My dear Friend, The important step is taken, and I am virtually a free man. * * * * *[22] What had I better do in these circumstances? I dare not write to her, I dare not write to her father, or else I would. She has shot me through with poisoned arrows, and I think another 'winged wound' would finish me. It is a pleasant sort of balm (as you express it) she has left in my heart! One thing I agree with you in, it will remain there for ever; but yet not very long. It festers, and consumes me. If it were not for my little boy, whose face I see struck blank at the news, looking through the world for pity and meeting with contempt instead, I should soon, I fear, settle the question by my death.[23] That recollection is the only thought that brings my wandering reason to an anchor; that stirs the smallest interest in me; or gives me fortitude to bear up against what I am doomed to feel for the *ungrateful*. Otherwise, I am dead to every thing but the sense of what I have lost. She was my life – it is gone from me, and I am grown spectral! If I find myself in a place I am acquainted with, it reminds me of her, of the way in which I thought of her,

> – and carved on every tree
> The soft, the fair, the inexpressive she![24]

If it is a place that is new to me, it is desolate, barren of all interest; for nothing touches me but what has a reference to her. If the clock strikes, the sound jars me; a million of hours will not bring back peace to my breast. The light startles me; the darkness terrifies me. I seem falling into a pit, without a hand to help me. She has deceived me, and the earth fails from under my feet; no object in nature is substantial, real, but false and hollow, like her faith on which I built my trust. She came (I knew not how) and sat by my side and was folded in my arms, a vision of love and joy, as if she had dropped from the Heavens to bless me by some especial dispensation of a favouring Providence, and make me amends for all; and now without any fault of mine but too much fondness, she has vanished from me, and I am left to perish. My heart is torn out of me, with every feeling for which I wished to live. The whole is like a dream, an effect of enchantment; it torments me, and it drives me mad. I lie down with it; I rise up with it; and see no chance of repose. I grasp at a shadow, I try to undo the past, and weep with rage and pity over my own weakness and misery. I spared her again and again (fool that I was) thinking what she allowed from me was love, friendship, sweetness, not wantonness. How could I doubt it, looking in her face, and hearing her words, like sighs breathed from the gentlest of all bosoms? I had hopes, I had prospects to come, the flattery of something like fame, a pleasure in writing, health even would have come back with her smile – she has blighted all, turned all to poison and childish tears. Yet the barbed arrow is in my heart – I can neither endure it, nor draw it out; for with it flows my life's-blood. I had conversed too long with abstracted truth to trust myself with the immortal thoughts of love. *That S. L. might have been mine, and now never can* – these are the two sole propositions that for ever stare me in the face, and look ghastly in at my poor brain. I am in some sense proud that I can feel this dreadful passion – it gives me a kind of rank in the kingdom of love – but I could have wished it had been for an object that at least could have understood its value and pitied its excess.[25] You say her not coming to the door when you went is a proof – yes, that her complement is at present full! That is the reason she doesn't want me there, lest I should discover the new affair – wretch that I am! Another has possession of her, oh Hell! I'm satisfied of it from her manner, which had a wanton insolence in it. Well might I run wild when I received no letters from her. I foresaw, I felt my fate. The gates of Paradise were once open to me too, and I blushed to enter but with the golden keys of love! I would die; but her lover – my love of her – ought not to die. When I am dead, who will love her as I have done? If she should be in misfortune, who will comfort her? when she is old, who will look in her face, and bless her? Would there be any harm in calling upon M——, to know confidentially if he thinks it worth my while to make her an offer the instant it is in my power? Let me have an answer, and save me, if possible, *for* her and *from* myself.[26]

Letter VIII

My dear Friend, Your letter raised me for a moment from the depths of despair; but not hearing from you yesterday or today (as I hoped) I have had a relapse.[27] You say I want to get rid of her. I hope you are more right in your conjectures about her than in this about me. Oh no! believe it, I love her as I do my own soul; my very heart is wedded to her (be she what she may) and I would not hesitate a moment between her and 'an angel from Heaven'. I grant all you say about my self-tormenting folly: but has it been without cause? Has she not refused me again and again with a mixture of scorn and resentment, after going the utmost lengths with a man for whom she now disclaims all affection; and what security can I have for her reserve with others, who will not be restrained by feelings of delicacy towards her, and whom she has probably preferred to me for their want of it. '*She can make no more confidences*' – these words ring for ever in my ears, and will be my death-watch. They can have but one meaning, be sure of it – she always expressed herself with the exactest propriety. That was one of the things for which I loved her – shall I live to hate her for it? My poor fond heart, that brooded over her and the remains of her affections as my only hope of comfort upon earth, cannot brook this new degradation. Who is there so low as me? Who is there besides (I ask) after the homage I have paid her and the caresses she has lavished on me, so vile, so abhorrent to love, to whom such an indignity could have happened? When I think of this (and I think of nothing else) it stifles me. I am pent up in burning, fruitless desires, which can find no vent or object. Am I not hated, repulsed, derided by her whom alone I love or ever did love? I cannot stay in any place, and seek in vain for relief from the sense of her contempt and her ingratitude. I can settle to nothing: what is the use of all I have done? Is it not that very circumstance (my thinking beyond my strength, my feeling more than I need about so many things) that has withered me up, and made me a thing for Love to shrink from and wonder at? Who could ever feel that peace from the touch of her dear hand that I have done; and is it not torn from me for ever? My state is this, that I shall never lie down again at night nor rise up in the morning in peace, nor ever behold my little boy's face with pleasure while I live unless I am restored to her favour. Instead of that delicious feeling I had when she was heavenly-kind to me, and my heart softened and melted in its own tenderness and her sweetness, I am now enclosed in a dungeon of despair. The sky is marble to my thoughts; nature is dead around me, as hope is within me; no object can give me one gleam of satisfaction now, nor the prospect of it in time to come.[28] I wander by the sea-side; and the eternal ocean and lasting despair and her face are before me. Slighted by her, on whom my heart by its last fibre hung, where shall I turn? I wake with her by my side, not as my sweet bedfellow, but as the corpse of my love, without a heart in her bosom, cold, insensible, or struggling from me; and the worm gnaws me, and the sting of unrequited love, and the canker of a hopeless, endless sorrow. I have lost the taste of my food by feverish anxiety; and my favourite beverage, which used to refresh me when I got up, has no moisture in it.[29] Oh! cold, solitary, sepulchral breakfasts, compared with those which I promised myself with her; or which I made when she had been standing an hour by my side, my guardian-angel, my wife, my sister, my sweet friend, my Eve, my all; and had blest me with her seraph kisses! Ah! what I suffer at present only shows what I have enjoyed. But 'the girl is a good girl, if there is goodness in human nature'. I thank you for those words; and I will fall down and worship you, if you can prove them true: and I would not do much less for him that proves her a demon. She is one or the other, that's certain; but I fear the worst. Do let me know if anything has passed: suspense is my greatest punishment. I am going into the country to see if I can work a little in the three weeks I have yet to stay here. Write on the receipt of this, and believe me ever your unspeakably obliged friend.

To Edinburgh

'Stony-hearted' Edinburgh![30] What art thou to me? The dust of thy streets mingles with my tears and blinds me. City of palaces, or of tombs – a quarry, rather than the habitation of men! Art thou like London, that populous hive, with its sunburnt, well-baked, brick-built houses – its public edifices, its theatres, its bridges, its squares, its ladies, and its pomp, its throng of wealth, its outstretched magnitude, and its mighty heart that never lies still?[31] Thy cold grey walls reflect back the leaden melancholy of the soul. The square, hard-edged, unyielding faces of thy inhabitants have no sympathy to impart. What is it to me that I look along the level line of thy tenantless streets, and meet perhaps a lawyer like a grasshopper chirping and skipping, or the daughter of a Highland laird, haughty, fair, and freckled? Or why should I look down your boasted Prince's Street, with the beetle-browed Castle on one side, and the Calton Hill with its proud monument at the further end, and the ridgy steep of Salisbury Crag, cut off abruptly by Nature's boldest hand, and Arthur's Seat overlooking all, like a lioness watching her cubs? Or shall I turn to the far-off Pentland Hills, with Craig-Crook nestling beneath them, where lives the prince of critics and the king of men?[32] Or cast my eye unsated over the Firth of Forth, that from my window of an evening (as I read of Amy and her love)[33] glitters like a broad golden mirror in the sun, and kisses the winding shores of kingly Fife? Oh no! But to thee, to thee I turn, North Berwick-Law,[34] with thy blue cone rising out of summer seas; for thou art the beacon of my banished thoughts, and dost point my way to her, who is my heart's true home. The air is too thin for me, that has not the breath of Love in it; that is not embalmed by her sighs!

A Thought

I am not mad, but my heart is so; and raves within me, fierce and untameable, like a panther in its den, and tries to get loose to its lost mate, and fawn on her hand, and bend lowly at her feet.

Another

Oh! thou dumb heart, lonely, sad, shut up in the prison-house of this rude form, that hast never found a fellow but for an instant, and in very mockery of thy misery, speak, find bleeding words to express thy thoughts, break thy dungeon-gloom, or die pronouncing thy Infelice's name![35]

Another

Within my heart is lurking suspicion, and base fear, and shame and hate; but above all, tyrannous love sits throned, crowned with her graces, silent and in tears.

Letter IX

My dear P——, You have been very kind to me in this business; but I fear even your indulgence for my infirmities is beginning to fail.[36] To what a state am I reduced, and for what? For fancying a little artful vixen to be an angel and a saint, because she affected to look like one, to hide her rank thoughts and deadly purposes. Has she not murdered me under the mask of the tenderest friendship? And why? Because I have loved her with unutterable love, and sought to make her my wife. You say it is my own 'outrageous conduct' that has estranged her: nay, I have been *too gentle* with her. I ask you first in candour whether the ambiguity of her behaviour with respect to me, sitting and fondling a man (circumstanced as I was) sometimes for half a day together, and then declaring she had no love for him beyond common regard, and professing never to marry, was not enough to excite my suspicions, which the different exposures from the conversations below-stairs were not calculated to allay? I ask you what you yourself would have felt or done, if loving her as I did, you had heard what I did, time after time? Did not her mother own to one of the grossest charges (which I shall not repeat)[37] – and is such indelicacy to be reconciled with her pretended character (that character with which I fell in love, and to which I *made love*) without supposing her to be the greatest hypocrite in the world? My unpardonable offence has been that I took her at her word, and was willing to believe her the precise little puritanical person she set up for. After exciting her wayward desires by the fondest embraces and the purest kisses, as if she had been 'made my wedded wife yestreen',[38] or was to become so tomorrow (for that was always my feeling with respect to her) – I did not proceed to gratify them, or to follow up my advantage by any action which should declare, 'I think you a common adventurer, and will see whether you are so or not!' Yet any one but a credulous fool like me would have made the experiment, with whatever violence to himself, as a matter of life and death; for I had every reason to distrust appearances. Her conduct has been of a piece from the beginning. In the midst of her closest and falsest endearments, she has always (with one or two exceptions) disclaimed the natural inference to be drawn from them, and made a verbal reservation, by which she might lead me on in a Fool's Paradise, and make me the tool of her levity, her avarice, and her love of intrigue as long as she liked, and dismiss me whenever it suited her. This, you see, she has done, because my intentions grew serious, and if complied with, would deprive her of *the pleasures of a single life*! Offer marriage to this 'tradesman's daughter, who has as nice a sense of honour as any one can have';[39] and like Lady Bellaston in *Tom Jones*, she *cuts* you immediately in a fit of abhorrence and alarm.[40] Yet she seemed to be of a different mind formerly, when struggling from me in the height of our first intimacy, she exclaimed – 'However I might agree to my own ruin, I never will consent to bring disgrace upon my family!' That I should have spared the traitress after expressions like this, astonishes me when I look back upon it. Yet if it were all to do over again, I know I should act just the same part. Such is her power over me! I cannot run the least risk of offending her – I love her so. When I look in her face, I cannot doubt her truth! Wretched being that I am! I have thrown away my heart and soul upon an unfeeling girl; and my life (that might have been so happy, had she been what I thought her) will soon follow either voluntarily, or by the force of grief, remorse, and disappointment. I cannot get rid of the reflection for an instant, nor even seek relief from its galling pressure. Ah! what a heart she has lost! All the love and affection of my whole life were centred in her, who alone, I thought, of all women had found out my true character, and knew how to value my tenderness. Alas! alas! that this, the only hope, joy, or comfort I ever had, should turn to a mockery, and hang like an ugly film over the remainder of my days! – I was at Roslin Castle yesterday. It lies low in a rude, but sheltered valley, hid from the vulgar gaze, and powerfully reminds one of the old song. The straggling fragments of the russet ruins, suspended smiling and graceful in the air as if they would linger out another century to please the curious beholder, the green larch-trees trembling between with the blue sky and white silver clouds, the wild mountain plants starting out here and there, the date of the year on an old low doorway, but still more, the beds of flowers in orderly decay, that seem to have no hand to tend them, but keep up a sort of traditional remembrance of civilisation in former ages, present altogether a delightful and amiable subject for contemplation. The exquisite beauty of the scene, with the thought of what I should feel, should I ever be restored to her, and have to lead her through such places as my adored, my angel-wife, almost drove me beside myself. For this picture, this ecstatic vision, what have I of late instead as the image of the reality? Demoniacal possessions. I see the young witch seated in another's lap, twining her serpent arms round him, her eye glancing and her cheeks on fire – why does not the hideous thought choke me?[41] Or why do I not go and find out the truth at once? The moonlight streams over the silver waters: the bark is in the bay that might waft me to her, almost with a wish. The mountain-breeze sighs out her name: old ocean with a world of tears murmurs back my woes! Does not my heart yearn to be with her; and shall I not follow its bidding? No, I must wait till I am free; and then I will take my Freedom (a glad prize) and lay it at her feet and tell her my proud love of her that would not brook a rival in her dishonour, and that would have her all or none, and gain her or lose myself for ever! You see by this letter the way I am in, and I hope you will excuse it as the picture of a half-disordered mind. The least respite from my uneasiness (such as I had yesterday) only brings the contrary reflection back upon me, like a flood; and by letting me see the happiness I have lost, makes me feel, by contrast, more acutely what I am doomed to bear.

Letter X[42]

Dear Friend, Here I am at St Bees once more, amid the scenes which I greeted in their barrenness in winter; but which have now put on their full green attire that shows luxuriant to the eye, but speaks a tale of sadness to this heart widowed of its last, its dearest, its only hope! Oh! lovely Bees-Inn! here I composed a volume of law-cases, here I wrote my enamoured follies to her, thinking her human, and that all below was not the fiend's[43] – here I got two cold, sullen answers from the little witch, and here I was ——[44] and I was damned. I thought the revisiting the old haunts would have soothed me for a time, but it only brings back the sense of what I have suffered for her and of her unkindness the more strongly, till I cannot endure the recollection. I eye the Heavens in dumb despair, or vent my sorrows in the desert air. 'To the winds, to the waves, to the rocks I complain' – you may suppose with what effect! I fear I shall be obliged to return. I am tossed about (backwards and forwards) by my passion, so as to become ridiculous. I can now understand how it is that mad people never remain in the same place – they are moving on for ever, *from themselves*!

Do you know, you would have been delighted with the effect of the Northern twilight on this romantic country as I rode along last night? The hills and groves and herds of cattle were seen reposing in the grey dawn of midnight, as in a moonlight without shadow. The whole wide canopy of Heaven shed its reflex light upon them, like a pure crystal mirror. No sharp points, no petty details, no hard contrasts – every object was seen softened yet distinct, in its simple outline and natural tones, transparent with an inward light, breathing its own mild lustre. The landscape altogether was like an airy piece of mosaic-work, or like one of Poussin's broad massy landscapes or Titian's lovely pastoral scenes. Is it not so, that poets see nature, veiled to the sight, but revealed to the soul in visionary grace and grandeur! I confess the sight touched me; and might have removed all sadness except mine. So (I thought) the light of her celestial face once shone into my soul, and wrapped me in a heavenly trance. The sense I have of beauty raises me for a moment above myself, but depresses me the more afterwards, when I recollect how it is thrown away in vain admiration, and that it only makes me more susceptible of pain from the mortifications I meet with. Would I had never seen her! I might then not indeed have been happy, but at least I might have passed my life in peace, and have sunk into forgetfulness without a pang. The noble scenery in this country mixes with my passion, and refines, but does not relieve it. I was at Stirling Castle not long ago. It gave me no pleasure. The declivity seemed to me abrupt, not sublime; for in truth I did not shrink back from it with terror. The weather-beaten towers were stiff and formal: the air was damp and chill: the river winded its dull, slimy way like a snake along the marshy grounds: and the dim misty tops of Ben Leddi, and the lovely Highlands (woven fantastically of thin air) mocked my embraces and tempted my longing eyes like her, the sole queen and mistress of my thoughts! I never found my contemplations on this subject so subtilised and at the same time so desponding as on that occasion. I wept myself almost blind, and I gazed at the broad golden sunset through my tears that fell in showers. As I trod the green mountain turf, oh! how I wished to be laid beneath it – in one grave with her – that I might sleep with her in that cold bed, my hand in hers, and my heart for ever still – while worms should taste her sweet body, that I had never tasted! There was a time when I could bear solitude; but it is too much for me at present. Now I am no sooner left to myself than I am lost in infinite space, and look round me in vain for support or comfort. She was my stay, my hope: without her hand to cling to, I stagger like an infant on the edge of a precipice. The universe without her is one wide, hollow abyss, in which my harassed thoughts can find no resting-place. I must break off here; for the *hysterica passio*[45] – comes upon me, and threatens to unhinge my reason.

Letter XI

My dear and good Friend, I am afraid I trouble you with my querulous epistles, but this is probably the last. Tomorrow or the next day decides my fate with respect to the divorce, when I expect to be a free man.[46] In vain! Was it not for her and to lay my freedom at her feet, that I consented to this step which has cost me infinite perplexity, and now to be discarded for the first pretender that came in her way! If so, I hardly think I can survive it. You who have been a favourite with women, do not know what it is to be deprived of one's only hope, and to have it turned to shame and disappointment. There is nothing in the world left that can afford me one drop of comfort – *this* I feel more and more. Everything is to me a mockery of pleasure, like her love. The breeze does not cool me: the blue sky does not cheer me. I gaze only on her face averted from me – alas! the only face that ever was turned fondly to me! And why am I thus treated? Because I wanted her to be mine for ever in love or friendship, and did not push my gross familiarities as far as I might. 'Why can you not go on as we have done, and say nothing about the word, *forever*?' Was it not plain from this that she even then meditated an escape from me to some less sentimental lover? 'Do you allow anyone else to do so?' I said to her once, as I was toying with her. 'No, not now!' was her answer; that is, because there was nobody else in the house to take freedoms with her. I was very well as a stopgap, but I was to be nothing more. While the coast was clear, I had it all my own way: but the instant C—— came, she flung herself at his head in the most barefaced way,[47] ran breathless up stairs before him, blushed when his foot was heard, watched for him in the passage, and was sure to be in close conference with him when he went down again. It was then my mad proceedings commenced. No wonder. Had I not reason to be jealous of every appearance of familiarity with others, knowing how easy she had been with me at first, and that she only grew shy when I did not take farther liberties? What has her character to rest upon but her attachment to me, which she now denies, not modestly, but impudently? Will you yourself say that if she had all along no particular regard for me, she will not do as much or more with other more likely men? 'She has had', she says, 'enough of my conversation', so it could not be that! Ah! my friend, it was not to be supposed I should ever meet even with the outward demonstrations of regard from any woman but a common trader in the endearments of love! I have tasted the sweets of the well-practised illusion, and now feel the bitterness of knowing what a bliss I am deprived of, and must ever be deprived of. Intolerable conviction! Yet I might, I believe, have won her by other methods; but some demon held my hand. How indeed could

I offer her the least insult when I worshipped her very footsteps; and even now pay her divine honours from my inmost heart, whenever I think of her, abased and brutalised as I have been by that Circean cup of kisses,[48] of enchantments, of which I have drunk! I am choked, withered, dried up with chagrin, remorse, despair, from which I have not a moment's respite, day or night. I have always some horrid dream about her, and wake wondering what is the matter that 'she is no longer the same to me as ever?' I thought at least we should always remain dear friends, if nothing more – did she not talk of coming to live with me only the day before I left her in the winter? But 'she's gone, I am abused, and my revenge must be to *love* her!'[49] – Yet she knows that one line, one word would save me, the cruel, heartless destroyer! I see nothing for it but madness, unless Friday brings a change, or unless she is willing to let me go back. You must know I wrote to her to that purpose, but it was a very quiet, sober letter, begging pardon, and professing reform for the future, and all that. What effect it will have, I know not. I was forced to get out of the way of her answer, till Friday came.

Ever yours.

To S. L.

My dear Miss L——, *Evil to them that evil think,* is an old saying; and I have found it a true one. I have ruined myself by my unjust suspicions of you. Your sweet friendship was the balm of my life; and I have lost it, I fear for ever, by one fault and folly after another. What would I give to be restored to the place in your esteem, which, you assured me, I held only a few months ago! Yet I was not contented, but did all I could to torment myself and harass you by endless doubts and jealousy. Can you not forget and forgive the past, and judge of me by my conduct in future? Can you not take all my follies in the lump, and say like a good, generous girl, 'Well, I'll think no more of them?' In a word, may I come back, and try to behave better? A line to say so would be an additional favour to so many already received by

Your obliged friend,
And sincere well-wisher.

Letter XII to C. P——

I have no answer from her. I'm mad. I wish you to call on M—— in confidence, to say I intend to make her an offer of my hand, and that I will write to her father to that effect the instant I am free, and ask him whether he thinks it will be to any purpose, and what he would advise me to do.

Unaltered Love

Love is not love that alteration finds:
Oh no! it is an ever-fixed mark,
That looks on tempests and is never shaken.[50]

Shall I not love her for herself alone, in spite of fickleness and folly? To love her for her regard to me, is not to love her, but myself. She has robbed me of herself: shall she also rob me of my love of her? Did I not live on her smile? Is it less sweet because it is withdrawn from me? Did I not adore her every grace? Does she bend less enchantingly, because she has turned from me to another? Is my love then in the power of fortune, or of her caprice? No, I will have it lasting as it is pure; and I will make a Goddess of her, and build a temple to her in my heart, and worship her on indestructible altars, and raise statues to her: and my homage shall be unblemished as her unrivalled symmetry of form; and when that fails, the memory of it shall survive; and my bosom shall be proof to scorn, as hers has been to pity; and I will pursue her with an unrelenting love, and sue to be her slave, and tend her steps without notice and without reward; and serve her living, and mourn for her when dead. And thus my love will have shown itself superior to her hate; and I shall triumph and then die. This is my idea of the only true and heroic love! Such is mine for her.

Perfect Love

Perfect love has this advantage in it, that it leaves the possessor of it nothing farther to desire. There is one object (at least) in which the soul finds absolute content, for which it seeks to live, or dares to die. The heart has as it were filled up the moulds of the imagination. The truth of passion keeps pace with and outvies the extravagance of mere language. There are no words so fine, no flattery so soft, that there is not a sentiment beyond them, that it is impossible to express, at the bottom of the heart where true love is. What idle sounds the common phrases, *adorable creature, angel, divinity,* are? What a proud reflection it is to have a feeling answering to all these, rooted in the breast, unalterable, unutterable, to which all other feelings are light and vain! Perfect love reposes on the object of its choice, like the halcyon on the wave; and the air of heaven is around it.

From C.P., Esq.

London, July 4th, 1822

I have seen M——! Now, my dear H., let me entreat and adjure you to take what I have to tell you, *for what it is worth* – neither for less, nor more. In the first place, I have learned nothing decisive from him. This, as you will at once see, is, as far as it goes, good. I am either to hear from him, or see him again in a day or two; but I thought you would like to know what passed inconclusive as it was – so I write without delay, and in great haste to save a post. I found him frank, and even friendly in his manner to me, and in his views respecting you. I think that he is sincerely sorry for your situation; and he feels that the person who has placed you in that situation, is not much less awkwardly situated herself; and he professes that he would willingly do what he can for the good of both. But he sees great difficulties attending the affair – which he frankly professes to consider as an altogether unfortunate one. With respect to the marriage, he seems to see the most formidable objections to it, on both sides; but yet he by no means decidedly says that it cannot, or that it ought not to take place. These, mind you, are his own feelings on the subject: but the most important point I learn from him is this, that he is not prepared to use his influence either way – that the rest of the family are of the same way of feeling; and that, in fact, the thing must and does entirely rest with herself. To learn this was, as you see, gaining a great point. When I then endeavoured to ascertain whether he knew anything decisive as to what are her views on the subject, I found that he did not. He has an opinion on the subject, and he didn't scruple to tell me what it was; but he has no positive knowledge. In short, he believes, from what he learns from herself (and he had purposely seen her on the subject, in consequence of my application to him) that she is at present indisposed to the marriage; but he is not prepared to say positively that she will not consent to it.

Now all this, coming from him in the most frank and unaffected manner, and without any appearance of cant, caution, or reserve, I take to be most important as it respects your views, whatever they may be; and certainly much more favourable to them (I confess it) than I was prepared to expect, supposing them to remain as they were. In fact, as I said before, the affair rests entirely with herself. They are none of them disposed either to further the marriage, or throw any insurmountable obstacles in the way of it; and what is more important than all, they are evidently by no means *certain* that she may not, at some future period, consent to it; or they would, for her sake as well as their own, let you know as much flatly, and put an end to the affair at once.

Seeing in how frank and straightforward a manner he received what I had to say to him, and replied to it, I proceeded to ask him what were *his* views, and what were likely to be *hers* (in case she did not consent) as to whether you should return to live in the house; – but I added, without waiting for his answer, that if she intended to persist in treating you as she had done for some time past, it would be worse than madness for you to think of returning. I added that, in case you did return, all you would expect from her would be that she would treat you with civility and kindness – that she would continue to evince that friendly feeling towards you, that she had done for a great length of time, etc. To this, he said, he could really give no decisive reply, but that he should be most happy if, by any intervention of his, he could conduce to your comfort; but he seemed to think that for you to return on any express understanding that she should behave to you in any particular manner, would be to place her in a most awkward situation. He went somewhat at length into this point, and talked very reasonably about it; the result, however, was that he would not throw any obstacles in the way of your return, or of her treating you as a friend, etc., nor did it appear that he believed she would refuse to do so. And, finally, we parted on the understanding that he would see them on the subject, and ascertain what could be done for the comfort of all parties: though he was of opinion that if you could make up your mind to break off the acquaintance altogether, it would be the best plan of all. I am to hear from him again in a day or two. Well, what do you say to all this? Can you turn it to any thing but good – comparative good? If you would know what I say to it, it is this: – she is still to be won by wise and prudent conduct on your part; she was always to have been won by such;

– and if she is lost, it has been (not, as you sometimes suppose, because you have not carried that unwise, may I not say *unworthy*? conduct still farther, but) because you gave way to it at all. Of course I use the terms 'wise' and 'prudent' with reference to your object. Whether the pursuit of that object is wise, only yourself can judge. I say she has all along been to be won, and she still is to be won; and all that stands in the way of your views at this moment is your past conduct. They are all of them, every soul, frightened at you; they have *seen* enough of you to make them so; and they have doubtless heard ten times more than they have seen, or than anyone else has seen. They are all of them, including M—— (and particularly she herself) frightened out of their wits, as to what might be your treatment of her if she were yours; and they dare not trust you – they will not trust you, at present.[51] I do not say that they will trust you, or rather that *she* will, for it all depends on her, when you have gone through a probation, but I am sure that she will not trust you till you have. You will, I hope, not be angry with me when I say that she would be a fool if she did. If she were to accept you at present, and without knowing more of you, even I should begin to suspect that she had an unworthy motive for doing it. Let me not forget to mention what is perhaps as important a point as any, as it regards the marriage. I of course stated to M—— that when you are free, you are prepared to make her a formal offer of your hand; but I begged him, if he was certain that such an offer would be refused, to tell me so plainly at once, that I might endeavour, in that case, to dissuade you from subjecting yourself to the pain of such a refusal. *He would not tell me that he was certain.* He said his opinion was that she would not accept your offer, but still he seemed to think that there would be no harm in making it! – One word more, and a very important one. He once, and without my referring in the slightest manner to that part of the subject, spoke of her as a *good girl,* and *likely to make any man an excellent wife*! Do you think if she were a bad girl (and if she were, he must know her to be so) he would have dared to do this, under these circumstances? – And once, in speaking of *his* not being a fit person to set his face against 'marrying for love', he added 'I did so myself, and out of that house; and I have had reason to rejoice at it ever since.' And mind (for I anticipate your cursed suspicions) I'm certain, at least, if manner can entitle one to be certain of any thing, that he said all this spontaneously, and without any understood motive; and I'm certain, too, that he knows you to be a person that it would not do to play any tricks of this kind with. I believe – (and all this would never have entered my thoughts, but that I know it will enter yours) I believe that even if they thought (as you have sometimes supposed they do) that she needs whitewashing, or making an honest woman of, you would be the last person they would think of using for such a purpose, for they know (as well as I do) that you couldn't fail to find out the trick in a month, and would turn her into the street the next moment, though she were twenty times your wife – and that, as to the consequences of doing so, you would laugh at them, even if you couldn't escape from them – I shall lose the post if I say more.

Believe me,

Ever truly your friend,

C. P.

Letter XIII

My dear P——, You have saved my life. If I do not keep friends with her now, I deserve to be hanged, drawn, and quartered. She is an angel from Heaven, and you cannot pretend I ever said a word to the contrary! The little rogue must have liked me from the first, or she never could have stood all these hurricanes without slipping her cable. What could she find in me? 'I have mistook my person all this while', etc.[52] Do you know I saw a picture, the very pattern of her, the other day, at Dalkeith Palace (*Hope finding Fortune in the Sea*),[53] just before this blessed news came, and the resemblance drove me almost out of my senses. Such delicacy, such fulness, such perfect softness, such buoyancy, such grace! If it is not the very image of her, I am no judge. You have the face to doubt my making the best husband in the world; you might as well doubt it if I was married to one of the Houris of Paradise.[54] She is a saint, an angel, a love. If she deceives me again, she kills me. But I will have such a kiss when I get back, as shall last me twenty years. May God bless her for not utterly disowning and destroying me! What an exquisite little creature it is, and how she holds out to the last in her system of consistent contradictions! Since I wrote to you about making a formal proposal, I have had her face constantly before me, looking so like some faultless marble statue, as cold, as fixed and graceful as ever statue did; the expression (nothing was ever like *that*!) seemed to say – 'I wish I could love you better than I do, but still I will be yours.' No, I'll never believe again that she will not be mine; for I think she was made on purpose for me. If there's anyone else that understands that turn of her head as I do, I'll give her up without scruple. I have made up my mind to this, never to dream of another woman, while she even thinks it worth her while to *refuse to have me.* You see I am not hard to please, after all. Did M—— know of the intimacy that had subsisted between us? Or did you hint at it? I think it would be a *clencher*, if he did. How ought I to behave when I go back? Advise a fool, who had nearly lost a Goddess by his folly. The thing was, I could not think it possible she would ever like *me*. Her taste is singular, but not the worse for that. I'd rather have her love, or liking (call it what you will) than empires. I deserve to call her mine; for nothing else *can* atone for what I've gone through for her. I hope your next letter will not reverse all, and then I shall be happy till I see her, – one of the blest when I do see her, if she looks like my own beautiful love. I may perhaps write a line when I come to my right wits. – Farewell at present, and thank you a thousand times for what you have done for your poor friend.

P.S. I like what M—— said about her sister, much. There are good people in the world: I begin to see it, and believe it.

Letter the Last

Dear P——, Tomorrow is the decisive day that makes me or mars me.[55] I will let you know the result by a line added to this. Yet what signifies it, since either way I have little hope there, 'whence alone my hope cometh'![56] You must know I am strangely in the dumps at this present writing. My reception with her is doubtful, and my fate is then certain. The hearing of your happiness has, I own, made me thoughtful.[57] It is just what I proposed to her to do – to have crossed the Alps with me, to sail on sunny seas, to bask in Italian skies, to have visited Vevai and the rocks of Meillerie, and to have repeated to her on the spot the story of Julia and St Preux,[58] and to have shown her all that my heart had stored up for her – but on my forehead alone is written – REJECTED! Yet I too could have adored as fervently, and loved as tenderly as others, had I been permitted. You are going abroad, you say, happy in making happy. Where shall I be? In the grave, I hope, or else in her arms. To me, alas! there is no sweetness out of her sight, and that sweetness has turned to bitterness, I fear; that gentleness to sullen scorn!

Still I hope for the best. If she will but *have* me, I'll make her love me: and I think her not giving a positive answer looks like it, and also shows that there is no one else. Her holding out to the last also, I think, proves that she was never to have been gained but with honour. She's a strange, almost an inscrutable girl: but if I once win her consent, I shall kill her with kindness.[59] Will you let me have a sight of *somebody*[60] before you go? I should be most proud. I was in hopes to have got away by the steam-boat tomorrow, but owing to the business not coming on till then, I cannot; and may not be in town for another week, unless I come by the mail, which I am strongly tempted to do. In the latter case I shall be *there,* and visible on Saturday evening. Will you look in and see about eight o'clock? I wish much to see you and her and J.H.[61] and my little boy once more; and then, if she is not what she once was to me, I care not if I die that instant. I will conclude here till tomorrow, as I am getting into my old melancholy. –

It is all over, and I am my own man, and yours ever –

Part III

Addressed to J. S. K——[1]

My dear K——, It is all over, and I know my fate. I told you I would send you word, if anything decisive happened; but an impenetrable mystery hung over the affair till lately. It is at last (by the merest accident in the world) dissipated; and I keep my promise, both for your satisfaction, and for the ease of my own mind.

You remember the morning when I said 'I will go and repose my sorrows at the foot of Ben Lomond' – and when from Dumbarton Bridge its giant-shadow, clad in air and sunshine, appeared in view. We had a pleasant day's walk.[2] We passed Smollett's monument on the road (somehow these poets touch one in reflection more than most military heroes) – talked of old times; you repeated Logan's beautiful verses to the cuckoo,* which I wanted to compare with Wordsworth's, but my courage failed me; you then told me some passages of an early attachment which was suddenly broken off; we considered together which was the most to be pitied, a disappointment in love where the attachment was mutual or one where there has been no return, and we both agreed, I think, that the former was best to be endured, and that to have the consciousness of it a companion for life was the least evil of the two, as there was a secret sweetness that took off the bitterness and the sting of regret, and 'the memory of what once had been' atoned, in some measure, and at intervals, for what 'never more could be'.[3] In the other case, there was nothing to look back to with tender satisfaction, no redeeming trait, not even a possibility of turning it to good. It left behind it not cherished sighs, but stifled pangs. The

* Sweet bird, thy bower is ever green,
  Thy sky is ever clear;
Thou hast no sorrow in thy song,
  No winter in thy year.

So they begin. It was the month of May; the cuckoo sang shrouded in some woody copse; the showers fell between whiles; my friend repeated the lines with native enthusiasm in a clear manly voice, still resonant of youth and hope. Mr Wordsworth will excuse me, if in these circumstances I declined entering the field with his profounder metaphysical strain, and kept my preference to myself.

galling sense of it did not bring moisture into the eyes, but dried up the heart ever after. One had been my fate, the other had been yours!

You startled me every now and then from my reverie by the robust voice, in which you asked the country people (by no means prodigal of their answers) – 'If there was any trout-fishing in those streams?' – and our dinner at Luss set us up for the rest of our day's march. The sky now became overcast; but this, I think, added to the effect of the scene. The road to Tarbet is superb. It is on the very verge of the lake – hard, level, rocky, with low stone bridges constantly flung across it, and fringed with birch trees, just then budding into spring, behind which, as through a slight veil, you saw the huge shadowy form of Ben Lomond. It lifts its enormous but graceful bulk direct from the edge of the water without any projecting lowlands, and has in this respect much the advantage of Skiddaw. Loch Lomond comes upon you by degrees as you advance, unfolding and then withdrawing its conscious beauties like an accomplished coquet. You are struck with the point of a rock, the arch of a bridge, the Highland huts (like the first rude habitations of men) dug out of the soil, built of turf, and covered with brown heather, a sheepcote, some straggling cattle feeding half-way down a precipice; but as you advance farther on, the view expands into the perfection of lake scenery. It is nothing (or your eye is caught by nothing) but water, earth, and sky. Ben Lomond waves to the right, in its simple majesty, cloud-capped or bare, and descending to a point at the head of the lake, shows the Trossachs beyond, tumbling about their blue ridges like woods waving; to the left is the Cobbler, whose top is like a castle shattered in pieces and nodding to its ruin; and at your side rise the shapes of round pastoral hills, green, fleeced with herds, and retiring into mountainous bays and upland valleys, where solitude and peace might make their lasting home, if peace were to be found in solitude! That it was not always so, I was a sufficient proof; for there was one image that alone haunted me in the midst of all this sublimity and beauty, and turned it to a mockery and a dream!

The snow on the mountain would not let us ascend; and being weary of waiting and of being visited by the guide every two hours to let us know that the weather would not do, we returned, you homewards, and I to London –

Italiam, Italiam![4]

You know the anxious expectations with which I set out: – now hear the result.

As the vessel sailed up the Thames, the air thickened with the consciousness of being near her, and I 'heaved her name pantingly forth'.[5] As I approached the house, I could not help thinking of the lines –

> How near am I to a happiness,
> That earth exceeds not! Not another like it.
> The treasures of the deep are not so precious
> As are the conceal'd comforts of a man
> Lock'd up in woman's love. I scent the air
> Of blessings when I come but near the house.
> What a delicious breath true love sends forth!
> The violet-beds not sweeter. Now for a welcome
> Able to draw men's envies upon man:
> A kiss now that will hang upon my lip,
> As sweet as morning dew upon a rose,
> And full as long![6]

I saw her, but I saw at the first glance that there was something amiss. It was with much difficulty and after several pressing entreaties that she was prevailed on to come up into the room; and when she did, she stood at the door, cold, distant, averse; and when at length she was persuaded by my repeated remonstrances to come and take my hand, and I offered to touch her lips, she turned her head and shrunk from my embraces, as if quite alienated or mortally offended. I asked what it could mean? What had I done in her absence to have incurred her displeasure? Why had she not written to me? I could get only short, sullen, disconnected answers, as if there was something labouring in her mind which she either could not or would not impart. I hardly knew how to bear this first reception after so long an absence, and so different from the one my sentiments towards her merited; but I thought it possible it might be prudery (as I had returned without having actually accomplished what I went about)[7] or that she had taken offence at something in my letters. She saw how much I was hurt. I asked her, 'If she was altered since I went away?' – 'No'. 'If there was any one else who had been so fortunate as to gain her favourable opinion?' – 'No, there was no one else.' 'What was it then? Was it anything in my letters? Or had I displeased her by letting Mr P—— know she wrote to me?' – 'No, not at all; but she did not apprehend my last letter required any answer, or she would have replied to it.' All this appeared to me very unsatisfactory and evasive; but I could get no more from her, and was obliged to let her go with a heavy, foreboding heart. I however found that C—— was gone, and no one else had been there, of whom I had cause to be jealous. 'Should I see her on the morrow?' – 'She believed so, but she could not promise.' The next morning she did not appear with the breakfast as usual. At this I grew somewhat uneasy. The little Bonaparte, however, was placed in its old position on the mantlepiece, which I considered as a sort of recognition of old times. I saw her once or twice casually; nothing particular happened till the next day, which was Sunday. I took occasion to go into the parlour for the newspaper, which she gave me with a gracious smile, and seemed tolerably frank and cordial. This of course acted as a spell upon me. I walked out with my little boy, intending to go and dine out at one or two places, but I found that I still contrived to bend my steps towards her, and I went back to take tea at home. While we were out, I talked to William about Sarah, saying that she too was unhappy, and asking him to make it up with her. He said, if she was unhappy, he would not bear her malice any more. When she came up with the tea-things, I said to her, 'William has something to say to you – I believe he wants to be friends.' On which he said in his abrupt, hearty manner, 'Sarah, I'm sorry if I've ever said anything to vex you' – so they shook hands, and she said, smiling affably – '*Then* I'll think no more of it!' I added – 'I see you've brought me back my little Bonaparte' – She answered with tremulous softness – 'I told you I'd keep it safe for you!' – as if her pride and pleasure in doing so had been equal, and she had, as it were, thought of nothing during my absence but how to greet me with this proof of her fidelity on my return. I cannot describe her manner. Her words are few and simple; but you can have no idea of the exquisite, unstudied, irresistible graces with which she accompanies them, unless you can suppose a Greek statue to smile, move, and speak. Those lines in Tibullus seem to have been written on purpose for her –

> Quicquid agit quoquo vestigià vertit.
> Componit furtim, subsequiturque decor.[8]

Or what do you think of those in a modern play, which might actually have been composed with an eye to this little trifler –

– See with what a waving air she goes
Along the corridor. How like a fawn!
Yet statelier. No sound (however soft)
Nor gentlest echo telleth when she treads,
But every motion of her shape doth seem
Hallowed by silence. So did Hebe grow
Among the gods a paragon! Away, I'm grown
The very fool of Love![9]

The truth is, I never saw anything like her, nor I never shall again. How then do I console myself for the loss of her? Shall I tell you, but you will not mention it again? I am foolish enough to believe that she and I, in spite of every thing, shall be sitting together over a sea-coal fire, a comfortable good old couple, twenty years hence! But to my narrative. –

I was delighted with the alteration in her manner, and said, referring to the bust – 'You know it is not mine, but yours; I gave it you; nay, I have given you all – my heart, and whatever I possess, is yours! She seemed good-humouredly to decline this *carte blanche* offer, and waved, like a thing of enchantment, out of the room. False calm! – Deceitful smiles! – Short interval of peace, followed by lasting woe! I sought an interview with her that same evening. I could not get her to come any farther than the door. 'She was busy – she could hear what I had to say there.' 'Why do you seem to avoid me as you do? Not one five minutes' conversation, for the sake of old acquaintance? Well, then, for the sake of *the little image*!' The appeal seemed to have lost its efficacy; the charm was broken; she remained immoveable. 'Well, then I must come to you, if you will not run away.' I went and sat down in a chair near the door, and took her hand, and talked to her for three quarters of an hour; and she listened patiently, thoughtfully, and seemed a good deal affected by what I said. I told her how much I had felt, how much I had suffered for her in my absence, and how much I had been hurt by her sudden silence, for which I knew not how to account. I could have done nothing to offend her while I was away; and my letters were, I hoped, tender and respectful. I had had but one thought ever present with me; her image never quitted my side, alone or in company, to delight or distract me. Without her I could have no peace, nor ever should again, unless she would behave to me as she had done formerly. There was no abatement of my regard to her; why was she so changed? I said to her, 'Ah! Sarah, when I think that it is only a year ago that you were everything to me I could wish, and that now you seem lost to me for ever, the month of May (the name of which ought to be a signal for joy and hope) strikes chill to my heart. How different is this meeting from that delicious parting, when you seemed never weary of repeating the proofs of your regard and tenderness, and it was with difficulty we tore ourselves asunder at last! I am ten thousand times fonder of you than I was then, and ten thousand times more unhappy.' 'You have no reason to be so; my feelings towards you are the same as they ever were.' I told her 'She was my all of hope or comfort: my passion for her grew stronger every time I saw her.' She answered, 'She was sorry for it; for *that* she never could return.' I said something about looking ill: she said in her pretty, mincing, emphatic way, 'I despise looks!' So, thought I, it is not that; and she says there's no one else: it must be some strange air she gives herself, in consequence of the approaching change in my circumstances. She has been probably advised not to give up till all is fairly over, and then she will be my own sweet girl again. All this time she was standing just outside the door, my hand in hers (would that they could have grown together!) she was dressed in a loose morning-gown, her hair curled beautifully; she stood with her profile to me, and looked down the whole time. No expression was ever more soft or perfect. Her whole attitude, her whole form, was dignity and bewitching grace. I said to her, 'You look like a queen, my love, adorned with your own graces!' I grew idolatrous, and would have kneeled to her. She made a movement, as if she was displeased. I tried to draw her towards me. She wouldn't. I then got up, and offered to kiss her at parting. I found she obstinately refused. This stung me to the quick. It was the first time in her life she had ever done so. There must be some new bar between us to produce these continued denials; and she had not even esteem enough left to tell me so. I followed her half-way downstairs, but to no purpose, and returned into my room, confirmed in my most dreadful surmises. I could bear it no longer. I gave way to all the fury of disappointed hope and jealous passion. I was made the dupe of trick and cunning, killed with cold, sullen scorn; and, after all the agony I had suffered, could obtain no explanation why I was subjected to it. I was still to be tantalised, tortured, made the cruel sport of one, for whom I would have sacrificed all. I tore the locket which contained her hair (and which I used to wear continually in my bosom, as the precious token of her dear regard) from my neck, and trampled it in pieces. I then dashed the little Bonaparte on the ground, and stamped upon it, as one of her instruments of mockery. I could not stay in the room; I could not leave it; my rage, my despair were uncontrollable. I shrieked curses on her name, and on her false love; and the scream I uttered (so pitiful and so piercing was it, that the sound of it terrified me) instantly brought the whole house, father, mother, lodgers and all, into the room. They thought I was destroying her and myself. I had gone into the bedroom, merely to hide away from myself, and as I came out of it, raging-mad with the new sense of present shame and lasting misery, Mrs E—— said, 'She's in there! He has got her in there!' thinking the cries had proceeded from her, and that I had been offering her violence. 'Oh! no,' I said, 'She's in no danger from me; I am not the person'; and tried to burst from this scene of degradation. The mother endeavoured to stop me, and said, 'For God's sake, don't go out, Mr ——! For God's sake, don't!' Her father, who was not, I believe, in the secret, and was therefore justly scandalised at such outrageous conduct, said angrily, 'Let him go! Why should he stay?' I however sprang down stairs, and as they called out to me, 'What is it? – What has she done to you?' I answered, 'She has murdered me! – She has destroyed me for ever! – She has doomed my soul to perdition!' I rushed out of the house, thinking to quit it forever; but I was no sooner in the street, than the desolation and the darkness became greater, more intolerable; and the eddying violence of my passion drove me back to the source, from whence it sprung. This unexpected explosion, with the conjectures to which it would give rise, could not be very agreeable to the *precieuse* or her family; and when I went back, the father was waiting at the door, as if anticipating this sudden turn of my feelings, with no friendly aspect. I said, 'I have to beg pardon, Sir; but my mad fit is over, and I wish to say a few words to you in private.' He seemed to hesitate, but some uneasy forebodings on his own account, probably, prevailed over his resentment; or, perhaps (as philosophers have a desire to know the cause of thunder) it was a natural curiosity to know what circumstances of provocation had given rise to such an extraordinary scene of confusion. When we reached my room, I requested him to be seated. I said, 'It is true, Sir, I have lost my peace of mind for ever, but at present I am quite calm and collected, and I wish to explain to you why I have behaved in so extravagant a way, and to ask for your advice and intercession.' He appeared satisfied, and I went on. I had no chance either of exculpating myself, or of probing the question to the bottom, but by stating the naked truth, and therefore I said at once, 'Sarah told me, Sir (and I never shall forget the way in which she told me, fixing her dove's eyes upon me, and looking a thousand tender reproaches for the loss of that good opinion, which she held dearer than all the world) she told me, Sir, that as you one day passed the door, which stood ajar, you saw her in an attitude which a good deal startled you; I mean sitting in my lap, with her arms round my neck, and mine twined round her in the fondest manner. What I wished to ask was, whether this was actually the case, or whether it was a mere invention of her own, to enhance the sense of my obligations to her; for I begin to doubt everything?' – 'Indeed, it was so; and very much surprised and hurt I was to see it.' 'Well then, Sir, I can only say, that as you saw her sitting then, so she had been sitting for the last year and a half, almost every day of her life, by the hour together; and you may judge yourself, knowing what a nice modest-looking girl she is, whether, after having been admitted to such intimacy with so sweet a creature, and for so long a time, it is not enough to make any one frantic to be received by her as I have been since my return, without any provocation given or cause assigned for it.' The old man answered very seriously, and, as I think, sincerely, 'What you now tell me, Sir, mortifies and shocks me as much as it can do yourself. I had no idea such a thing was possible. I was much pained at what I saw; but I thought it an accident, and that it would never happen again.' 'It was a constant habit; it has happened a hundred times since, and a thousand before. I lived on her caresses as my daily food, nor can I live without them.' So I told him the whole story,[10] 'what conjurations, and what mighty magic I won his daughter with',[11] to be anything but *mine for life*. Nothing could well exceed his astonishment and apparent mortification. 'What I had said', he owned, had left a weight upon his mind that he should not easily get rid of.' I told him, 'For myself, I never could recover the blow I had received. I thought, however, for her own sake, she ought to alter her present behaviour. Her marked neglect and dislike, so far from justifying, left her former intimacies without excuse; for nothing could reconcile them to propriety, or even a pretence to common decency, but either love, or friendship so strong and pure that it could put on the guise of love. She was certainly a singular girl. Did she think it right and becoming to be free with strangers, and strange to old friends?' I frankly declared, 'I did not see how it was in human nature for any one who was not rendered callous to such familiarities by bestowing them indiscriminately on every one, to grant the extreme and continued indulgences she had done to me, without either liking the man at first, or coming to like him in the end, in spite of herself. When my addresses had nothing, and could have nothing honourable in them, she gave them every encouragement; when I wished to make them honourable, she treated them with the utmost contempt. The terms we had been all along on were such as if she had been to be my bride next day. It was only when I wished her actually to become so, to ensure her own character and my happiness, that she shrunk back with precipitation and panic-fear. There seemed to me something wrong in all this; a want both of common propriety, and I might say, of natural feeling; yet, with all her faults, I loved her, and ever should, beyond any other human being. I had drank in the poison of her sweetness too long ever to be cured of it; and though I might find it to be poison in the end, it was still in my veins. My only ambition was to be permitted to live with her, and to die in her arms. Be she what she would, treat me how she would, I felt that my soul was wedded to hers; and were she a mere lost creature, I would try to snatch her from perdition, and marry her tomorrow if she would have me. That was the question – "Would she have me, or would she not?"' He said he could not tell; but should not attempt to put any constraint upon her inclinations, one way or other. I acquiesced, and added, that 'I had brought all this upon myself, by acting contrary to the suggestions of my friend, Mr ——, who had desired me to take no notice whether she came near me or kept away, whether she smiled or frowned, was kind or contemptuous – all you have to do, is to wait patiently for a month till you are your own man, as you will be in all probability; then make her an offer of your hand, and if she refuses, there's an end of the matter.' Mr L. said, 'Well, Sir, and I don't think you can follow a better advice!' I took this as at least a sort of negative encouragement, and so we parted.

To the Same

(in continuation)

My dear Friend, The next day I felt almost as sailors must do after a violent storm over-night, that has subsided towards daybreak. The morning was a dull and stupid calm, and I found she was unwell, in consequence of what had happened. In the evening I grew more uneasy, and determined on going into the country for a week or two. I gathered up the fragments of the locket of her hair, and the little bronze statue, which were strewed about the floor, kissed them, folded them up in a sheet of paper, and sent them to her, with these lines written in pencil on the outside – '*Pieces of a broken heart, to be kept in remembrance of the unhappy. Farewell.*' No notice was taken; nor did I expect any. The following morning I requested Betsey to pack up my box for me, as I should go out of town the next day, and at the same time wrote a note to her sister to say, I should take it as a favour if she would please to accept of the enclosed copies of the *Vicar of Wakefield, The Man of Feeling,* and *Nature and Art,*[12] in lieu of three volumes of my own writings, which I had given her on different occasions, in the course of our acquaintance. I was piqued, in fact, that she should have these to show as proofs of my weakness, and as if I thought the way to win her was by plaguing her with my own performances. She sent me word back that the books I had sent were of no use to her, and that I should have those I wished for in the afternoon; but that she could not before, as she had lent them to her sister, Mrs M——. I said, 'very well'; but observed (laughing) to Betsey, 'It's a bad rule to give and take; so, if Sarah won't have these books, you must; they are very pretty ones, I assure you.' She curtsied and took them, according to the family custom. In the afternoon, when I came back to tea, I found the little girl on her knees, busy in packing up my things, and a large paper parcel on the table, which I could not at first tell what to make of. On opening it, however, I soon found what it was. It contained a number of volumes which I had given her at different times (among others, a little Prayer-Book, bound in crimson velvet, with green silk linings; she kissed it twenty times when she received it, and said it was the prettiest present in the world, and that she would show it to her aunt, who would be proud of it) – and all these she had returned together. Her name in the title-page was cut out of them all. I doubted at the instant whether she had done this before or after I had sent for them back, and I have doubted of it since; but there is no occasion to suppose her *ugly all over with hypocrisy*.[13] Poor little thing! She has enough to answer for, as it is. I asked Betsey if she could carry a message for me, and she said '*Yes*'. 'Will you tell your sister, then, that I did not want all these books; and give my love to her, and say that I shall be obliged if she will still keep these that I have sent back, and tell her that it is only those of my own writing that I think unworthy of her.' What do you think the little imp made answer? She raised herself on the other side of the table where she stood, as if inspired by the genius of the place, and said – 'AND THOSE ARE THE ONES THAT SHE PRIZES THE MOST!' If there were ever words spoken that could revive the dead, those were the words. 'Let me kiss them, and forget that my ears have heard aught else!' I said, 'Are you sure of that?' and she said, 'Yes, quite sure'. I told her, 'If I could be, I should be very different from what I was.' And I became so that instant, for these casual words carried assurance to my heart of her esteem – that once implied, I had proofs enough of her fondness. Oh! how I felt at that moment! Restored to love, hope, and joy, by a breath which I had caught by the merest accident, and which I might have pined in absence and mute despair for want of hearing! I did not know how to contain myself; I was childish, wanton, drunk with pleasure. I gave Betsey a twenty-shilling note which I happened to have in my hand, and on her asking 'What's this for, Sir?' I said, 'It's for you. Don't you think it worth that to be made happy? You once made me very wretched by some words I heard you drop, and now you have made me as happy; and all I wish you is, when you grow up, that you may find some one to love you as well as I do your sister, and that you may love better than she does me!' I continued in this state of delirium or dotage all that day and the next, talked incessantly, laughed at every thing, and was so extravagant, nobody could tell what was the matter with me. I murmured her name; I blest her; I folded her to my heart in delicious fondness; I called her by my own name; I worshipped her: I was mad for her. I told P—— I should laugh in her face, if ever she pretended not to like me again. Her mother came in and said, she hoped I should excuse Sarah's coming up. 'Oh, Ma'am', I said, 'I have no wish to see her; I feel her at my heart; she does not hate me after all, and I wish for nothing. Let her come when she will, she is to me welcomer than light, than life; but let it be in her own sweet time, and at her own dear pleasure.' Betsey also told me she was 'so glad to get the books back'. I, however, sobered and wavered (by degrees) from seeing nothing of her, day after day; and in less than a week I was devoted to the Infernal Gods. I could hold out no longer than the Monday evening following. I sent a message to her; she returned an ambiguous answer; but she came up. Pity me, my friend, for the shame of this recital. Pity me for the pain of having ever had to make it! If the spirits of mortal creatures, purified by faith and hope, can (according to the highest assurances) ever, during thousands of years of smooth-rolling eternity and balmy, sainted repose, forget the pain, the toil, the anguish, the helplessness, and the despair they have suffered here, in this frail being, then may I forget that withering hour, and her, that fair, pale form that entered, my inhuman betrayer, and my only earthly love! She said, 'Did you wish to speak to me, Sir?' I said, 'Yes, may I not speak to you? I wanted to see you and be friends.' I rose up, offered her an armchair which stood facing, bowed on it, and knelt to her adoring. She said (going) 'If that's all, I have nothing to say.' I replied, 'Why do you treat me thus? What have I done to become thus hateful to you?' *Answer*, 'I always told you I had no affection for you.' You may suppose this was a blow, after the imaginary honeymoon in which I had passed the preceding week. I was stunned by it; my heart sunk within me. I contrived to say, 'Nay, my dear girl, not always neither; for did you not once (if I might presume to look back to those happy, happy times), when you were sitting on my knee as usual, embracing and embraced, and I asked if you could not love me at last, did you not make answer, in the softest tones that ever man heard, *'I could easily say so, whether I did or not; you should judge by my actions!'* Was I to blame in taking you at your word, when every hope I had depended on your sincerity? And did you not say since I came back, *'Your feelings to me were the same as ever'*? Why then is your behaviour so different?' S. 'Is it nothing, your exposing me to the whole house in the way you did the other evening?' H. 'Nay, that was the consequence of your cruel reception of me, not the cause of it. I had better have gone away last year, as I proposed to do, unless you would give some pledge of your fidelity; but it was your own offer that I should remain. "Why should I go?" you said, "Why could we not go on the same as we had done, and say nothing about the word *forever*?"' S. 'And how did you behave when you returned?' H. 'That was all forgiven when we last parted, and your last words were, "I should find you the same as ever" when I came home? Did you not that very day enchant and madden me over again by the purest kisses and embraces, and did I not go from you (as I said) adoring, confiding, with every assurance of mutual esteem and friendship?' S. 'Yes, and in your absence I found that you had told my aunt what had passed between us.' H. 'It was to induce her to extort your real sentiments from you, that you might no longer make a secret of your true regard for me, which your actions (but not your words) confessed.' S. 'I own I have been guilty of improprieties, which you have gone and repeated, not only in the house, but out of it; so that it has come to my ears from various quarters, as if I was a light character. And I am determined in future to be guided by the advice of my relations, and particularly of my aunt, whom I consider as my best friend, and keep every lodger at a proper distance.' You will find hereafter that her favourite lodger, whom she visits daily, had left the house; so that she might easily make and keep this vow of extraordinary self-denial. Precious little dissembler! Yet her aunt, her best friend, says, 'No, Sir, no; Sarah's no hypocrite!' which I was fool enough to believe; and yet my great and unpardonable offence is to have entertained passing doubts on this delicate point. I said, Whatever errors I had committed, arose from my anxiety to have everything explained to her honour: my conduct showed that I had that at heart, and that I built on the purity of her character as on a rock. My esteem for her amounted to adoration. 'She did not want adoration'. It was only when any thing happened to imply that I had been mistaken, that I committed any extravagance, because I could not bear to think her short of perfection. 'She was far from perfection', she replied, with an air and manner (oh, my God!) as near it as possible. 'How could she accuse me of a want of regard to her? It was but the other day, Sarah', I said to her, 'when that little circumstance of the books happened, and I fancied the expressions your sister dropped proved the sincerity of all your kindness to me – you don't know how my heart melted within me at the thought, that after all, I might be dear to you. New hopes sprung up in my heart, and I felt as Adam must have done when his Eve was created for him!' 'She had heard enough of that sort of conversation', (moving towards the door). This, I own, was the unkindest cut of all. I had, in that case, no hopes whatever. I felt that I had expended words in vain, and that the conversation below stairs (which I told you of when I saw you)[14] had spoiled her taste for mine. If the allusion had been classical I should have been to blame; but it was scriptural, it was a sort of religious courtship, and Miss L. is religious!

> At once he took his Muse and dipt her
> Right in the middle of the Scripture.[15]

It would not do – the lady could make neither head nor tail of it. This is a poor attempt at levity. Alas! I am sad enough. 'Would she go and leave me so? If it was only my own behaviour, I still did not doubt of success. I knew the sincerity of my love, and she would be convinced of it in time. If that was all, I did not care: but tell me true, is there not a new attachment that is the real cause of your estrangement? Tell me, my sweet friend, and before you tell me, give me your hand (nay, both hands) that I may have something to support me under the dreadful conviction.' She let me take her hands in mine, saying, 'She supposed there could be no objection to that', – as if she acted on the suggestions of others, instead of following her own will – but still avoided giving me any answer. I conjured her to tell me the worst, and kill me on the spot. Any thing was better than my present state. I said, 'Is it Mr C——?' She smiled, and said with gay indifference, 'Mr C—— was here a very short time.' 'Well, then, was it Mr ——?' She hesitated, and then replied faintly, 'No'. This was a mere trick to mislead; one of the profoundnesses of Satan, in which she is an adept. 'But', she added hastily, 'she could make no more confidences.' 'Then', said I, 'you have something to communicate.' 'No; but she had once mentioned a thing of the sort, which I had hinted to her mother, though it signified little.' All this while I was in tortures. Every word, every half-denial, stabbed me. 'Had she any tie?' 'No, I have no tie.' 'You are not going to be married soon?' 'I don't intend ever to marry at all!' 'Can't you be friends with me as of old?' 'She could give no promises.' 'Would she make her own terms?' 'She would make none.' – 'I was sadly afraid the *little image* was dethroned from her heart, as I had dashed it to the ground the other night.' – 'She was neither desperate nor violent.' I did not answer – 'But deliberate and deadly', – though I might; and so she vanished in this running fight of question and answer, in spite of my vain efforts to detain her. The cockatrice, I said, mocks me: so she has always done. The thought was a dagger to me. My head reeled, my heart recoiled within me. I was stung with scorpions; my flesh crawled; I was choked with rage; her scorn scorched me like flames; her air (her heavenly air) withdrawn from me, stifled me, and left me gasping for breath and being. It was a fable. She started up in her own likeness, a serpent in place of a woman. She had fascinated, she had stung me, and had returned to her proper shape, gliding from me after inflicting the mortal wound, and instilling deadly poison into every pore; but her form lost none of its original brightness by the change of character, but was all glittering, beauteous, voluptuous grace. Seed of the serpent or of the woman, she was divine! I felt that she was a witch, and had bewitched me. Fate had enclosed me round about. *I* was transformed too, no longer human (any more than she, to whom I had knit myself) my feelings were marble; my blood was of molten lead; my thoughts on fire. I was taken out of myself, wrapped into another sphere, far from the light of day, of hope, of love. I had no natural affection left; she had slain me, but no other thing had power over me. Her arms embraced another; but her mock-embrace, the phantom of her love, still bound me, and I had not a wish to escape. So I felt then, and so perhaps shall feel till I grow old and die, nor have any desire that my years should last longer than they are linked in the chain of those amorous folds, or than her enchantments steep my soul in oblivion of all other things! I started to find myself alone – for ever alone, without a creature to love me. I looked round the room for help; I saw the tables, the chairs, the places where she stood or sat, empty, deserted, dead. I could not stay where I was; I had no one to go to but to the parent-mischief, the preternatural hag, that had 'drugged this posset'[16] of her daughter's charms and falsehood for me, and I went down and (such was my weakness and helplessness) sat with her for an hour, and talked with her of her daughter, and the sweet days we had passed together, and said I thought her a good girl, and believed that if there was no rival, she still had a regard for me at the bottom of her heart; and how I liked her all the better for her coy, maiden airs: and I received the assurance over and over that there was no one else; and that Sarah (they all knew) never stayed five minutes with any other lodger, while with me she would stay by the hour together, in spite of all her father could say to her (what were her motives, was best known to herself!) and while we were talking of her, she came bounding into the room, smiling with smothered delight at the consummation of my folly and her own art; and I asked her mother whether she thought she looked as if she hated me, and I took her wrinkled, withered, cadaverous, clammy hand at parting, and kissed it. Faugh!

I will make an end of this story; there is something in it discordant to honest ears. I left the house the next day,[17] and returned to Scotland in a state so near to frenzy that I take it the shades sometimes ran into one another. R——[18] met me the day after I arrived, and will tell you the way I was in. I was like a person in a high fever; only mine was in the mind instead of the body. It had the same irritating, uncomfortable effect on the bye-standers. I was incapable of any application, and don't know what I should have done, had it not been for the kindness of ——.[19] I came to see you, to 'bestow some of my tediousness upon you', but you were gone from home. Everything went on well as to the law business; and as it approached to a conclusion, I wrote to my good friend P—— to go to M——, who had married her sister, and ask him if it would be worth my while to make her a formal offer, as soon as I was free, as, with the least encouragement, I was ready to throw myself at her feet; and to know, in case of refusal, whether I might go back there and be treated as an old friend. Not a word of answer could be got from her on either point, notwithstanding every importunity and entreaty; but it was the opinion of M—— that I might go and try my fortune. I did so with joy, with something like confidence. I thought her giving no positive answer implied a chance, at least, of the reversion of her favour, in case I behaved well. All was false, hollow, insidious. The first night after I got home, I slept on down.[20] In Scotland, the flint had been my pillow. But now I slept under the same roof with her. What softness, what balmy repose in the very thought! I saw her that same day and shook hands with her, and told her how glad I was to see her; and she was kind and comfortable, though still cold and distant. Her manner was altered from what it was the last time. She still absented herself from the room, but was mild and affable when she did come. She was pale, dejected, evidently uneasy about something, and had been ill. I thought it was perhaps her reluctance to yield to my wishes, her pity for what I suffered; and that in the struggle between both, she did not know what to do. How I worshipped her at these moments! We had a long interview the third day, and I thought all was doing well. I found her sitting at work in the window-seat of the front parlour; and on my asking if I might come in, she made no objection. I sat down by her; she let me take her hand; I talked to her of indifferent things, and of old times. I asked her if she would put some new frills on my shirts? – 'With the greatest pleasure'. If she could get *the little image* mended? 'It was broken in three pieces, and the sword was gone, but she would try.' I then asked her to make up a plaid silk which I had given her in the winter, and which she said would make a pretty summer gown. I so longed to see her in it! – 'She had little time to spare, but perhaps might!' Think what I felt, talking peaceably, kindly, tenderly with my love, – not passionately, not violently. I tried to take pattern by her patient meekness, as I thought it, and to subdue my desires to her will. I then sued to her, but respectfully, to be admitted to her friendship – she must know I was as true a friend as ever woman had – or if there was a bar to our intimacy from a dearer attachment, to let me know it frankly, as I showed her all my heart. She drew out her handkerchief and wiped her eyes 'of tears which sacred pity had engendered there.'[21] Was it so or not? I cannot tell. But so she stood (while I pleaded my cause to her with all the earnestness, and fondness in the world) with the tears trickling from her eyelashes, her head stooping, her attitude fixed, with the finest expression that ever was seen of mixed regret, pity, and stubborn resolution; but without speaking a word, without altering a feature. It was like a petrifaction of a human face in the softest moment of passion. 'Ah!' I said, 'how you look! I have prayed again and again while I was away from you, in the agony of my spirit, that I might but live to see you look so again, and then breathe my last!' I entreated her to give me some explanation. In vain! At length she said she must go, and disappeared like a spirit. That week she did all the little trifling favours I had asked of her. The frills were put on, and she sent up to know if I wanted any more done. She got the Bonaparte mended. This was like healing old wounds indeed! How? As follows, for thereby hangs the conclusion of my tale. Listen.

I had sent a message one evening to speak to her about some special affairs of the house, and received no answer. I waited an hour expecting her, and then went out in great vexation at my disappointment. I complained to her mother a day or two after, saying I thought it so unlike Sarah's usual propriety of behaviour, that she must mean it as a mark of disrespect. Mrs L—— said, 'La! Sir, you're always fancying things. Why, she was dressing to go out, and she was only going to get the little image you're both so fond of mended; and it's to be done this evening. She has been to two or three places to see about it, before she could get anyone to undertake it.' My heart, my poor fond heart, almost melted within me at this news. I answered, 'Ah! Madam, that's always the way with the dear creature. I am finding fault with her and thinking the hardest things of her; and at that very time she's doing something to show the most delicate attention, and that she has no greater satisfaction than in gratifying my wishes!' On this we had some farther talk, and I took nearly the whole of the lodgings at a hundred guineas a year, that (as I said) she might have a little leisure to sit at her needle of an evening, or to read if she chose, or to walk out when it was fine. She was not in good health, and it would do her good to be less confined. I would be the drudge and she should no longer be the slave. I asked nothing in return. To see her happy, to make her so, was to be so myself. This was agreed to. I went over to Blackheath that evening, delighted as I could be after all I had suffered, and lay the whole of the next morning on the heath under the open sky, dreaming of my earthly Goddess. This was Sunday. That evening I returned, for I could hardly bear to be for a moment out of the house where she was, and the next morning she tapped at the door – it was opened – it was she – she hesitated and then came forward: she had got the little image in her hand, I took it, and blest her from my heart. She said 'They had been obliged to put some new pieces to it.' I said 'I didn't care how it was done, so that I had it restored to me safe, and by her.' I thanked her and begged to shake hands with her. She did so, and as I held the only hand in the world that I never wished to let go, I looked up in her face, and said 'Have pity on me, have pity on me, and save me if you can!' Not a word of answer, but she looked full in my eyes, as much as to say, 'Well, I'll think of it; and if I can, I will save you!' We talked about the expense of repairing the figure. 'Was the man waiting?' – 'No, she had fetched it on Saturday evening.' I said I'd give her the money in the course of the day, and then shook hands with her again in token of reconciliation; and she went waving out of the room, but at the door turned round and looked full at me, as she did the first time she beguiled me of my heart. This was the last.

All that day I longed to go down stairs to ask her and her mother to set out with me for Scotland on Wednesday, and on Saturday I would make her my wife. Something withheld me. In the evening,[22] however, I could not rest without seeing her, and I said to her younger sister, 'Betsey, if Sarah will come up now, I'll pay her what she laid out for me the other day.' – 'My sister's gone out, Sir', was the answer. What again! thought I, that's somewhat sudden. I told P—— her sitting in the window-seat of the front parlour boded me no good. It was not in her old character. She did not use to know there were doors or windows in the house – and now she goes out three times in a week. It is to meet some one, I'll lay my life on't. 'Where is she gone?' – 'To my grandmother's, Sir'. 'Where does your grandmother live now?' – 'At Somers Town'.[23] I immediately set out to Somers Town. I passed one or two streets, and at last turned up King Street, thinking it most likely she would return that way home. I passed a house in King Street where I had once lived, and had not proceeded many paces, ruminating on chance, and change and old times, when I saw her coming towards me. I felt a strange pang at the sight, but I thought her alone. Some people before me moved on, and I saw another person with her. *The murder was out*. It was a tall, rather well-looking young man, but I did not at first recollect him. We passed at the crossing of the street without speaking. Will you believe it, after all that had past between us for two years, after what had passed in the last half-year, after what had passed that very morning, she went by me without even changing countenance, without expressing the slightest emotion, without betraying either shame or pity or remorse or any other feeling that any other human being but herself must have shown in the same situation. She had no time to prepare for acting a part, to suppress her feelings – the truth is, she has not one natural feeling in her bosom to suppress. I turned and looked – they also turned and looked – and as if by mutual consent, we both retrod our steps and passed again, in the same way. I went home. I was stifled. I could not stay in the house, walked into the street and met them coming towards home. As soon as he had left her at the door (I fancy she had prevailed with him to accompany her, dreading some violence) I returned, went up stairs, and requested an interview. Tell her, I said, I'm in excellent temper and good spirits, but I must see her! She came smiling, and I said 'Come in, my dear girl, and sit down, and tell me all about it, how it is and who it is.' – 'What', she said, 'do you mean Mr C——?' 'Oh', said I, 'then it is he! Ah! you rogue, I always suspected there was something between you, but you know you denied it lustily: why did you not tell me all about it at the time, instead of letting me suffer as I have done? But, however, no reproaches. I only wish it may all end happily and honourably for you, and I am satisfied. But', I said, 'you know you used to tell me, you despised looks.' – 'She didn't think Mr C—— was so particularly handsome.' 'No, but he's very well to pass, and a well-grown youth into the bargain.' Pshaw! let me put an end to the fulsome detail. I found he had lived over the way, that he had been lured thence, no doubt, almost a year before, that they had first spoken in the street, and that he had never once hinted at marriage, and had gone away, because (as he said) they were too much together, and that it was better for her to meet him occasionally out of doors. 'There could be no harm in them walking together.' 'No, but you may go somewhere afterwards.' – 'One must trust to one's principle for that.' Consummate hypocrite! * * * * * * I told her Mr M——, who had married her sister, did not wish to leave the house. I, who would have married her, did not wish to leave it. I told her I hoped I should not live to see her come to shame, after all my love of her; but put her on her guard as well as I could, and said, after the lengths she had permitted herself with me, I could not help being alarmed at the influence of one over her, whom she could hardly herself suppose to have a tenth part of my esteem for her!! She made no answer to this, but thanked me coldly for my good advice, and rose to go. I begged her to sit a few minutes, that I might try to recollect if there was anything else I wished to say to her, perhaps for the last time; and then, not finding anything, I bade her good night, and asked for a farewell kiss. Do you know she refused; so little does she understand what is due to friendship, or love, or honour! We parted friends, however, and I felt deep grief, but no enmity against her. I thought C—— had pressed his suit after I went, and had prevailed. There was no harm in that – a little fickleness or so, a little overpretension to unalterable attachment – but that was all. She liked him better than me – it was my hard hap, but I must bear it. I went out to roam the desert streets, when, turning a corner, whom should I meet but her very lover? I went up to him and asked for a few minutes' conversation on a subject that was highly interesting to me and I believed not indifferent to him: and in the course of four hours' talk, it came out that for three months previous to my quitting London for Scotland, she had been playing the same game with him as with me – that he breakfasted first, and enjoyed an hour of her society, and then I took my turn, so that we never jostled; and this explained why, when he came back sometimes and passed my door, as she was sitting in my lap, she coloured violently, thinking if her lover looked in, what a *dénouement* there would be. He could not help again and again expressing his astonishment at finding that our intimacy had continued unimpaired up to so late a period after he came, and when they were on the most intimate footing. She used to deny positively to him that there was anything between us, just as she used to assure me with impenetrable effrontery that 'Mr C—— was nothing to her, but merely a lodger.' All this while she kept up the farce of her romantic attachment to her old lover, vowed that she never could alter in that respect, let me go to Scotland on the solemn and repeated assurance that there was no new flame, that there was no bar between us but this shadowy love – I leave her on this understanding, she becomes more fond or more intimate with her new lover; he quitting the house (whether tired out or not, I can't say) – in revenge she ceases to write to me, keeps me in wretched suspense, treats me like something loathsome to her when I return to enquire the cause, denies it with scorn and impudence, destroys me and shows no pity, no desire to soothe or shorten the pangs she has occasioned by her wantonness and hypocrisy, and wishes to linger the affair on to the last moment, going out to keep an appointment with another while she pretends to be obliging me in the tenderest point (which C—— himself said was too much) ... What do you think of all this? Shall I tell you my opinion? But I must try to do it in another letter.

To the Same

(in conclusion)

I did not sleep a wink all that night; nor did I know till the next day the full meaning of what had happened to me. With the morning's light, conviction glared in upon me that I had not only lost her for ever – but every feeling I had ever had towards her – respect, tenderness, pity – all but my fatal passion, was gone. The whole was a mockery, a frightful illusion. I had embraced the false Florimel instead of the true;[24] or was like the man in the *Arabian Nights* who had married a *ghoul*.[25] How different was the idea I once had of her? Was this she,

– Who had been beguiled – she who was made
Within a gentle bosom to be laid –
To bless and to be blessed – to be heart-bare
To one who found his bettered likeness there –
To think for ever with him, like a bride. –
To haunt his eye, like taste personified –
To double his delight, to share his sorrow,
And like a morning beam, wake to him every morrow?[26]

I saw her pale, cold form glide silent by me, dead to shame as to pity. Still I seemed to clasp this piece of witchcraft to my bosom; this lifeless image, which was all that was left of my love, was the only thing to which my sad heart clung. Were she dead, should I not wish to gaze once more upon her pallid features? She is dead to me; but what she once was to me, can never die! The agony, the conflict of hope and fear, of adoration and jealousy is over; or it would, ere long, have ended with my life. I am no more lifted now to Heaven, and then plunged in the abyss; but I seem to have been thrown from the top of a precipice, and to lie grovelling, stunned, and stupefied. I am melancholy, lonesome, and weaker than a child. The worst is, I have no prospect of any alteration for the better: she has cut off all possibility of a reconcilement at any future period. Were she even to return to her former pretended fondness and endearments, I could have no pleasure, no confidence in them. I can scarce make out the contradiction to myself. I strive to think she always was what I now know she is; but I have great difficulty in it, and can hardly believe but she still is what she so long *seemed*. Poor thing! I am afraid she is little better off herself; nor do I see what is to become of her, unless she throws off the mask at once, and *runs amuck* at infamy. She is exposed and laid bare to all those whose opinion she set a value upon. Yet she held her head very high, and must feel (if she feels any thing) proportionably mortified. A more complete experiment on character was never made.[27] If I had not met her lover immediately after I parted with her, it would have been nothing. I might have supposed she had changed her mind in my absence, and had given him the preference as soon as she felt it, and even shown her delicacy in declining any farther intimacy with me. But it comes out that she had gone on in the most forward and familiar way with both at once – (she could not change her mind in passing from one room to another) – told both the same bare-faced and unblushing falsehoods, like the commonest creature; received presents from me to the very last, and wished to keep up the game still longer, either to gratify her humour, her avarice, or her vanity in playing with my passion, or to have me as a *dernier resort*, in case of accidents. Again, it would have been nothing, if she had not come up with her demure, well-composed, wheedling looks that morning, and then met me in the evening in a situation, which (she believed) might kill me on the spot with no more feeling than a common courtesan shows, who *bilks*[28] a customer, and passes him, leering up at her bully, the moment after. If there had been the frailty of passion, it would have been excusable; but it is evident she is a practised, callous jilt, a regular lodging-house decoy, played off by her mother upon the lodgers, one after another, applying them to her different purposes, laughing at them in turns, and herself the probable dupe and victim of some favourite gallant in the end. I know all this; but what do I gain by it, unless I could find some one with her shape and air, to supply the place of the lovely apparition? That a professed wanton should come and sit on a man's knee, and put her arms round his neck, and caress him, and seem fond of him, means nothing, proves nothing, no one concludes anything from it; but that a pretty, reserved, modest, delicate-looking girl should do this, from the first hour to the last of your being in the house, without intending anything by it, is new, and, I think, worth explaining. It was, I confess, out of my calculation, and may be out of that of others. Her unmoved indifference and self-possession all the while, show that it is her constant practice. Her look even, if closely examined, bears this interpretation. It is that of studied hypocrisy or startled guilt, rather than of refined sensibility or conscious innocence. 'She defied anyone to read her thoughts', she once told me. 'Do they then require concealing?' I imprudently asked her. The command over herself is surprising. She never once betrays herself by any momentary forgetfulness, by any appearance of triumph or superiority to the person who is her dupe, by any levity of manner in the plenitude of her success; it is one faultless, undeviating, consistent, consummate piece of acting. Were she a saint on earth, she could not seem more like one. Her hypocritical high-flown pretensions, indeed, make her the worse: but still the ascendancy of her will, her determined perseverance in what she undertakes to do, has something admirable in it, approaching to the heroic. She is certainly an extraordinary girl! Her retired manner, and invariable propriety of behaviour made me think it next to impossible she could grant the same favours indiscriminately to everyone that she did to me. Yet this now appears to be the fact. She must have done the very same with C——, invited him into the house to carry on a closer intrigue with her, and then commenced the double game with both together. She always 'despised looks'. This was a favourite phrase with her, and one of the hooks which she baited for me. Nothing could win her but a man's behaviour and sentiments. Besides, she could never like another – she was a martyr to disappointed affection – and friendship was all she could even extend to any other man. All the time, she was making signals, playing off her pretty person, and having occasional interviews in the street with this very man, whom she could only have taken so sudden and violent a liking to from his looks, his personal appearance, and what she probably conjectured of his circumstances. Her sister had married a counsellor –

the Miss F——'s, who kept the house before, had done so too – and so would she. 'There was a precedent for it.' Yet if she was so desperately enamoured of this new acquaintance, if he had displaced *the little image* from her breast, if he was become her *second* 'unalterable attachment' (which I would have given my life to have been) why continue the same unwarrantable familiarities with me to the last, and promise that they should be renewed on my return (if I had not unfortunately stumbled upon the truth to her aunt) and yet keep up the same refined cant about her old attachment all the time, as if it was that which stood in the way of my pretensions, and not her faithlessness to it? 'If one swerves from one, one shall swerve from another' – was her excuse for not returning my regard. Yet that which I thought a prophecy, was I suspect a history. She had swerved twice from her avowed engagements, first to me, and then from me to another. If she made a fool of me, what did she make of her lover? I fancy he has put that question to himself. I said nothing to him about the amount of the presents which is another damning circumstance, that might have opened my eyes long before; but they were shut by my fond affection, which 'turned all to favour and to prettiness'.[29] She cannot be supposed to have kept up an appearance of old regard to me, from a fear of hurting my feelings by her desertion; for she not only showed herself indifferent to, but evidently triumphed in my sufferings, and heaped every kind of insult and indignity upon them. I must have incurred her contempt and resentment by my mistaken delicacy at different times; and her manner, when I have hinted at becoming a reformed man in this respect, convinces me of it. 'She hated it!' She always hated whatever she liked most. She 'hated Mr C——'s red slippers', when he first came! One more count finishes the indictment. She not only discovered the most hardened indifference to the feelings of others; she has not shown the least regard to her own character, or shame when she was detected. When found out, she seemed to say, 'Well, what if I am? I have played the game as long as I could; and if I could keep it up no longer, it was not for want of good will!' Her colouring once or twice is the only sign of grace she has exhibited. Such is the creature on whom I had thrown away my heart and soul – one who was incapable of feeling the commonest emotions of human nature, as they regarded herself or any one else. 'She had no feelings with respect to herself', she often said. She in fact knows what she is, and recoils from the good opinion or sympathy of others, which she feels to be founded on a deception; so that my over-weening opinion of her must have appeared like irony, or direct insult. My seeing her in the street has gone a good way to satisfy me. Her manner there explains her manner indoors to be conscious and overdone; and besides, she looks but indifferently. She is diminutive in stature, and her measured step and timid air do not suit these public airings. I am afraid she will soon grow common to my imagination, as well as worthless in herself.[30] Her image seems fast 'going into the wastes of time',[31] like a weed that the wave bears farther and farther from me. Alas! thou poor hapless weed, when I entirely lose sight of thee, and for ever, no flower will ever bloom on earth to glad my heart again!

THE END

The Journal of F., March 4–16, 1823

The text of Hazlitt's unpublished diary of the testing of Sarah Walker has been taken from Appendix A of *The Letters of William Hazlitt*, edited by H. M. Sikes and W. H. Bonner, New York University Press, New York, 1978. It also incorporates Stanley Jones's proposed emendations as published in *The Library*, Series 5, Vol. 26 (1971), pp. 325–6.

In the concluding paragraph of *Liber Amoris* 'H.' professed himself convinced of 'S.'s duplicity (after having seen her in the street with her 'other' lover, C——) and sets about consigning her to the oblivion of the past. In real life, however, the break was not so clear-cut. In a bid to escape from Sarah, the essayist moved out of Southampton Buildings in late September 1822. But he was back by early March of the following year, in spirit if not in body, having enlisted a young friend of his, 'F.', to take up residence there and 'try her'. The unpublished diary that Hazlitt kept of 'F.'s campaign, which lasted from 4–16 March 1823, is a short but disturbing document. It gives further proof, if proof were needed, of the increasingly punitive nature of Hazlitt's obsession, and its timing suggests a late, abortive attempt to extract the 'dark truth' about Sarah's character before the fast-approaching publication of *Liber Amoris*.

March 4. Mr F. goes to No. 9 S[outhampton] B[uildings] at my request to see the lodgings. Sees Mrs W[alker] who is very communicative – says there is no one but herself and *her daughter* – her eldest daughter married one of the Mr Roscoes of Liverpool – gentlemen generally staid there two or three years – the gentleman that last occupied the front room staid there three years – a Mr Crombie (no, the last person that occupied it was a Mr T[omkins], who did not stay there quite so long) She concluded Mr F. from the country and let the front-room, second-floor, to him at 15s. a week. The back-room (my poor room) was empty at 14s. a week.

March 5. Goes. Is introduced into the back-parlour – meets Miss shawled and bonnetted going out to meet T[omkins]. Mrs W. has my name up as having lodged there and says that except when I am at Salisbury, I lodge there still – speaks of the quantity of money I got by my writings, and of several I had given her daughter – She returns and takes off her bonnet and shawl, throws them down on Mr F.'s great-coat which he had put in a chair. This is her first move, thus putting these little matters together and mingling persons by proxy. She then went out and gave one of her set looks at the door.

March 6. The next morning she comes up to light his fire, and he wanting his pantaloons brushed, she comes to take them out of his hands, as he gives them to her naked at the door. She is not dressed to wait at breakfast, but is very graceful and smiling, and repulses a kiss very gently. She afterwards expressly forgives this freedom, and is backwards and forwards all day. On his asking for a newspaper or a book, she brings him up the *Round Table*,[1] with my name and sincere regards written in the title-page.

March 7. This morning she is dressed to wait on the gentleman. The day before it was too early. Nothing occurs, but she regularly answers the bell, yet does not bring up the things that are wanted, smirks and backs out of the room in her marked manner. A circumstance happened decisive of her lying character. Mr F. going into the parlour for his umbrella met her going out to meet T. her mother repeating the old cant that it was too late to go to Mr Roscoe's. She however went, and her father after her, probably to watch and entrap T. But F. going upstairs again found Betsey in the room and on telling her the bed was not made, she said 'her sister told her it was, but not turned down'. This was no doubt a lie to keep the job to herself and be there on his return.

March 7. At night Miss was gone to bed, and on being asked next morning whether she did not retire sooner than usual, said, 'She sometimes went to bed earlier and sometimes later'. This was just like one of her common place answers on all occasions. Mr F. went down for a glass of water, and the brother (Cajah as they call him) was there. He observed Mr H. always drank water and they didn't like it at the Southampton Arms. He continued, 'I was rather an odd man, a little flighty,' he believed, and added smiling, 'I was in love'. F. did not ask him with whom, but said that the whole was a regularly understood thing, that there was nothing singular in gentlemen being *in love* in that house.

March 8, Saturday. Mr F. got a paper and lent it to the Father to read. Saw Miss several times. In the evening pressed her to stay for tea which she declined, but he followed her to the door, and kissed her several times on the stair case, at which she laughed. While this passed he had hold of one hand, and the other was at liberty, but she did not once attempt to raise it so as to make even a show of resistance. This is what she calls 'being determined to keep *every* lodger at a proper distance'. Her aunt must know that she has not stuck to her advice.

March 9. Miss was seen in close conference with T[omkins] on Saturday night opposite her own door. I wondered what divine music he poured into her ear, to which my words were harsh discord. What, I thought, would I not give to hear those words of that honeyed breath that sinks into her heart, that I might despair and feel how just has been her preference! The next moments were enough. I had a specimen of that sort of conversation to which 'her ear she seriously inclines'.[2] Not T[omkins's] but my man's. F. insisted on her drinking tea with him, declaring he would not sit alone, that he was not used to that sort of thing, and that if she did not stay, he would not have any tea at all, and would take his hat and walk out. By that terrible threat she was awed, she did not 'show an independent spirit', and let the gentleman go, but said if she *must* stop she would sit on the chair next the door instead of the one next to him. Wonderful delicacy! F. then got up and shut the door that she might not be exposed to the draught, and Emma[3] who was waiting on the stairs went down to announce this new arrangement. 'Sarah, they all knew never staid five minutes with any lodger but me.' She then poured out F.'s tea and the talk commenced. F. asked her which of the Essays in the *Round Table* was a favourite with her, to which she seemed at a loss for an answer. He said he thought that on Methodism was a good one and asked what she thought of the remark that 'David was the first Methodist'?[4] She laughed and said 'Mr H. was full of his remarks.' F. answered 'Did she mean on the ladies?' 'No – Mr H. thought very little about the ladies – indeed she believed he cared very little about them.' F. 'In a prose writer this was not so necessary, but a poet could hardly do without them. What did she think of Mr Moore's *Loves of the Angels*?'[5] 'She thought it very impious to make angels fall in love with women.' 'Had she any of Lord Byron's works.' She had read *Cain*, which she thought very fine (I think I know which part). Had she read *Don Juan*? 'No, for her sister said it was impious.' At which F. repeated the word 'Impious' and laughed, at which she laughed. 'Had Mr F. read any of Mr Proctor's poetry?' He could not say. On which she explained 'Mr Barry Cornwall's.' Oh yes. Had she. Yes: she had *Marcian Colonna* and *Mirandola* and had seen *Mirandola*.[6] Mr Proctor was a particular friend of Mr Hazlitt's, and had very gentle and pleasing manners. Miss Foote played Isadora when she saw it: she was a pretty girl but no actress. She liked Miss Stephens as a singer, her voice was very clear and good but her acting was deficient. 'Did she like going to the play?' 'She was fond of tragedy, but did not think comedy worth going to see.' – She had not been to Drury Lane: this was a hint that she should like to go. We shall see. And so she cackled on with her new gallant; T[omkins] being in the street with her every night and I in hell for this grinning, chattering idiot. F. said he is sure she is quite incapable of understanding any such works, and shut up her lips with me for fear of being found out for what she is, a little mawkish simpleton. So that it was more stupidity than unkindness. She rose to go in about ten minutes and then being pressed sat down again for another quarter of an hour, and then said she must go to her sister's to take her the child. F. kissed her and let her go. I thought no lodger was ever to kiss her again but T. The next morning she came up to answer the breakfast bell but being in her bed gown would not come in, but ran up with the breakfast things in ten minutes, dressed all in her best things. Decoy! Damned, treble damned idiot! [several words inked out] When shall I burn her out of my thoughts? – Yet I like to hear about her – that she had her bed-gown or her ruff on, that she stood or sat, or made some insipid remark, is to me a visitation from Heaven – to know that she is a whore or an idiot is better than nothing. Were I in Hell my only consolation would be to learn of her. In Heaven to see her would be my only reward.

March 10. In the evening Betsey waited at tea, her sister, she said, being busy. Mr F. went down afterwards and sat with the family in the back parlour first opposite to her and then next to her. She said little, but laughed and smiled and seemed quite at her ease. Oh low life! God deliver me from thee! This was with a person, a perfect stranger to her, and whose only introduction was that he obtruded himself upon her and her friends without ceremony and without respect, under the pretext that he was too dull to sit alone.

T[omkins] [name inked out], a lover of different stamp, will not even be seen with her or come near the house. So that she reasons by the familiar and the distant – all but true regard which requires a return which she cannot feel. Me, poor, tortured worm, she rejected on this account. I asked F. how she looked. He said 'She had more flesh on her bones than her mother.' On rising to go upstairs, he saw three books piled on the drawers, and on going toward them, Mrs W. said they were the books he had asked Sarah to lend him. One of mine and two of Proctor's. He was going to take them, but said he thought he had better not, as he wanted a good night's rest, and they might prevent him. Mrs W. accorded with this, intending her daughter to bring them up in the morning. *N.B.* Mrs W. among other things stated that Mr H[azlitt] had been in the neighbourhood the other evening at a literary party in Castle Street.

March 11. She came up with the books, dressed. F. asked her to point out a passage in *Marcian Colonna* which she liked. She declined this, and said she admired the whole. She in fact I daresay had not read a word of it. He then read some of it, and on her coming up again pretended it was so serious it had made him sentimental and melancholy so that he should be obliged to turn to Mr Moore. He then said he would to look at *Mirandola* but he was afraid of venturing on a tragedy – so hoped Miss would point out a passage. So she took the book and turning to the place where there was the description of herself,[7] said – 'This was Mr H.'s favourite passage.' F. said he could hardly believe his eyes when he saw it, for she seemed perfectly unmoved. He then read it and said he thought it very pretty; but could not reconcile what she said of its being my favourite passage with her declaring the day before that I cared very little about the ladies, as it was all about love. She hesitated awhile and then repeated that she didn't think I did, adding 'I don't think Mr H.'s love lasts long.' Incomparable piece of clockwork! To suppose that any man could count upon her remarks beforehand is ridiculous. She is not good or bad, she is defective in certain faculties that belong to human nature, and acts upon others, because you can make no impression on her. I was only wrong in not pulling up her petticoats, yet F. says he thinks it would be impossible to offer her rudeness, if he did not know beforehand what she was. 'Being a thing majestical, it were a violence' etc.[8] He kissed her heartily and put his arms round her neck going away, at which she seemed as pleased as punch. In the evening she brought up the tea-things but said significantly she wouldn't stop then, as there was nobody in the house but her father. He went down just before he came to me and found she was gone out as far as Fleet Street to get M—— some coffee. That is, to meet Tomkins. If she has two, why not three? One of them thought her a saint! Her sister was sitting downstairs with her child in the afternoon when Mr F. bolted into the room for his umbrella and as she had her back to him, he mistook her for Mrs W. and said 'How do you do, Mam.' She seemed a little dissatisfied at such familiarity, but the other said, 'It's only my sister' and handed him the umbrella, quite sweetly. Who could suppose that under such a manner there was a heart of marble or that a mask could smile? Mrs Roscoe was doubtless ashamed and hurt after the blow-up with me on account of having shattered the attachment to Tomkins to see this new affair in such friendliness. She perhaps doesn't wish her little girl to see her aunt a little whore in the street a few years hence.

March 12. The little idiot came up with the breakfast, dressed as usual, or rather varied, that is, she had a cap on and a shawl, which I gave her on. F. had got his *Marcian Colonna* lying on the chair beside him and when she came in, read her some lines, and asked if she remembered them. No: but she had the whole. He then asked her to look at them, and for that purpose she came round the table to his side, and on his asking her, she sat down. After looking them over, the book was laid aside, and he laid his hand upon her thigh, to which she made not the slightest objection. He then put his arm round her neck, and began to play with her necklace and paddle in her neck, all which she took smilingly, being determined to keep every lodger at a proper distance, having been guilty of improprieties enough with me. He told her she would make a pretty nun. That, she said, she was sure she never should be. She was not made to be shut up. F. asked her if she ever went out, and she said very seldom and only in the neighbourhood, to her sister. In the afternoon this conversation was resumed in the parlour downstairs while her mother was in bed in the inner room and she was mending a stocking; and she then declared she did not like to be confined to the conversation of her own sex, although she believed the nuns had leave to talk with their Confessors. F. observed that one Confessor was hardly enough for fifty or sixty nuns. 'No!' 'If', he said, 'there was a Confessor for every Nun?' 'That indeed!' said the lady of individual attachments. Half a dozen would do better. F. then asked her to go to the play. She said, she was afraid her mother would object to her going with a stranger. 'Phoo! nonsense that was nothing: she really *must* go. She should have her choice of any part of the house, except the one shilling gallery. He supposed her ambition was not so high as that'. 'No, her ambition was not so high, and laughed at this as an excellent jest.' 'But any part of the boxes: in the pit they would be equally exposed'. It was left undetermined and tonight we are to see. I think I am exculpated by all this. I asked F. if he wanted to take a girl into keeping would he allow her half a guinea a week to be his whore? and he said, No, for one might get girls that would have some conversation in them for that, and she had not. He thought at first she would not talk, but now he was convinced she could not. F. asked what was to be done if she consented to come to bed with him. I said 'Why you had better proceed.' He did not seem to like the idea of getting her with child, and I supposed he didn't like to have a child by a monster, which he said was really his feeling. In this child-getting business we are however reckoning without our host, for she has evidently some evasion for that. It remains to be seen what her theory and practice on this subject are. F. speaking of Mr F[ollett] said, he seemed out of sorts the other evening. She said, Mr F[ollett] knew his ill-humours had no effect upon her. And added, 'We have not had the pleasure of seeing you in an ill-humour yet.' F. answered, 'Supposed I was to give you a specimen? She said, I hope not till *I* give you cause.' Mr F. hearing F[ollett] above-stairs called out 'Who's that?' F[ollett] said 'Sir?' on which the other replied gruffly, 'Oh, it was not you I wanted to see, but somebody else.' So that she is perhaps thus breaking this poor man's heart and probably his wife's, and thus feels very happy that his ill-humours have no effect upon her.

March 14. F. got her between his legs so that she came in complete contact with him. She made no resistance nor complaint. She retired a step or two and he followed and then she retreated a little further like the Squire and the Dove in Spenser.[9] He said 'I'll half kill you with kissing, if I catch you.' 'But you must catch me first', she said, and bounded down stairs and stood looking up and laughing at the first landing place. By God, there isn't such another charming provoking devil in the world. F. is I think already in love and thinks she likes him and I shan't be able to get him to move. She didn't go to the play the other night but was backwards and forwards with her sist[er] all the evening as an excuse. Yesterday he says he could make nothing of her. They had a parley in the evening. She didn't come up with the tea-things, but on ringing afterwards, she answered the bell. She would not come in: she could hear where she was—her old word. F. got up and sat near her. He began to say he was sorry he staid out at night and was afraid she thought him wild. She said she was not his keeper. He then said he could learn to live by himself but wanted something to kiss and fondle and thought they should make good company. She asked if [he thought that would be] proper. Oh! he said, hang propriety. What, she said, you would not hang propriety! [She half hangs it and cuts it down again.] Would it be seemly? Oh, he said, as to seemly, there was nobody to see them but themselves. While this delicate negotiation was going on, she kept smiling and hemming all the time and at last said she must go now. But she would come and sit with him when they were gone to bed? She made no promises and there it stands. F. swears he'll put it home to her today: but I doubt she has already disarmed him.

Saturday, March 15. She did not come up in the morning and nothing was done but that as she put down the curtains at night, he kissed her and saying he was determined to give her a good tickling for her tricks in running away from him the day before, put his hand between her legs without ceremony. She only said, 'Let me go, Sir,' and retiring to the door, asked if he would have the fire lighted. She did not come up again. She was altered in her manner, and probably begins to smoke something.[10] In lighting F. upstairs she waits for him to go first, and on his insisting on her leading the way, they had a regular scamper for it, he all the way tickling her legs behind. Yet she expressed no resentment nor shame. This is she who murdered me that she might keep every lodger at a proper distance. I met Tomkins in the street who looks badly. I fancy we are all in for it; and poor F. will be over head and ears in love with her in another week.

March 16. Saw nothing of her in the morning, but asked her to tea – answered 'she never drank tea with gentlemen,' and was high. F. was in despair when returning home at dusk, he meets my lady with her muff moving along Lincoln's Inn Fields by herself. He saw [her] turn at the corner of Queen Street to go down towards the New Inn. Followed her – asked to accompany – she refused – and on his offering to take her arm, stood stock still, immoveable, inflexible – like herself and on his saying he could not then press her and offering his hand, she gave it him, and then went on to her lover. I also am her lover and will live and die for her only, since she can be true to anyone. F. met her brother at the door and said, 'I just met your sister.' 'Why she is gone to her grandmother's.' Let her [and then cross hatched up the right side of the page is:] lie to hell with her tongue. She is as true as heaven wished her heart and lips to be. My [own?] fair hell.

The Fight

This justly celebrated piece was first published in the *New Monthly Magazine* in February 1822 under the name 'Phantastes' and then later reprinted by Hazlitt's son in the *Literary Remains* of 1836.

The match between Tom Hickman – the 'Gas-man' – and Bill Neat was like most Regency boxing matches, a noisy and bloody affair; noisy because it was attended by a huge crowd cheering and betting vigorously throughout; bloody because it was a straight bare-knuckle contest with no round restriction. Pugilism was illegal in Hazlitt's time, which meant that news of a major match was seldom advertised in advance. Information would circulate informally, by word of mouth, and thousands of people would then travel long distances in coaches or on foot to reach the appointed venue. The battle between Neat and Gas took place on a small patch of ground near Hungerford in Berkshire on 11 December 1821, and in Hazlitt's account at least half the interest and pleasure of the occasion lay in the heroic struggle to get there.

Contained in the endnotes to this edition are three short passages from the original manuscript that were later removed in proof. Each of these carry personal references to Hazlitt's growing obsession with Sarah Walker. Even in the published version of the essay there are a number of allusions to the affair. Think of the opening dedication addressed to the 'fairest of the fair [who] kill [more] with poisoned baits than ever fell in the ring'. Think also of Hazlitt's 'particular satisfaction' at discovering that his friend Pigott (P.G. Patmore) had brought a volume of Rousseau's *Nouvelle Héloïse* to the ringside, proving that 'a love of the FANCY' (i.e. boxing) was in no way incompatible with 'the cultivation of sentiment'.

– The *fight*, the *fight's* the thing,
Wherein I'll catch the conscience of the king.[1]

Where there's a will, there's a way. – I said so to myself, as I walked down Chancery Lane, about half-past six o'clock on Monday the

10th of December, to inquire at Jack Randall's where the fight the next day was to be; and I found 'the proverb' nothing 'musty' in the present instance. I was determined to see this fight, come what would, and see it I did, in great style. It was my *first fight*, yet it more than answered my expectations. Ladies! it is to you I dedicate this description; nor let it seem out of character for the fair to notice the exploits of the brave. Courage and modesty are the old English virtues; and may they never look cold and askance on one another! Think, ye fairest of the fair, loveliest of the lovely kind, ye practisers of soft enchantment, how many more ye kill with poisoned baits than ever fell in the ring; and listen with subdued air and without shuddering, to a tale tragic only in appearance, and sacred to the FANCY![2]

I was going down Chancery Lane, thinking to ask at Jack Randall's where the fight was to be, when looking through the glass-door of the Hole in the Wall,[3] heard a gentleman asking the same question *at* Mrs Randall, as the author of *Waverley* would express it. Now Mrs Randall stood answering the gentleman's question, with the authenticity of the lady of the Champion of the Light Weights. Thinks I, I'll wait till this person comes out, and learn from him how it is. For to say a truth, I was not fond of going into this house of call for heroes and philosophers, ever since the owner of it (for Jack is no gentleman) threatened once upon a time to kick me out of doors for wanting a mutton-chop at his hospitable board, when the conqueror in thirteen battles was more full of *blue ruin*[4] than of good manners. I was the more mortified at this repulse, inasmuch as I had heard Mr James Simpkins, hosier in the Strand, one day when the character of the Hole in the Wall was brought in question, observe – 'The house is a very good house, and the company quite genteel: I have been there myself!' Remembering this unkind treatment of mine host, to which mine hostess was also a party, and not wishing to put her in unquiet thoughts at a time jubilant like the present, I waited at the door, when, who should issue forth but my friend Joe Toms,[5] and turning suddenly up Chancery Lane with that quick jerk and impatient stride which distinguishes a lover of the FANCY, I said, 'I'll be hanged if that fellow is not going to the fight, and is on his way to get me to go with him.' So it proved in effect, and we agreed to adjourn to my lodgings to discuss measures with that cordiality which makes old friends like new, and new friends like old, on great occasions. We are cold to others only when we are dull in ourselves, and have neither thoughts nor feelings to impart to them. Give a man a topic in his head, a throb of pleasure in his heart, and he will be glad to share it with the first person he meets. Toms and I, though we seldom meet, were an *alter idem*[6] on this memorable occasion, and had not an idea that we did not candidly impart; and 'so carelessly did we fleet the time', that I wish no better, when there is another fight, than to have him for a companion on my journey down, and to return with my friend Jack Pigott,[7] talking of what was to happen or of what did happen, with a noble subject always at hand, and liberty to digress to others whenever they offered. Indeed, on my repeating the lines from Spenser in an involuntary fit of enthusiasm,

> What more felicity can fall to creature,
> Than to enjoy delight with liberty?[8]

my last-named ingenious friend stopped me by saying that this, translated into the vulgate, meant *'Going to see a fight'*.

Joe Toms and I could not settle about the method of going down. He said there was a caravan, he understood, to start from Tom Belcher's at two,[9] which would go there right out and back again the next day. Now I never travel all night, and said I should get a cast to Newbury by one of the mails. Joe swore the thing was impossible, and I could only answer that I had made up my mind to it. In short, he seemed to me to waver, said he only came to see if I was going, had letters to write, a cause coming on the day after, and faintly said at parting (for I was bent on setting out that moment) – 'Well, we meet at Philippi!'[10] I made the best of my way to Piccadilly. The mail coach stand was bare. 'They are all gone', said I – 'this is always the way with me – in the instant I lose the future – if I had not stayed to pour out that last cup of tea, I should have been just in time' – and cursing my folly and ill-luck together, without inquiring at the coach-office whether the mails were gone or not, I walked on in despite, and to punish my own dilatoriness and want of determination. At any rate, I would not turn back: I might get to Hounslow, or perhaps farther, to be on my road the next morning. I passed Hyde Park Corner (my Rubicon), and trusted to fortune.[11] Suddenly I heard the clattering of a Brentford stage, and the fight rushed full upon my fancy. I argued (not unwisely) that even a Brentford coachman was better company than my own thoughts (such as they were just then), and at his invitation mounted the box with him. I immediately stated my case to him – namely, my quarrel with myself for missing the Bath or Bristol mail, and my determination to get on in consequence as well as I could, without any disparagement or insulting comparison between longer or shorter stages. It is a maxim with me that stage-coaches, and consequently stage-coachmen, are respectable in proportion to the distance they have to travel: so I said nothing on that subject to my Brentford friend. Any incipient tendency to an abstract proposition, or (as he might have construed it) to a personal reflection of this kind, was however nipped in the bud; for I had no sooner declared indignantly that I had missed the mails, than he flatly denied that they were gone along, and lo! at the instant three of them drove by in rapid, provoking, orderly succession, as if they would devour the ground before them. Here again I seemed in the contradictory situation of the man in Dryden who exclaims,

> I follow Fate, which does too hard pursue![12]

If I had stopped to inquire at the White Horse Cellar,[13] which would not have taken me a minute, I should now have been driving down the road in all the dignified unconcern and *ideal* perfection of mechanical conveyance. The Bath mail I had set my mind upon, and I had missed it, as I missed every thing else, by my own absurdity, in putting the will for the deed, and aiming at ends without employing means. 'Sir', said he of the Brentford, 'the Bath mail will be up presently, my brother-in-law drives it, and I will engage to stop him if there is a place empty.' I almost doubted my good genius; but, sure enough, up it drove like lightning, and stopped directly at the call of the Brentford Jehu. I would not have believed this possible, but the brother-in-law of a mail-coach driver is himself no mean man. I was transferred without loss of time from the top of one coach to that of the other, desired the guard to pay my fare to the Brentford coachman for me as I had no change, was accommodated with a greatcoat, put up my umbrella to keep off a drizzling mist, and we began to cut through the air like an arrow. The mile-stones disappeared one after another, the rain kept off; Tom Turtle,[14] the trainer, sat before me on the coach-box, with whom I exchanged civilities as a gentleman going to the fight; the passion that had transported me an hour before was subdued to pensive regret and conjectural musing on the next day's battle; I was promised a place inside at Reading, and upon the whole, I thought myself a lucky fellow. Such is the force of imagination! On the outside of any other coach on the 10th of December, with a Scotch mist drizzling through the cloudy moonlight air, I should have been cold, comfortless, impatient, and, no doubt, wet through; but seated on the Royal mail, I felt warm and comfortable, the air did me good, the ride did me good, I was pleased with the progress we had made, and confident that all would go well through the journey. When I got inside at Reading, I found Turtle and a stout valetudinarian, whose costume bespoke him one of the FANCY, and who had risen from a three months' sick bed to get into the mail to see the fight. They were intimate, and we fell into a lively discourse. My friend the trainer was confined in his topics to fighting dogs and men, to bears and badgers; beyond this he was 'quite chap-fallen',[15] had not a word to throw at a dog, or indeed very wisely fell asleep, when any other game was started. The whole art of training (I, however, learnt from him) consists in two things, exercise and abstinence, abstinence and exercise, repeated alternately and without end. A yolk of an egg with a spoonful of rum in it is the first thing in a morning, and then a walk of six miles till breakfast. This meal consists of a plentiful supply of tea and toast and beefsteaks. Then another six or seven miles till dinner-time, and another supply of solid beef or mutton with a pint of porter, and perhaps, at the utmost, a couple of glasses of sherry. Martin trains on water, but this increases his infirmity on another very dangerous side. The Gas-man takes now and then a chirping glass (under the rose) to console him, during a six weeks' probation, for the absence of Mrs Hickman – an agreeable woman, with (I understand) a pretty fortune of two hundred pounds. How matter presses on me! What stubborn things are facts! How inexhaustible is nature and art! 'It is well', as I once heard Mr Richmond[16] observe, 'to see a variety.' He was speaking of cock-fighting as an edifying spectacle. I cannot deny but that one learns more of what *is* (I do not say of what *ought to be*) in this desultory, mode of practical study, than from reading the same book twice over, even though it should be a moral treatise. Where was I? I was sitting at dinner with the candidate for the honours of the ring, 'where good digestion waits on appetite, and health on both'.[17] Then follows an hour of social chat and native glee; and afterwards, to another breathing over heathy hill or dale. Back to supper, and then to bed, and up by six again – Our hero

Follows so the ever-running sun
With profitable *ardour* –[18]

to the day that brings him victory or defeat in the green fairy circle. Is not this life more sweet than mine? I was going to say; but I will not libel any life by comparing it to mine, which is (at the date of these presents) bitter as coloquintida and the dregs of aconitum![19]

The invalid in the Bath mail soared a pitch above the trainer, and did not sleep so sound, because he had 'more figures and more fantasies'. We talked the hours away merrily. He had faith in surgery, for he had had three ribs set right, that had been broken in a *turn-up* at Belcher's, but thought physicians old women, for they had no antidote in their catalogue for brandy. An indigestion is an excellent common-place for two people that never met before. By way of ingratiating myself, I told him the story of my doctor, who, on my earnestly representing to him that I thought his regimen had done me harm, assured me that the whole pharmacopeia contained nothing comparable to the prescription he had given me; and, as a proof of its undoubted efficacy, said that, 'he had had one gentleman with my complaint under his hands for the last fifteen years'. This anecdote made my companion shake the rough sides of his three great coats with boisterous laughter; and Turtle, starting out of his sleep, swore he knew how the fight would go, for he had had a dream about it. Sure enough the rascal told us how the three first rounds went off, but 'his dream', like others, 'denoted a foregone conclusion'. He knew his men. The moon now rose in silver state, and I ventured, with some hesitation, to point out this object of placid beauty, with the blue serene beyond, to the man of science, to which his ear he 'seriously inclined', the more as it gave promise *d'un beau jour* for the morrow, and showed the ring undrenched by envious showers, arrayed in sunny smiles. Just then, all going on well, I thought on my friend Toms, whom I had left behind, and said innocently, 'There was a blockhead of a fellow I left in town, who said there was no possibility of getting down by the mail, and talked of going by a caravan from Belcher's at two in the morning, after he had written some letters.' 'Why', said he of the lapels, 'I should not wonder if that was the very person we saw running about like mad from one coach-door to another, and asking if any one had seen a friend of his, a gentleman going to the fight, whom he had missed stupidly enough by staying to write a note.' 'Pray, Sir', said my fellow-traveller, 'had he a plaid-cloak on?' – 'Why, no', said I, 'not at the time I left him, but he very well might afterwards, for he offered to lend me one.' The plaid-cloak and the letter decided the thing. Joe, sure enough, was in the Bristol mail, which preceded us by about fifty yards. This was droll enough. We had now but a few miles to our place of destination, and the first thing I did on alighting at Newbury, both coaches stopping at the same time, was to call out, 'Pray, is there a gentleman in that mail of the name of Toms?' 'No', said Joe, borrowing something of the vein of Gilpin,[20] 'for I have just got out.' 'Well!' says he, 'this is lucky; but you don't know how vexed I was to miss you; for', added he, lowering his voice, 'do you know when I left you I went to Belcher's to ask about the caravan, and Mrs Belcher said very obligingly she couldn't tell about that, but there were two gentlemen who had taken places by the mail and were gone on in a landau, and she could frank us. It's a pity I didn't meet with you; we could then have got down for nothing. But *mum's the word.*' It's the devil for any one to tell me a secret, for it's sure to come out in print. I do not care so much to gratify a friend, but the public ear is too great a temptation to me.

Our present business was to get beds and a supper at an inn; but this was no easy task. The public-houses were full, and where you saw a light at a private house, and people poking their heads out of the casement to see what was going on, they instantly put them in and shut the window, the moment you seemed advancing with a suspicious overture for accommodation. Our guard and coachman thundered away at the outer gate of the Crown for some time without effect – such was the greater noise within; – and when the doors were unbarred, and we got admittance, we found a party assembled in the kitchen round a good hospitable fire, some sleeping, others drinking, others talking on politics and on the fight. A tall English yeoman (something like Matthews[21] – in the face, and quite as great a wag)

> A lusty man to ben an abbot able, –[22]

was making such a prodigious noise about rent and taxes, and the price of corn now and formerly, that he had prevented us from being heard at the gate. The first thing I heard him say was to a shuffling fellow who wanted to be off a bet for a shilling glass of brandy and water – 'Confound it, man, don't be *insipid*!' Thinks I, that is a good phrase. It was a good omen. He kept it up so all night, nor flinched with the approach of morning. He was a fine fellow, with sense, wit, and spirit, a hearty body and a joyous mind, free-spoken, frank, convivial – one of that true English breed that went with Harry the Fifth to the siege of Harfleur – 'standing like greyhounds in the slips', etc. We ordered tea and eggs (beds were soon found to be out of the question) and this fellow's conversation was *sauce piquante.* It did one's heart good to see him brandish his oaken towel[23] and to hear him talk. He made mince-meat of a drunken, stupid, red-faced, quarrelsome, *frowsy* farmer, whose nose 'he moralised into a thousand similes', making it out a firebrand like Bardolph's. 'I'll tell you what, my friend', says he, 'the landlady has only to keep you here to save fire and candle. If one was to touch your nose, it would go off like a piece of charcoal.' At this the other only grinned like an idiot, the sole variety in his purple face being his little peering grey eyes and yellow teeth; called for another glass, swore he would not stand it; and after many attempts to provoke his humorous antagonist to single combat, which the other turned off (after working him up to a ludicrous pitch of choler) with great adroitness, he fell quietly asleep with a glass of liquor in his hand, which he could not lift to his head. His laughing persecutor made a speech over him, and turning to the opposite side of the room, where they were all sleeping in the midst of this 'loud and furious fun', said, 'There's a scene, by G–d, for Hogarth to paint. I think he and Shakespeare were our two best men at copying life.' This confirmed me in my good opinion of him. Hogarth, Shakespeare, and Nature, were just enough for him (indeed for any man) to know. I said, 'You read Cobbett, don't you? At least', says I, 'you talk just as well as he writes.'[24] He seemed to doubt this. But I said, 'We have an hour to spare: if you'll get pen, ink, and paper, and keep on talking, I'll write down what you say; and if it doesn't make a capital *Political Register*, I'll forfeit my head. You have kept me alive tonight, however. I don't know what I should have done without you.' He did not dislike this view of the thing, nor my asking if he was not about the size of Jem Belcher; and told me soon afterwards, in the confidence of friendship, that 'the circumstance which had given him nearly the greatest concern in his life, was Cribb's beating Jem after he had lost his eye by racket-playing.'[25] The morning dawns; that dim but yet clear light appears, which weighs like solid bars of metal on the sleepless eyelids; the guests drop down from their chambers one by one – but it was too late to think of going to bed now (the clock was on the stroke of seven), we had nothing for it but to find a barber's (the pole that glittered in the morning sun lighted us to his shop), and then a nine miles' march to Hungerford. The day was fine, the sky was blue, the mists were retiring from the marshy ground, the path was tolerably dry, the sitting-up all night had not done us much harm – at least the cause was good; we talked of this and that with amicable difference, roving and sipping of many subjects, but still invariably we returned to the fight. At length, a mile to the left of Hungerford, on a gentle eminence, we saw the ring surrounded by covered carts, gigs, and carriages, of which hundreds had passed us on the road; Toms gave a youthful shout, and we hastened down a narrow lane to the scene of action.

Reader, have you ever seen a fight? If not, you have a pleasure to come, at least if it is a fight like that between the Gas-man and Bill Neate. The crowd was very great when we arrived on the spot; open carriages were coming up, with streamers flying and music playing, and the country-people were pouring in over hedge and ditch in all directions, to see their hero beat or be beaten. The odds were still on Gas, but only about five to four. Gully[26] had been down to try Neate, and had backed him considerably, which was a damper to the sanguine confidence of the adverse party. About two hundred thousand pounds were pending. The Gas says, he has lost £3000 which were promised him by different gentlemen if he had won. He had presumed too much on himself, which had made others presume on him. This spirited and formidable young fellow seems to have taken for his motto the old maxim, that 'there are three things necessary to success in life – *Impudence! Impudence! Impudence!*[27] It is so in matters of opinion, but not in the FANCY, which is the most practical of all things, though even here confidence is half the battle, but only half. Our friend had vapoured and swaggered too much, as if he wanted to grin and bully his adversary out of the fight. 'Alas! the Bristol man was not so tamed!' – 'This is *the grave-digger*' (would Tom Hickman exclaim in the moments of intoxication from gin and success, showing his tremendous right hand), 'this will send many of them to their long homes; I haven't done with them yet!' Why should he – though he had licked four of the best men within the hour, yet why should he threaten to inflict dishonourable chastisement on my old master Richmond, a veteran going off the stage, and who has borne his sable honours meekly? Magnanimity, my dear Tom, and bravery, should be inseparable. Or why should he go up to his antagonist, the first time he ever saw him at the Fives Court, and measuring him from head to foot with a glance of contempt, as Achilles surveyed Hector, say to him, 'What, are you Bill Neate? I'll knock more blood out of that great carcass of thine, this day fortnight, than you ever knock'd out of a bullock's!' It was not manly, 'twas not fighter-like. If he was sure of the victory (as he was not), the less said about it the better. Modesty should accompany the FANCY as its shadow. The best men were always the best behaved. Jem Belcher, the Game Chicken[28] (before whom the Gas-man could not have lived) were civil, silent men. So is Cribb, so is Tom Belcher, the most elegant of sparrers, and not a man for every one to take by the nose. I enlarged on this topic in the mail (while Turtle was asleep), and said very wisely (as I thought) that impertinence was a part of no profession. A boxer was bound to beat his man, but not to thrust his fist, either actually or by implication, in every one's face. Even a highwayman, in the way of trade, may blow out your brains, but if he uses foul language at the same time, I should say he was no gentleman. A boxer, I would infer, need not be a blackguard or a coxcomb, more than another. Perhaps I press this point too much on a fallen man – Mr Thomas Hickman has by this time learnt that first of all lessons, 'That man was made to mourn'. He has lost nothing by the late fight but his presumption; and that every man may do as well without! By an over-display of this quality, however, the public had been prejudiced against him, and the *knowing-ones* were taken in. Few but those who had bet on him wished Gas to win. With my own prepossessions on the subject, the result of the 11th of December appeared to me as fine a piece of poetical justice as I had ever witnessed. The difference of weight between the two combatants (14 stone to 12) was nothing to the sporting men. Great, heavy, clumsy, long-armed Bill Neate kicked the beam in the scale of the Gas-man's vanity. The amateurs were frightened at his big words, and thought that they would make up for the difference of six feet and five feet nine. Truly, the FANCY are not men of imagination. They judge of what has been, and cannot conceive of any thing that is to be. The Gas-man had won hitherto; therefore he must beat a man half as big again as himself – and that to a certainty. Besides, there are as many feuds, factions, prejudices, pedantic notions in the FANCY as in the state or in the schools. Mr Gully is almost the only cool, sensible man among them, who exercises an unbiased discretion, and is not a slave to his passions in these matters. But enough of reflections, and to our tale. The day, as I have said, was fine for a December morning. The grass was wet, and the ground miry, and ploughed up with multitudinous feet, except that, within the ring itself, there was a spot of virgin-green closed in and unprofaned by vulgar tread, that shone with dazzling brightness in the mid-day sun. For it was now noon, and we had an hour to wait. This is the trying time. It is then the heart sickens, as you think what the two champions are about, and how short a time will determine their fate. After the first blow is struck, there is no opportunity for nervous apprehensions; you are swallowed up in the immediate interest of the scene – but

> Between the acting of a dreadful thing
> And the first motion, all the interim is
> Like a phantasma, or a hideous dream.[29]

I found it so as I felt the sun's rays clinging to my back, and saw the white wintry clouds sink below the verge of the horizon. 'So', I thought, 'my fairest hopes have faded from my sight! – so will the Gas-man's glory, or that of his adversary, vanish in an hour.' The *swells* were parading in their white box-coats, the outer ring was cleared with some bruises on the heads and shins of the rustic assembly (for the *cockneys* had been distanced by the sixty-six miles); the time drew near, I had got a good stand; a bustle, a buzz, ran through the crowd, and from the opposite side entered Neate, between his second and bottle-holder. He rolled along, swathed in his loose great coat, his knock-knees bending under his huge bulk; and, with a modest cheerful air, threw his hat into the ring. He then just looked round, and began quietly to undress; when from the other side there was a similar rush and an opening made, and the Gas-man came forward with a conscious air of anticipated triumph, too much like the cock-of-the-walk. He strutted about more than became a hero, sucked oranges with a supercilious air and threw away the skin with a toss of his head, and went up and looked at Neate, which was an act of supererogation. The only sensible thing he did was, as he strode away from the modern Ajax, to fling out his arms, as if he wanted to try whether they would do their work that day. By this time they had stripped, and presented a strong contrast in appearance. If Neate was like Ajax, 'with Atlantean shoulders, fit to bear'[30] the pugilistic reputation of all Bristol, Hickman might be compared to Diomed, light, vigorous, elastic, and his back glistened in the sun, as he moved about, like a panther's hide. There was now a dead pause – attention was awe-struck. Who at that moment, big with a great event, did not draw his breath short – did not feel his heart throb? All was ready. They tossed up for the sun, and the Gas-man won. They were led up to the *scratch* – shook hands, and went at it.

In the first round every one thought it was all over. After making play a short time, the Gas-man flew at his adversary like a tiger, struck five blows in as many seconds, three first, and then following him as he staggered back, two more, right and left, and down he fell, a mighty ruin. There was a shout, and I said, 'There is no standing this.' Neate seemed like a lifeless lump of flesh and bone, round which the Gas-man's blows played with the rapidity of electricity or lightning, and you imagined he would only be lifted up to be knocked down again. It was as if Hickman held a sword or a fire in that right hand of his, and directed it against an unarmed body. They met again, and Neate seemed, not cowed, but particularly cautious. I saw his teeth clenched together and his brows knit close against the sun. He held out both his arms at full length straight before him, like two sledge-hammers, and raised his left an inch or two higher. The Gas-man could not get over this guard – they struck mutually and fell, but without advantage on either side. It was the same in the next round; but the balance of power was thus restored – the fate of the battle was suspended. No one could tell how it would end. This was the only moment in which opinion was divided; for, in the next, the Gas-man aiming a mortal blow at his adversary's neck, with his right hand, and failing from the length he had to reach, the other returned it with his left at full swing, planted a tremendous blow on his cheek-bone and eyebrow, and made a red ruin of that side of his face. The Gas-man went down, and there was another shout – a roar of triumph as the waves of fortune rolled tumultuously from side to side. This was a settler. Hickman got up, and 'grinned horrible a ghastly smile',[31] yet he was evidently dashed in his opinion of himself; it was the first time he had ever been so punished; all one side of his face was perfect scarlet, and his right eye was closed in dingy blackness, as he advanced to the fight, less confident, but still determined. After one or two rounds, not receiving another such remembrancer, he rallied and went at it with his former impetuosity. But in vain. His strength had been weakened, – his blows could not tell at such a distance, – he was obliged to fling himself at his adversary, and could not strike from his feet; and almost as regularly as he flew at him with his right hand, Neate warded the blow, or drew back out of its reach, and felled him with the return of his left. There was little cautious sparring – no half-hits – no tapping and trifling, none of the *petit-maîtreship* of the art – they were almost all knock-down blows: – the fight was a good stand up fight. The wonder was the half-minute time. If there had been a minute or more allowed between each round, it would have been intelligible how they should by degrees recover strength and resolution; but to see two men smashed to the ground, smeared with gore, stunned, senseless, the breath beaten out of their bodies; and then, before you recover from the shock, to see them rise up with new strength and courage, stand steady to inflict or receive mortal offence, and rush upon each other 'like two clouds over the Caspian'[32] – this is the most astonishing thing of all: – this is the high and heroic state of man! From this time forward the event became more certain every round; and about the twelfth it seemed as if it must have been over. Hickman generally stood with his back to me; but in the scuffle, he had changed positions, and Neate just then made a tremendous lunge at him, and hit him full in the face. It was doubtful whether he would fall backwards or forwards; he hung suspended for a second or two, and then fell back, throwing his hands in the air, and with his face lifted up to the sky. I never saw any thing more terrific than his aspect just before he fell. All traces of life, of natural expression, were gone from him. His face was like a human skull, a death's head, spouting blood. The eyes were filled with blood, the nose streamed with blood, the mouth gaped blood. He was not like an actual man, but like a preternatural, spectral appearance, or like one of the figures in Dante's *Inferno*. Yet he fought on after this for several rounds, still striking the first desperate blow, and Neate standing on the defensive, and using the same cautious guard to the last, as if he had still all his work to do; and it was not till the Gas-man was so stunned in the seventeenth or eighteenth round, that his senses forsook him, and he could not come to time, that the battle was declared over.* Ye who despise the FANCY, do something to show as much *pluck*, or as much self-possession as this, before you assume a superiority which you have never given a single proof of by any one action in the whole course of your lives! – When the Gas-man came to himself, the first words he uttered were, 'Where am I? What is the

* Scroggins said of the Gas-man, that he thought he was a man of that courage, that if his hands were cut off, he would still fight on with the stumps – like that of Widrington, –

> – In doleful dumps,
> Who, when his legs were smitten off
> Still fought upon his stumps.[33]

matter?' 'Nothing is the matter, Tom, – you have lost the battle, but you are the bravest man alive.' And Jackson[34] whispered to him, 'I am collecting a purse for you, Tom.' – Vain sounds, and unheard at that moment! Neate instantly went up and shook him cordially by the hand, and seeing some old acquaintance, began to flourish with his fists, calling out, 'Ah, you always said I couldn't fight – What do you think now?' But all in good humour, and without any appearance of arrogance; only it was evident Bill Neate was pleased that he had won the fight. When it was over, I asked Cribb if he did not think it was a good one? He said, '*Pretty well!*' The carrier-pigeons now mounted into the air, and one of them flew with the news of her husband's victory to the bosom of Mrs Neate. Alas, for Mrs Hickman!

Mais au revoir, as Sir Fopling Flutter says.[35] I went down with Toms; I returned with Jack Pigott, whom I met on the ground. Toms is a rattle-brain; Pigott is a sentimentalist. Now, under favour, I am a sentimentalist too – therefore I say nothing, but that the interest of the excursion did not flag as I came back.[36] Pigott and I marched along the causeway leading from Hungerford to Newbury, now observing the effect of a brilliant sun on the tawny meads or moss-coloured cottages, now exulting in the fight, now digressing to some topic of general and elegant literature. My friend was dressed in character for the occasion, or like one of the FANCY; that is, with a double portion of great coats, clogs, and over-hauls: and just as we had agreed with a couple of country-lads to carry his superfluous wearing-apparel to the next town, we were overtaken by a return post-chaise, into which I got, Pigott preferring a seat on the bar. There were two strangers already in the chaise, and on their observing they supposed I had been to the fight, I said I had, and concluded they had done the same. They appeared, however, a little shy and sore on the subject; and it was not till after several hints dropped, and questions put, that it turned out that they had missed it. One of these friends had undertaken to drive the other there in his gig: they had set out, to make sure work, the day before at three in the afternoon. The owner of the one-horse vehicle scorned to ask his way, and drove right on to Bagshot, instead of turning off at Hounslow: there they stopped all night, and set off the next day across the country to Reading, from whence they took coach, and got down within a mile or two of Hungerford, just half an hour after the fight was over. This might be safely set down as one of the miseries of human life. We parted with these two gentlemen who had been to see the fight, but had returned as they went, at Wolhampton, where we were promised beds (an irresistible temptation, for Pigott had passed the preceding night at Hungerford as we had done at Newbury), and we turned into an old bow-windowed parlour with a carpet and a snug fire; and after devouring a quantity of tea, toast, and eggs, sat down to consider, during an hour of philosophic leisure, what we should have for supper. In the midst of an Epicurean deliberation between a roasted fowl and mutton chops with mashed potatoes, we were interrupted by an inroad of Goths and Vandals – *O procul este profani*[37] – not real flash-men, but interlopers, noisy pretenders, butchers from Tothill-fields, brokers from Whitechapel, who called immediately for pipes and tobacco, hoping it would not be disagreeable to the gentlemen, and began to insist that it was *a cross*. Pigott withdrew from the smoke and noise into another room, and left me to dispute the point with them for a couple of hours *sans intermission* by the dial.[38] The next morning we rose refreshed; and on observing that Jack had a pocket volume in his hand, in which he read in the intervals of our discourse, I inquired what it was, and learned to my particular satisfaction that it was a volume of the *New Eloise*.[39] Ladies, after this, will you contend that a love for the FANCY is incompatible with the cultivation of sentiment?[40] – We jogged on as before, my friend setting me up in a genteel drab great coat and green silk handkerchief (which I must say became me exceedingly), and after stretching our legs for a few miles, and seeing Jack Randall, Ned Turner, and Scroggins, pass on the top of one of the Bath coaches, we engaged with the driver of the second to take us to London for the usual fee. I got inside, and found three other passengers. One of them was an old gentleman with an aquiline nose, powdered hair, and a pigtail, and who looked as if he had played many a rubber at the Bath rooms. I said to myself, he is very like Mr Windham; I wish he would enter into conversation, that I might hear what fine observations would come from those finely-turned features. However, nothing passed, till, stopping to dine at Reading, some inquiry was made by the company about the fight, and I gave (as the reader may believe) an eloquent and animated description of it. When we got into the coach again, the old gentleman, after a graceful exordium, said, he had, when a boy, been to a fight between the famous Broughton and George Stevenson, who was called the *Fighting Coachman*, in the year 1770,[41] with the late Mr Windham. This beginning flattered the spirit of prophecy within me and rivetted my attention. He went on – 'George Stevenson was coachman to a friend of my father's. He was an old man when I saw him some years afterwards. He took hold of his own arm and said, "There was muscle here once, but now it is no more than this young gentleman's." He added, "Well, no matter; I have been here long, I am willing to go hence, and I hope I have done no more harm than another man."' 'Once', said my unknown companion, 'I asked him if he had ever beat Broughton? He said Yes; that he had fought with him three times, and the last time he fairly beat him, though the world did not allow it. "I'll tell you how it was, master. When the seconds lifted us up in the last round, we were so exhausted that neither of us could stand, and we fell upon one another, and as Master Broughton fell uppermost, the mob gave it in his favour, and he was said to have won the battle. But," says he, "the fact was, that as his second (John Cuthbert) lifted him up, he said to him, 'I'll fight no more, I've had enough'; which," says Stevenson, "you know gave me the victory. And to prove to you that this was the case, when John Cuthbert was on his death-bed, and they asked him if there was anything on his mind which he wished to confess, he answered, 'Yes, that there was one thing he wished to set right, for that certainly Master Stevenson won that last fight with Master Broughton; for he whispered him as he lifted him up in the last round of all, that he had had enough.'"' 'This', said the Bath gentleman, 'was a bit of human nature'; and I have written this account of the fight on purpose that it might not be lost to the world. He also stated as a proof of the candour of mind in this class of men, that Stevenson acknowledged that Broughton could have beat him in his best day; but that he (Broughton) was getting old in their last rencounter. When we stopped in Piccadilly, I wanted to ask the gentleman some questions about the late Mr Windham, but had not courage. I got out, resigned my coat and green silk handkerchief to Pigott (loth to part with these ornaments of life), and walked home in high spirits.

P.S. Toms called upon me the next day, to ask me if I did not think the fight was a complete thing? I said I thought it was. I hope he will relish my account of it.

On Great and Little Things

Published in the very same issue of *The New Monthly Magazine* as 'The Fight' (February 1822) but advertised as 'Table-Talk No II' and signed 'T.'

Liber Amoris and Related Writings tells the story of a breakdown, and this breakdown was as much public as private. In fact, the two fed into one another, as Hazlitt attempted to console himself for the fall of Bonaparte and the difficulties of freelance authorship by investing all his hopes in the image of Sarah Walker. Hazlitt's obsession with Sarah is referred to only once in 'On Great and Little Things' but the entire matrix of the essay is unconsciously structured by it.

The greatest irritant of the human will, he says, is not the sublime force of necessity but the 'petty, incessant, insect warfare' of little things: 'the more contemptible the object or the obstructions in the way to it, the more are we provoked at being hindered by them'. Having mulled over the mind's obsession with the humble and the inconsequential, the essay then takes an unexpectedly autobiographical turn, with Hazlitt the middle-class author suddenly confessing to a life-long weakness for servant girls 'with their red elbows, hard hands, black stockings and mob-caps'. 'I have written love-letters to such in my time,' he writes, 'the simpletons only laughed and said that "those were not the sort of things to gain the affection"'. There follows a long, lingering lament on the part of the lovelorn middle-aged intellectual, which gives way only reluctantly to a revealing passage on the imagination's ambition to raise the little into the great: 'poets choose mistresses who have the fewest charms, that they may make something out of nothing'. The concluding paragraph then looks forward to that extraordinary fascination with 'the magnificence even of small things' that lies at the heart of *Liber Amoris*.

These little things are great to little man.

GOLDSMITH[1]

The great and the little have, no doubt, a real existence in the nature of things: but they both find pretty much the same level in the mind of man. It is a common measure, which does not always accommodate itself to the size and importance of the objects it represents. It has a certain interest to spare for certain things (and no more) according to its humour and capacity; and neither likes to be stinted in its allowance, nor to muster up an unusual share of sympathy, just as the occasion may require. Perhaps if we could recollect distinctly, we should discover that the two things that have affected us most in the course of our lives have been, one of them of the greatest, and the other of the smallest possible consequence. To let that pass as too fine a speculation, we know well enough that very trifling circumstances do give us great and daily annoyance, and as often prove too much for our philosophy and forbearance, as matters of the highest moment. A lump of soot spoiling a man's dinner, a plate of toast falling in the ashes, the being disappointed of a ribbon to a cap or a ticket for a ball, have led to serious and almost tragical consequences. Friends not unfrequently fall out and never meet again for some idle misunderstanding, 'some trick not worth an egg', who have stood the shock of serious differences of opinion and clashing interests in life; and there is an excellent paper in *The Tatler*[2] to prove that if a married couple do not quarrel about some point in the first instance not worth contesting, they will seldom find an opportunity afterwards to quarrel about a question of real importance. Grave divines, great statesmen, and deep philosophers are put out of their way by very little things: nay, discreet, worthy people, without any pretensions but to good-nature and common sense, readily surrender the happiness of their whole lives sooner than give up an opinion to which they have committed themselves, though in all likelihood it was the mere turn of a feather which side they should take in the argument. It is the being baulked or thwarted in any thing that constitutes the grievance, the unpardonable affront, not the value of the thing to which we had made up our minds. Is it that we despise little things; that we are not prepared for them; that they take us in our careless, unguarded moments, and tease us out of our ordinary patience by their petty, incessant, insect warfare, buzzing about us and stinging us like gnats; so that we can neither get rid of nor grapple with them, whereas we collect all our fortitude and resolution to meet evils of greater magnitude? Or is it that there is a certain stream of irritability that is continually fretting upon the wheels of life, which finds sufficient food to play with in straws and feathers, while great objects are too much for it, either choke it up, or divert its course into serious and thoughtful interest? Some attempt might be made to explain this in the following manner.

One is always more vexed at losing a game of any sort by a single hole or ace, than if one has never had a chance of winning it. This is no doubt in part or chiefly because the prospect of success irritates the subsequent disappointment. But people have been known to pine and fall sick from holding the next number to the twenty thousand pound prize in the lottery. Now this could only arise from their being so near winning in fancy, from there seeming to be so thin a partition between them and success. When they were within one of the right number, why could they not have taken the next – it was so easy: this haunts their minds and will not let them rest, notwithstanding the absurdity of the reasoning. It is that the will here has a slight imaginary obstacle to surmount to attain its end: it should appear it had only an exceedingly trifling effort to make for this purpose, that it was absolutely in its power (had it known) to seize the envied prize, and it is continually harassing itself by making the obvious transition from one number to the other, when it is too late. That is to say, the will acts in proportion to its fancied power, to its superiority over immediate obstacles. Now in little or indifferent matters there seems no reason why it should not have its own way, and therefore a disappointment vexes it the more. It grows angry according to the insignificance of the occasion, and frets itself to death about an object, merely because from its very futility there can be supposed to be no real difficulty in the way of its attainment, nor any thing more required for this purpose than a determination of the will. The being baulked of this throws the mind off its balance, or puts it into what is called *a passion*; and as nothing but an act of voluntary power still seems necessary to get rid of every impediment, we indulge our violence more and more, and heighten our impatience by degrees into a sort of frenzy. The object is the same as it was, but we are no longer as we were. The blood is heated, the muscles are strained. The feelings are wound up to a pitch of agony with the vain strife. The temper is tried to the utmost it will bear.

The more contemptible the object or the obstructions in the way to it, the more are we provoked at being hindered by them. It looks like witchcraft. We fancy there is a spell upon us, so that we are hampered by straws and entangled in cobwebs. We believe that there is a fatality about our affairs. It is evidently done on purpose to plague us. A demon is at our elbow to torment and defeat us in every thing, even in the smallest things. We see him sitting and mocking us, and we rave and gnash our teeth at him in return. It is particularly hard that we cannot succeed in any one point, however trifling, that we set our hearts on. We are the sport of imbecility and mischance. We make another desperate effort, and fly out into all the extravagance of impotent rage once more. Our anger runs away with our reason, because, as there is little to give it birth, there is nothing to check it or recall us to our senses in the prospect of consequences. We take up and rend in pieces the mere toys of humour, as the gusts of wind take up and whirl about chaff and stubble. Passion plays the tyrant, in a grand tragic-comic style, over the Lilliputian difficulties and petty disappointments it has to encounter, gives way to all the fretfulness of grief and all the turbulence of resentment, makes a fuss about nothing because there is nothing to make a fuss about when an impending calamity, an irretrievable loss, would instantly bring it to its recollection, and tame it in its preposterous career. A man may be in a great passion and give himself strange airs at so simple a thing as a game at ball, for instance; may rage like a wild beast, and be ready to dash his head against the wall about nothing, or about that which he will laugh at the next minute, and think no more of ten minutes after, at the same time that a good smart blow from the ball, the effects of which he might feel as a serious inconvenience for a month, would calm him directly –

> Anon as patient as the female dove;
> His silence will sit drooping.[3]

The truth is, we pamper little griefs into great ones, and bear great ones as well as we can. We can afford to dally and play tricks with the one, but the others we have enough to do with, without any of the wantonness and bombast of passion – without the swaggering of Pistol, or the insolence of King Cambyses' vein.[4] To great evils we submit, we resent little provocations. I have before now been disappointed of a hundred pound job and lost half a crown at rackets on the same day, and been more mortified at the latter than the former. That which is lasting we share with the future, we defer the consideration of till tomorrow: that which belongs to the moment we drink up in all its bitterness, before the spirit evaporates. We probe minute mischiefs to the quick; we lacerate, tear, and mangle our bosoms with misfortune's finest, brittlest point, and wreak our vengeance on ourselves and it for good and all. Small pains are more manageable, more within our reach; we can fret and worry ourselves about them, can turn them into any shape, can twist and torture them how we please; a grain of sand in the eye, a thorn in the flesh only irritates the part, and leaves us strength enough to quarrel and get out of all patience with it; a heavy blows stuns and takes away all power of sense as well as of resistance. The great and mighty reverses of fortune, like the revolutions of nature, may be said to carry their own weight and reason along with them: they seem unavoidable and remediless, and we submit to them without murmuring as to a fatal necessity. The magnitude of the events, in which we may happen to be concerned, fills the mind, and carries it out of itself, as it were, into the page of history. Our thoughts are expanded with the scene on which we have to act, and lend us strength to disregard our own personal share in it. Some men are indifferent to the stroke of fate, as before and after earthquakes there is a calm in the air. From the commanding situation whence they have been accustomed to view things, they look down at themselves as only a part of the whole, and can abstract their minds from the pressure of misfortune, by the aid of its very violence. They are projected, in the explosion of events, into a different sphere, far from their former thoughts, purposes, and passions. The greatness of the change anticipates the slow effects of time and reflection: – they at once contemplate themselves from an immense distance, and look up with speculative wonder at the height on which they stood. Had the downfall been less complete, it would have been more galling and borne with less resignation, because there might still be a chance of remedying it by farther efforts and farther endurance – but *past cure, past hope.* It is chiefly this cause (together with something of constitutional character) which has enabled the greatest man in modern history to bear his reverses of fortune with gay magnanimity,[5] and to submit to the loss of the empire of the world with as little discomposure as if he had been playing a game at chess.* This does

* This essay was written in January, 1821.

not prove by our theory that he did not use to fly into violent passions with Talleyrand for plaguing him with bad news when things went wrong. He was mad at uncertain forebodings of disaster, but resigned to its consummation. A man may dislike impertinence, yet have no quarrel with necessity!

There is another consideration that may take off our wonder at the firmness with which the principals in great vicissitudes of fortune bear their fate, which is, that they are in the secret of its operations, and know that what to others appears chance-medley was unavoidable. The clearness of their perception of all the circumstances converts the uneasiness of doubt into certainty: they have not the qualms of conscience which their admirers have, who cannot tell how much of the event is to be attributed to the leaders, and how much to unforeseen accidents: they are aware either that the result was not to be helped, or that they did all they could to prevent it.

—— Si Pergama dextra
Defendi possent, etiam hac defensa fuissent.[6]

It is the mist and obscurity through which we view objects that makes us fancy they might have been, or might still be otherwise. The precise knowledge of antecedents and consequents makes men practical as well as philosophical Necessarians.[7] It is the want of this knowledge which is the principle and soul of gambling, and of all games of chance or partial skill. The supposition is, that the issue is uncertain, and that there is no positive means of ascertaining it. It is dependent on the turn of a die, on the tossing up of a halfpenny: to be fair, it must be a lottery; there is no knowing but by the event; and it is this which keeps the interest alive, and works up the passion little short of madness. There is all the agitation of suspense, all the alternation of hope and fear, of good and bad success, all the eagerness of desire, without the possibility of reducing this to calculation, that is, of subjecting the increased action of the will to a known rule, or restraining the excesses of passion within the bounds of reason. We see no cause beforehand why the run of the cards should not be in our favour: – we will hear of none afterwards why it should not have been so. As in the absence of all *data* to judge by, we wantonly fill up the blank with the most extravagant expectations, so, when all is over, we obstinately recur to the chance we had previously. There is nothing to tame us down to the event, nothing to reconcile us to our hard luck, for so we think it. We see no reason why we failed (and there was none, any more than why we should succeed) – we think that, reason apart, our will is the next best thing; we still try to have it our own way, and fret, torment, and harrow ourselves up with vain imaginations to effect impossibilities.* We play the game over again: we wonder how it was possible for us to fail. We turn our brain with straining at contradictions, and striving to make things what they are not, or in other words, to subject the course of nature to our fantastical wishes. '*If it had been so – if we had done such and such a thing*' – we try it in a thousand different ways, and are just as far off the mark as ever. We appealed to chance in the first instance, and yet, when it has decided against us, we will not give in, and sit down contented with our loss, but refuse to submit to any thing but reason, which has nothing to do with the matter. In drawing two straws, for example, to see which is the longest, there was no apparent necessity we should fix upon the wrong one, it was so easy to have fixed upon the other, nay, at one time we were going to do it – if we had – the mind thus runs back to what was so possible and feasible at one time, while the thing was pending, and would fain give a bias to causes so slender and insignificant, as the skittle-player bends his body to give a bias to the bowl he has already delivered from his hand, not considering that what is once determined, be the causes ever so trivial or evanescent, is in the individual instance unalterable. Indeed, to be a great philosopher, in the practical and most important sense of the term, little more seems necessary than to be convinced of the truth of the maxim, which the wise man repeated to the daughter of King Cophetua, *That if a thing is, it is*: and there is an end of it!

We often make life unhappy in wishing things to have turned out otherwise than they did, merely because that is possible to the imagination which is impossible in fact. I remember when L[amb]'s farce[8] was damned (for damned it was, that's certain) I used to dream every night for a month after (and then I vowed I would plague myself no more about it) that it was revived at one of the Minor or provincial theatres with great success, that such and such retrenchments and alterations had been made in it, and

* Losing gamesters thus become desperate, because the continued and violent irritation of the will against a run of ill luck drives it to extremity, and makes it bid defiance to common sense and every consideration of prudence or self-interest.

that it was thought *it might do at the other House*. I had heard indeed (this was told in confidence to L[amb]) that *Gentleman* Lewis was present on the night of its performance, and said, that if he had had it, he would have made it, by a few judicious curtailments, 'the most popular little thing that had been brought out for some time.' How often did I conjure up in recollection the full diapason of applause at the end of the Prologue, and hear my ingenious friend in the first row of the pit roar with laughter at his own wit! Then I dwelt with forced complacency on some part in which it had been doing well: then we would consider (in concert) whether the long, tedious opera of the *Travellers*,[9] which preceded it, had not tired people beforehand, so that they had not spirits left for the quaint and sparkling 'wit skirmishes' of the dialogue, and we all agreed it might have gone down after a Tragedy, except L[amb] himself, who swore he had no hopes of it from the beginning, and that he knew the name of the hero when it came to be discovered could not be got over. – *Mr H——*, thou wert damned! Bright shone the morning on the playbills that announced thy appearance, and the streets were filled with the buzz of persons asking one another if they would go to see *Mr H——*, and answering that they would certainly: but before night the gaiety, not of the author, but of his friends and the town was eclipsed, for thou wert damned! Hadst thou been anonymous, thou haply mightst have lived. But thou didst come to an untimely end for thy tricks, and for want of a better name to pass them off!

In this manner we go back to the critical minutes on which the turn of our fate, or that of any one else in whom we are interested, depended; try them over again with new knowledge and sharpened sensibility; and thus think to alter what is irrevocable, and ease for a moment the pang of lasting regret. So in a game at rackets*[10] (to compare small things with great) I think if at such a point I had followed up my success, if I had not been too secure or over-anxious in another part, if I had played for such an opening, in short, if I had done any thing but what I did and what has proved unfortunate in the result, the chances were all in my favour. But it is merely because I do not know what would have happened in the other case, that I interpret it so readily to my own advantage. I have

* Some of the poets in the beginning of the last century would often set out on a simile by observing – 'So in Arabia have I seen a Phoenix!' I confess my illustrations are of a more homely and humble nature.

sometimes lain awake a whole night, trying to serve out the last ball of an interesting game in a particular corner of the court, which I had missed from a nervous feeling. Rackets (I might observe for the sake of the uninformed reader) is, like any other athletic game, very much a thing of skill and practice: but it is also a thing of opinion, 'subject to all the skyey influences'.[11] If you think you can win, you can win. Faith is necessary to victory. If you hesitate in striking at the ball, it is ten to one but you miss it. If you are apprehensive of committing some particular error (such as striking the ball *foul*) you will be nearly sure to do it. While thinking of that which you are so earnestly bent upon avoiding, your hand mechanically follows the strongest idea, and obeys the imagination rather than the intention of the striker. A run of luck is a forerunner of success, and courage is as much wanted as skill. No one is however free from nervous sensations at times. A good player may not be able to strike a single stroke if another comes into the court that he has a particular dread of; and it frequently so happens that a player cannot beat another even, though he can give half the game to an equal player, because he has some associations of jealousy or personal pique against the first which he has not towards the last. *Sed haec hactenus*.[12] Chess is a game I do not understand, and have not comprehension enough to play at. But I believe, though it is so much less a thing of chance than science or skill, eager players pass whole nights in marching and countermarching their men and check-mating a successful adversary, supposing that at a certain point of the game, they had determined upon making a particular move instead of the one which they actually did make. I have heard a story of two persons playing at backgammon, one of whom was so enraged at losing his match at a particular point of the game, that he took the board and threw it out of the window. It fell upon the head of one of the passengers in the street, who came up to demand instant satisfaction for the affront and injury he had sustained. The losing gamester only asked him if he understood backgammon, and finding that he did, said, that if upon seeing the state of the game he did not excuse the extravagance of his conduct, he would give him any other satisfaction he wished for. The tables were accordingly brought, and the situation of the two contending parties being explained, the gentleman put up his sword, and went away perfectly satisfied. To return from this, which to some will seem a digression, and to others will serve as a confirmation of the doctrine I am insisting on.

It is not then the value of the object, but the time and pains bestowed upon it, that determines the sense and degree of our loss. Many men set their minds only on trifles, and have not a compass of soul to take an interest in any thing truly great and important beyond forms and *minutiae*. Such persons are really men of little minds, or may be complimented with the title of great children,

Pleased with a feather, tickled with a straw.[13]

Larger objects elude their grasp, while they fasten eagerly on the light and insignificant. They fidget themselves and others to death with incessant anxiety about nothing. A part of their dress that is awry keeps them in a fever of restlessness and impatience; they sit picking their teeth, or paring their nails, or stirring the fire, or brushing a speck of dirt off their coats, while the house or the world tumbling about their ears would not rouse them from their morbid insensibility. They cannot sit still on their chairs for their lives, though, if there were any thing for them to do, they would become immoveable. Their nerves are as irritable as their imaginations are callous and inert. They are addicted to an inveterate habit of littleness and perversity, which rejects every other motive to action or object of contemplation but the daily, teasing, contemptible, familiar, favourite sources of uneasiness and dissatisfaction. When they are of a sanguine instead of a morbid temperament, they become *quidnuncs* and virtuosos – collectors of caterpillars and odd volumes, makers of fishing-rods and curious in watch-chains. Will Wimble dabbled in this way, to his immortal honour.[14] But many others have been less successful. There are those who build their fame on epigrams or epitaphs, and others who devote their lives to writing the Lord's Prayer in little. Some poets compose and sing their own verses. Which character would they have us think most highly of – the poet or the musician? The Great is One. Some there are who feel more pride in sealing a letter with a head of Homer than ever that old blind bard did in reciting his *Iliad*. These raise a huge opinion of themselves out of nothing, as there are those who shrink from their own merits into the shade of unconquerable humility. I know one person at least, who would rather be the author of an unsuccessful farce than of a successful tragedy. Repeated mortification has produced an inverted ambition in his mind, and made failure the bitter test of desert. He cannot lift his drooping head to gaze on the gaudy crown of popularity placed within his reach, but casts a pensive, rivetted look downwards to the modest flowers which the multitude trample under their feet. If he had a piece likely to succeed, coming out under all advantages, he would damn it by some ill-timed, wilful jest, and lose the favour of the public, to preserve the sense of his personal identity. 'Misfortune', Shakespeare says, 'brings a man acquainted with strange bed-fellows':[15] and it makes our thoughts traitors to ourselves. It is a maxim with many – '*Take care of the pence, and the pounds will take care of themselves.*' Those only put it in practice successfully who think more of the pence than of the pounds. To such, a large sum is less than a small one. Great speculations, great returns are to them extravagant or imaginary: a few hundreds a year are something *snug* and comfortable. Persons who have been used to a petty, huckstering way of life cannot enlarge their apprehensions to a notion of any thing better. Instead of launching out into greater expense and liberality with the tide of fortune, they draw back with a fear of consequences, and think to succeed on a broader scale by dint of meanness and parsimony. My uncle Toby frequently caught Trim standing up behind his chair, when he had told him to be seated.[16] What the corporal did out of respect, others would do out of servility. The menial character does not wear out in three or four generations. You cannot keep some people out of the kitchen, merely because their grandfathers or grandmothers came out of it. A poor man and his wife walking along in the neighbourhood of Portland Place, he said to her peevishly, 'What is the use of walking along these fine streets and squares? Let us turn down some alley!' He felt he should be more at home there. L[amb] said of an old acquaintance of his, that when he was young, he wanted to be a tailor, but had not spirit! This is the misery of unequal matches. The woman cannot easily forget, or think that others forget, her origin; and with perhaps superior sense and beauty, keeps painfully in the background. It is worse when she braves this conscious feeling, and displays all the insolence of the upstart and affected fine-lady. But shouldst thou ever, my Infelice,[17] grace my home with thy loved presence, as thou hast cheered my hopes with thy smile, thou wilt conquer all hearts with thy prevailing gentleness, and I will show the world what Shakespeare's women were! – Some gallants set their hearts on princesses; others descend in imagination to women of quality; others are mad after opera-singers. For my part, I am shy even of actresses, and should not think of leaving my card with Madame V[estris].[18] I am for none of these *bonnes fortunes*; but for a list of humble beauties, servant-maids and shepherd-girls, with their red elbows, hard hands, black stockings and mob-caps, I could furnish out a gallery equal to Cowley's,[19] and paint them half as well. Oh! might I but attempt a description of some of them in poetic prose, Don Juan would forget his Julia, and Mr Davison might both print and publish this volume.[20] I agree so far with Horace, and differ with Montaigne.[21] I admire the Clementinas and Clarissas at a distance: the Pamelas and Fannys of Richardson and Fielding make my blood tingle.[22] I have written love-letters to such in my time, *d'un pathetique à faire fendre les rochers*, and with about as much effect as if they had been addressed to stone.[23] The simpletons only laughed, and said, that 'those were not the sort of things to gain the affections'. I wish I had kept copies in my own justification. What is worse, I have an utter aversion to *blue-stockings*. I do not care a fig for any woman that knows even what *an author* means. If I know that she has read any thing I have written, I cut her acquaintance immediately. This sort of literary intercourse with me passes for nothing. Her critical and scientific acquirements are *carrying coals to Newcastle*. I do not want to be told that I have published such or such a work. I knew all this before. It makes no addition to my sense of power. I do not wish the affair to be brought about in that way. I would have her read my soul: she should understand the language of the heart: she should know what I am, as if she were another self! She should love me for myself alone. I like myself without any reason: – I would have her do so too. This is not very reasonable. I abstract from my temptations to admire all the circumstances of dress, birth, breeding, fortune; and I would not willingly put forward my own pretensions, whatever they may be. The image of some fair creature is engraven on my inmost soul; it is on that I build my claim to her regard, and expect her to see into my heart, as I see her form always before me. Wherever she treads, pale primroses, like her face, vernal hyacinths, like her brow, spring up beneath her feet, and music hangs on every bough: but all is cold, barren, and desolate without her. Thus I feel and thus I think. But have I ever told her so? No. Or if I did, would she understand it? No. I 'hunt the wind, I worship a statue, cry aloud to the desert'.[24] To see beauty is not to be beautiful, to pine in love is not to be loved again. – I always was inclined to raise and magnify the power of Love. I thought that his sweet power should only be exerted to join together the loveliest forms and fondest hearts; that none but those in whom his Godhead shone outwardly, and was inly felt, should ever partake of his triumphs; and I stood and gazed at a distance, as unworthy to mingle in so bright a throng, and did not (even for a moment) wish to tarnish the glory of so fair a vision by being myself admitted into it. I say this was my notion once, but God knows it was one of the errors of my youth. For coming nearer to look, I saw the maimed, the blind, and the halt enter in, the crooked and the dwarf, the ugly, the old and impotent, the man of pleasure and the man of the world, the dapper and the pert, the vain and shallow boaster, the fool and the pedant, the ignorant and brutal, and all that is farthest removed from earth's fairest-born, and the pride of human life. Seeing all these enter the courts of Love, and thinking that I also might venture in under favour of the crowd, but finding myself rejected, I fancied (I might be wrong) that it was not so much because I was below, as above the common standard. I did feel, but I was ashamed to feel, mortified at my repulse, when I saw the meanest of mankind, the very scum and refuse, all creeping things and every obscene creature, enter in before me. I seemed a species by myself. I took a pride even in my disgrace: and concluded I had elsewhere my inheritance! The only thing I ever piqued myself upon was the writing the *Essay on the Principles of Human Action* – a work that no woman ever read, or would ever comprehend the meaning of. But if I do not build my claim to regard on the pretensions I have, how can I build it on those I am totally without? Or why do I complain and expect to gather grapes of thorns, or figs of thistles? Thought has in me cancelled pleasure; and this dark forehead, bent upon truth, is the rock on which all affection has split. And thus I waste my life in one long sigh; nor ever (till too late) beheld a gentle face turned gently upon mine! ... But no! not too late, if that face, pure, modest, downcast, tender, with angel sweetness, not only gladdens the prospect of the future, but sheds its radiance on the past, smiling in tears. A purple light hovers round my head. The air of love is in the room. As I look at my long-neglected copy of the *Death of Clorinda*,[25] golden gleams play upon the canvas, as they used when I painted it. The flowers of Hope and Joy springing up in my mind, recall the time when they first bloomed there. The years that are fled knock at the door and enter. I am in the Louvre once more. The sun of Austerlitz has not set.[26] It still shines here – in my heart; and he, the son of glory, is not dead, nor ever shall, to me. I am as when my life began. The rainbow is in the sky again. I see the skirts of the departed years.

All that I have thought and felt has not been in vain. I am not utterly worthless, unregarded; nor shall I die and wither of pure scorn. Now could I sit on the tomb of Liberty, and write a Hymn to Love. Oh! if I am deceived, let me be deceived still. Let me live in the Elysium of those soft looks; poison me with kisses, kill me with smiles; but still mock me with thy love!*

Poets choose mistresses who have the fewest charms, that they may make something out of nothing. They succeed best in fiction, and they apply this rule to love. They make a Goddess of any dowdy. As Don Quixote said, in answer to the matter of fact remonstrances of Sancho, that Dulcinea del Toboso answered the purpose of signalising his valour just as well as the 'fairest princess under sky',[27] so any of the fair sex will serve them to write about just as well as another. They take some awkward thing and dress her up in fine words, as children dress up a wooden doll in fine clothes. Perhaps, a fine head of hair, a taper waist, or some other circumstance strikes them, and they make the rest out according to their fancies. They have a wonderful knack of supplying deficiencies in the subjects of their idolatry out of the store-house of their imaginations. They presently translate their favourites to the skies, where they figure with Berenice's locks and Ariadne's crown. This predilection for the unprepossessing and insignificant, I take to arise not merely from a desire in poets to have some subject to exercise their inventive talents upon, but from their jealousy of any pretensions (even those of beauty in the other sex) that might interfere with the continual incense offered to their personal vanity.

Cardinal Mazarine never thought any thing of Cardinal de Retz,[28] after he told him that he had written for the last thirty years of his life with the same pen. Some Italian poet going to present a copy of verses to the Pope, and finding, as he was looking them over in the coach as he went, a mistake of a single letter in the printing, broke his heart of vexation and chagrin. A still more remarkable case of literary disappointment occurs in the history of a countryman of his, which I cannot refrain from giving here, as I find it related.[29] 'Anthony Codrus Urceus, a most learned and unfortunate Italian, born near Modena, 1446, was a striking instance', says his biographer, 'of the miseries men bring upon

* I beg the reader to consider this passage merely as a specimen of the mock-heroic style, and as having nothing to do with any real facts or feelings.

themselves by setting their affections unreasonably on trifles. This learned man lived at Forli, and had an apartment in the palace. His room was so very dark, that he was forced to use a candle in the day-time; and one day, going abroad without putting it out, his library was set on fire, and some papers which he had prepared for the press were burned. The instant he was informed of this ill news, he was affected even to madness. He ran furiously to the palace, and stopping at the door of his apartment, he cried aloud, "Christ Jesus! what mighty crime have I committed! Whom of your followers have I ever injured, that you thus rage with inexpiable hatred against me?" Then turning himself to an image of the Virgin Mary near at hand, "Virgin (says he) hear what I have to say, for I speak in earnest, and with a composed spirit: if I shall happen to address you in my dying moments, I humbly intreat you not to hear me, nor receive me into Heaven, for I am determined to spend all eternity in Hell!" Those who heard these blasphemous expressions endeavoured to comfort him; but all to no purpose: for, the society of mankind being no longer supportable to him, he left the city, and retired, like a savage, to the deep solitude of a wood. Some say that he was murdered there by ruffians: others, that he died at Bologna in 1500, after much contrition and penitence.'

Perhaps the censure passed at the outset of the anecdote on this unfortunate person is unfounded and severe, when it is said that he brought his miseries on himself 'by having set his affections unreasonably on trifles'. To others it might appear so: but to himself the labour of a whole life was hardly a trifle. His passion was not a causeless one, though carried to such frantic excess. The story of Sir Isaac Newton presents a strong contrast to the last-mentioned one, who on going into his study and finding that his dog Tray had thrown down a candle on the table, and burnt some papers of great value, contented himself with exclaiming, 'Ah! Tray, you don't know the mischief you have done!' Many persons would not forgive the overturning of a cup of chocolate so soon.

I remember hearing an instance some years ago of a man of character and property, who through unexpected losses had been condemned to a long and heart-breaking imprisonment, which he bore with exemplary fortitude. At the end of four years, by the interest and exertions of friends, he obtained his discharge with every prospect of beginning the world afresh, and had made his arrangements for leaving his irksome abode, and meeting his wife and family at a distance of two hundred miles by a certain day.

Owing to the miscarriage of a letter, some signature necessary to the completion of the business did not arrive in time, and on account of the informality which had thus arisen, he could not set out home till the return of the post, which was four days longer. His spirit could not brook the delay. He had wound himself up to the last pitch of expectation; he had, as it were, calculated his patience to hold out to a certain point, and then to throw down his load for ever, and he could not find resolution to resume it for a few hours beyond this. He put an end to the intolerable conflict of hope and disappointment in a fit of excruciating anguish. Woes that we have time to foresee and leisure to contemplate break their force by being spread over a larger surface, and borne at intervals; but those that come upon us suddenly, for however short a time, seem to insult us by their unnecessary and uncalled-for intrusion; and the very prospect of relief, when held out and then withdrawn from us, to however small a distance, only frets impatience into agony by tantalising our hopes and wishes; and to rend asunder the thin partition that separates us from our favourite object, we are ready to burst even the fetters of life itself!

I am not aware that any one has demonstrated how it is that a stronger capacity is required for the conduct of great affairs than of small ones. The organs of the mind, like the pupil of the eye, may be contracted or dilated to view a broader or a narrower surface, and yet find sufficient variety to occupy its attention in each. The material universe is infinitely divisible, and so is the texture of human affairs. We take things in the gross or in the detail, according to the occasion. I think I could as soon get up the budget of Ways and Means[30] for the current year, as be sure of making both ends meet, and paying my rent at quarter-day in a paltry huckster's shop. Great objects move on by their own weight and impulse: great power turns aside petty obstacles; and he, who wields it, is often but the puppet of circumstances, like the fly on the wheel that said, 'What a dust we raise!' It is easier to ruin a kingdom and aggrandise one's own pride and prejudices than to set up a green-grocer's stall. An idiot or a madman may do this at any time, whose word is law, and whose nod is fate. Nay, he whose look is obedience, and who understands the silent wishes of the great, may easily trample on the necks and tread out the liberties of a mighty nation, deriding their strength, and hating it the more from a consciousness of his own meanness. Power is not wisdom, it is true; but it equally ensures its own objects. It does not exact, but dispenses with talent. When a man creates this power, or new-moulds the state by sage counsels and bold enterprises, it is a different thing from overturning it with the levers that are put into his baby hands. In general, however, it may be argued that great transactions and complicated concerns ask more genius to conduct them than smaller ones, for this reason, *viz.* that the mind must be able either to embrace a greater variety of details in a more extensive range of objects, or must have a greater faculty of generalising, or a greater depth of insight into ruling principles, and so come at true results in that way. Bonaparte knew everything, even to the names of our cadets in the East India service; but he failed in this, that he did not calculate the resistance which barbarism makes to refinement. He thought that the Russians could not burn Moscow, because the Parisians could not burn Paris. The French think everything must be French. The Cossacks, alas! do not conform to etiquette: the rudeness of the seasons knows no rules of politeness! – Some artists think it a test of genius to paint a large picture,[31] and I grant the truth of this position, if the large picture contains more than a small one. It is not the size of the canvas, but the quantity of truth and nature put into it, that settles the point. It is a mistake, common enough on this subject, to suppose that a miniature is more finished than an oil-picture. The miniature is inferior to the oil-picture only because it is less finished, because it cannot follow nature into so many individual and exact particulars. The proof of which is, that the copy of a good portrait will always make a highly finished miniature (see for example Mr Bone's enamels[32]), whereas the copy of a good miniature, if enlarged to the size of life, will make but a very sorry portrait. Several of our best artists, who are fond of painting large figures, invert this reasoning. They make the whole figure gigantic, not that they may have room for nature, but for the motion of their brush (as if they were painting the side of a house), regarding the extent of canvas they have to cover as an excuse for their slovenly and hasty manner of getting over it; and thus, in fact, leave their pictures nothing at last but overgrown miniatures, but huge caricatures. It is not necessary in any case (either in a larger or a smaller compass) to go into details, so as to lose sight of the effect, and decompound the face into porous and transparent molecules, in the manner of Denner, who painted what he saw through a magnifying glass. The painter's eye need not be a microscope, but I contend that it should be a looking-glass, bright, clear, lucid. The *little* in art begins with insignificant parts, with what does not tell in connection with other parts. The true artist will paint not material points, but *moral quantities*. In a word, wherever there is feeling or expression in a muscle or a vein, there is grandeur and refinement too – I will conclude these remarks with an account of the manner in which the ancient sculptors combined great and little things in such matters. 'That the name of Phidias', says Pliny, 'is illustrious among all the nations that have heard of the fame of the Olympian Jupiter, no one doubts; but in order that those may know that he is deservedly praised who have not even seen his works, we shall offer a few arguments, and those of his genius only: nor to this purpose shall we insist on the beauty of the Olympian Jupiter, nor on the magnitude of the Minerva at Athens, though it is twenty-six cubits in height (about thirty-five feet), and is made of ivory and gold: but we shall refer to the shield, on which the battle of the Amazons is carved on the outer side: on the inside of the same is the fight of the Gods and Giants; and on the sandals, that between the Centaurs and Lapithae; so well did every part of that work display the powers of the art. Again, the sculptures on the pedestal he called the birth of Pandora: there are to be seen in number thirty Gods, the figure of Victory being particularly admirable: the learned also admire the figures of the serpent and the brazen sphinx, writhing under the spear. These things are mentioned, in passing, of an artist never enough to be commended, that it may be seen that he showed the same magnificence even in small things' – *Pliny's Natural History*, Book 36.

On the Disadvantages of Intellectual Superiority

Hazlitt wrote this in Scotland in February 1822 while waiting for his divorce. It was first published in the second volume of *Table-Talk* (1824).

An outspoken democrat in his politics, and a regular frequenter of the tavern and the fives court, Hazlitt liked to think of himself as a man of the people. But in this essay we find him complaining about the ridicule and suspicion with which he was often treated by working men and women. In his memoir *My Friends and Acquaintances* (1854) P.G. Patmore explains that Hazlitt 'always lived in furnished lodgings [...] of a very secondary class' fearing that more genteel landlords would object to his strange, solitary habits and irregular hours. 'Now, by keeping himself among a class of persons, to a certain degree removed from the vulgar,' Patmore muses, 'his name and pursuits would have secured him from personal disrespect, if they did not procure him the opposite; whereas in descending one or two steps lower in the scale, the effect of his intellectual pretensions was not merely nullified, but turned against him' (II, 311). In this essay Hazlitt contrasts the naïve idealism of scholars with the native chicanery of women and the working class. He has a half-ironic swipe at the Sarah Walkers of this world – chambermaids and wenches at lodging-houses – whom he regards as driven by 'trick, ignorance, and cunning'. This prepares the ground for the next essay in this collection, 'On the Knowledge of Character', in which the social and sexual prejudice that runs through his work in this period is even more strongly in evidence.

The chief disadvantage of knowing more and seeing farther than others, is not to be generally understood. A man is, in consequence of this, liable to start paradoxes, which immediately transport him beyond the reach of the common-place reader. A person speaking once in a slighting manner of a very original-minded man, received for answer – 'He strides on so far before you, that he dwindles in the distance!'

Petrarch complains, that 'Nature had made him different from other people' – *singular' d'altra genti*.[1] The great happiness of life is, to be neither better nor worse than the general run of those you meet with. If you are beneath them, you are trampled upon; if you are above them, you soon find a mortifying level in their indifference to what you particularly pique yourself upon. What is the use of being moral in a night-cellar, or wise in Bedlam? 'To be honest, as this world goes, is to be one man picked out of ten thousand.'[2] So says Shakespeare; and the commentators have not added that, under these circumstances, a man is more likely to become the butt of slander than the mark of admiration for being so. 'How now, thou particular fellow?'* is the common answer to all such out-of-the-way pretensions. By not doing as those at Rome do, we cut ourselves off from good-fellowship and society. We speak another language, have notions of our own, and are treated as of a different species. Nothing can be more awkward than to intrude with any such far-fetched ideas among the common herd, who will be sure to

> – Stand all astonied, like a sort of steers,
> 'Mongst whom some beast of strange and foreign race
> Unwares is chanced, far straying from his peers:
> So will their ghastly gaze betray their hidden fears.[3]

Ignorance of another's meaning is a sufficient cause of fear, and fear produces hatred: hence the suspicion and rancour entertained against all those who set up for greater refinement and wisdom than their neighbours. It is in vain to think of softening down this spirit of hostility by simplicity of manners, or by condescending to persons of low estate. The more you condescend, the more they will presume upon it; they will fear you less, but hate you more; and will be the more determined to take their revenge on you for a superiority as to which they are entirely in the dark, and of which you yourself seem to entertain considerable doubts. All the humility in the world will only pass for weakness and folly. They have no notion of such a thing. They always put their best foot forward; and argue that you would do the same if you had any such wonderful talents as people say. You had better, therefore, play off the great man at once – hector, swagger, talk big, and ride

* Jack Cade's salutation to one who tries to recommend himself by saying he can write and read. See *Henry VI*. Part Second.

the high horse over them: you may by this means extort outward respect or common civility; but you will get nothing (with low people) by forbearance and good nature but open insult or silent contempt. C[oleridge] always talks to people about what they don't understand: I, for one, endeavour to talk to them about what they do understand, and find I only get the more ill-will by it. They conceive I do not think them capable of any thing better; that I do not think it worth while, as the vulgar saying is, to *throw a word to a dog*. I once complained of this to C[oleridge], thinking it hard I should be sent to Coventry for not making a prodigious display. He said, 'As you assume a certain character, you ought to produce your credentials. It is a tax upon people's good nature to admit superiority of any kind, even where there is the most evident proof of it: but it is too hard a task for the imagination to admit it without any apparent ground at all.'

There is not a greater error than to suppose that you avoid the envy, malice, and uncharitableness, so common in the world, by going among people without pretensions. There are no people who have no pretensions; or the fewer their pretensions, the less they can afford to acknowledge yours without some sort of value received. The more information individuals possess, or the more they have refined upon any subject, the more readily can they conceive and admit the same kind of superiority to themselves that they feel over others. But from the low, dull, level sink of ignorance and vulgarity, no idea or love of excellence can arise. You think you are doing mighty well with them; that you are laying aside the buckram of pedantry and pretence, and getting the character of a plain, unassuming, good sort of fellow. It will not do. All the while that you are making these familiar advances, and wanting to be at your ease, they are trying to recover the wind of you. You may forget that you are an author, an artist, or what not – they do not forget that they are nothing, nor bate one jot of their desire to prove you in the same predicament. They take hold of some circumstance in your dress; your manner of entering a room is different from that of other people; you do not eat vegetables – that's odd; you have a particular phrase, which they repeat, and this becomes a sort of standing joke; you look grave, or ill; you talk, or are more silent than usual; you are in or out of pocket: all these petty, inconsiderable circumstances, in which you resemble, or are unlike other people, form so many counts in the indictment which is going on in their imaginations against you, and are so many contradictions in your character. In any one else they would pass unnoticed, but in a person of whom they had heard so much, they cannot make them out at all. Meanwhile, those things in which you may really excel, go for nothing, because they cannot judge of them. They speak highly of some book which you do not like, and therefore you make no answer. You recommend them to go and see some picture, in which they do not find much to admire. How are you to convince them that you are right? Can you make them perceive that the fault is in them, and not in the picture, unless you could give them your knowledge? They hardly distinguish the difference between a Correggio and a common daub. Does this bring you any nearer to an understanding? The more you know of the difference, the more deeply you feel it, or the more earnestly you wish to convey it, the farther do you find yourself removed to an immeasurable distance from the possibility of making them enter into views and feelings of which they have not even the first rudiments. You cannot make them see with your eyes, and they must judge for themselves.

Intellectual is not like bodily strength. You have no hold of the understanding of others but by their sympathy. Your knowing, in fact, so much more about a subject does not give you a superiority, that is, a power over them, but only renders it the more impossible for you to make the least impression on them. Is it then an advantage to you? It may be, as it relates to your own private satisfaction, but it places a greater gulf between you and society. It throws stumbling blocks in your way at every turn. All that you take most pride and pleasure in is lost upon the vulgar eye. What they are pleased with is a matter of indifference or of distaste to you. In seeing a number of persons turn over a portfolio of prints from different masters, what a trial it is to the patience, how it jars the nerves to hear them fall into raptures at some common-place flimsy thing, and pass over some divine expression of countenance without notice, or with a remark that it is very singular-looking? How useless is it in such cases to fret or argue, or remonstrate? Is it not quite as well to be without all this hypercritical, fastidious knowledge, and to be pleased or displeased as it happens, or struck with the first fault or beauty that is pointed out by others? I would be glad almost to change my acquaintance with pictures, with books, and, certainly, what I know of mankind, for any body's ignorance of them!

It is recorded in the life of some worthy (whose name I forget) that he was one of those 'who loved hospitality and respect': and I profess to belong to the same classification of mankind. Civility is with me a jewel. I like a little comfortable cheer, and careless, indolent chat. I hate to be always wise, or aiming at wisdom. I have enough to do with literary cabals, questions, critics, actors, essay-writing, without taking them out with me for recreation, and into all companies. I wish at these times to pass for a good-humoured fellow; and good-will is all I ask in return to make good company. I do not desire to be always posing myself or others with the questions of fate, free-will, fore-knowledge absolute, etc.[4] I must unbend sometimes. I must occasionally lie fallow. The kind of conversation that I affect most is what sort of a day it is, and whether it is likely to rain or hold up fine for tomorrow. This I consider as enjoying the *otium cum dignitate,* as the end and privilege of a life of study. I would resign myself to this state of easy indifference, but I find I cannot. I must maintain a certain pretension, which is far enough from my wish. I must be put on my defence, I must take up the gauntlet continually, or I find I lose ground. 'I am nothing, if not critical'. While I am thinking what o'clock it is, or how I came to blunder in quoting a well-known passage, as if I had done it on purpose, others are thinking whether I am not really as dull a fellow as I am sometimes said to be. If a drizzling shower patters against the windows, it puts me in mind of a mild spring rain, from which I retired twenty years ago, into a little public house near Wem in Shropshire, and while I saw the plants and shrubs before the door imbibe the dewy moisture, quaffed a glass of sparkling ale, and walked home in the dusk of evening, brighter to me than noon-day suns at present are! Would I indulge this feeling? In vain. They ask me what news there is, and stare if I say I don't know. If a new actress has come out, why must I have seen her? If a new novel has appeared, why must I have read it? I, at one time, used to go and take a hand at cribbage with a friend, and afterwards discuss a cold sirloin of beef, and throw out a few lack-a-daisical remarks, in a way to please myself, but it would not do long. I set up little pretension, and therefore the little that I did set up was taken from me. As I said nothing on that subject myself, it was continually thrown in my teeth that I was an author. From having me at this disadvantage, my friend wanted to peg on a hole or two in the game, and was displeased if I would not let him. If I won of him, it was hard he should be beat by an author. If he won, it would be strange if he did not understand the game better than I did. If I mentioned my favourite game of rackets, there was a general silence, as if this was my weak point. If I complained of being ill, it was asked why I made myself so? If I said such an actor had played a part well, the answer was, there was a different account in one of the newspapers. If any allusion was made to men of letters, there was a suppressed smile. If I told a humorous story, it was difficult to say whether the laugh was at me or at the narrative. The wife hated me for my ugly face: the servants because I could not always get them tickets for the play, and because they could not tell exactly what an author meant. If a paragraph appeared against any thing I had written, I found it was ready there before me, and I was to undergo a regular *roasting*. I submitted to all this till I was tired, and then I gave it up.

One of the miseries of intellectual pretensions is, that nine-tenths of those you come in contact with do not know whether you are an impostor or not. I dread that certain anonymous criticisms should get into the hands of servants where I go, or that my hatter or shoemaker should happen to read them, who cannot possibly tell whether they are well or ill founded. The ignorance of the world leaves one at the mercy of its malice. There are people whose good opinion or good will you want, setting aside all literary pretensions; and it is hard to lose by an ill report (which you have no means of rectifying) what you cannot gain by a good one. After a *diatribe* in the [*Quarterly Review*],[5] (which is taken in by a gentleman who occupies my old apartments on the first floor) my landlord brings me up his bill (of some standing), and on my offering to give him so much in money, and a note of hand for the rest, shakes his head, and says, he is afraid he could make no use of it. Soon after, the daughter comes in, and on my mentioning the circumstance carelessly to her, replies gravely, 'that indeed her father has been almost ruined by bills'. *This is the unkindest cut of all.* It is in vain for me to endeavour to explain that the publication in which I am abused is a mere government engine – an organ of a political faction. They know nothing about that. They only know such and such imputations are thrown out; and the more I try to remove them, the more they think there is some truth in them. Perhaps the people of the house are strong Tories – government-agents of some sort. Is it for me to enlighten their ignorance? If I say, I once wrote a thing called 'Prince Maurice's Parrot', and an 'Essay on the Regal Character', in the former of which allusion is made to a noble marquis, and in the latter to a great personage (so at least, I am told, it has been construed), and that Mr Croker has peremptory instructions to retaliate; they cannot conceive what connection there can be between me and such distinguished characters.[6] I can get no farther. Such is the misery of pretensions beyond your situation, and which are not backed by any external symbols of wealth or rank, intelligible to all mankind!

The impertinence of admiration is scarcely more tolerable than the demonstrations of contempt. I have known a person, whom I had never seen before, besiege me all dinner-time with asking, what articles I had written in the *Edinburgh Review*?[7] I was at last ashamed to answer to my splendid sins in that way. Others will pick out something not yours, and say, they are sure no one else could write it. By the first sentence they can always tell your style. Now I hate my style to be known; as I hate all *idiosyncrasy*. These obsequious flatterers could not pay me a worse compliment. Then there are those who make a point of reading every thing you write (which is fulsome); while others, more provoking, regularly lend your works to a friend, as soon as they receive them. They pretty well know your notions on the different subjects, from having heard you talk about them. Besides, they have a greater value for your personal character than they have for your writings. You explain things better in a common way, when you are not aiming at effect. Others tell you of the faults they have heard found with your last book, and that they defend your style in general from a charge of obscurity. A friend once told me of a quarrel he had had with a near relation, who denied that I knew how to spell the commonest words. These are comfortable confidential communications, to which authors, who have their friends and excusers, are subject. A gentleman told me, that a lady had objected to my use of the word *learneder*, as bad grammar. He said, that he thought it a pity that I did not take more care, but that the lady was perhaps prejudiced, as her husband held a government-office. I looked for the word, and found it in a motto from Butler. I was piqued, and desired him to tell the fair critic, that the fault was not in me, but in one who had far more wit, more learning, and loyalty than I could pretend to. Then, again, some will pick out the flattest thing of yours they can find, to load it with panegyrics; and others tell you (by way of letting you see how high they rank your capacity), that your best passages are failures. L[amb] has a knack of tasting (or as he would say, *palating*) the insipid: L[eigh H[unt] has a trick of turning away from the relishing morsels you put on his plate.

There is no getting the start of some people. Do what you will, they can do it better; meet with what success you may, their own good opinion stands them in better stead, and runs before the applause of the world. I once showed a person of this over-weening turn (with no small triumph I confess) a letter of a very flattering description I had received from the celebrated Count Stendhal, dated Rome.[8] He returned it with a smile of indifference, and said, he had had a letter from Rome himself the day before, from his friend S——! I did not think this 'germane to the matter'. G[o]dw[i]n pretends I never wrote any thing worth a farthing but my answers to Vetus, and that I fail altogether when I attempt to write an essay, or any thing in a short compass.[9]

What can one do in such cases? Shall I confess a weakness? The only set-off I know to these rebuffs and mortifications, is sometimes in an accidental notice or involuntary mark of distinction from a stranger. I feel the force of Horace's *digito monstrari* – I like to be pointed out in the street, or to hear people ask in Mr Powell's court, *which is Mr H——*? This is to me a pleasing extension of one's personal identity. Your name so repeated leaves an echo like music on the ear: it stirs the blood like the sound of a trumpet. It shows that other people are curious to see you: that they think of you, and feel an interest in you without your knowing it. This is a bolster to lean upon; a lining to your poor, shivering, threadbare opinion of yourself. You want some such cordial to exhausted spirits, and relief to the dreariness of abstract speculation. You are something; and, from occupying a place in the thoughts of others, think less contemptuously of yourself. You are the better able to run the gauntlet of prejudice and vulgar abuse. It is pleasant in this way to have your opinion quoted against yourself, and your own sayings repeated to you as good things. I was once talking with an intelligent man in the pit, and criticising Mr Knight's performance of Filch. 'Ah!' he said, 'little Simmons was the fellow to play that character.' He added, 'There was a most excellent remark made upon his acting it in the *Examiner* (I think it was) – *That he looked as if he had the gallows in one eye and a pretty girl in the other*.[10] I said nothing, but was in remarkably good humour the rest of the evening. I have seldom been in a company where fives-playing has been talked of, but some one has asked, in the course of it, 'Pray did any one ever see an account of one Cavanagh, that appeared some time back in most of the papers? Is it known who wrote it?'[11] These are trying moments. I had a triumph over a person, whose name I will not mention, on the following occasion. I happened to be saying something about Burke, and was expressing my opinion of his talents in no measured terms, when this gentleman interrupted me by saying, he thought, for his part, that Burke had been greatly overrated, and then added, in a careless way, 'Pray did you read a character of him in the last number of the [*Edinburgh Review*]?'[12] 'I wrote it!' – I could not resist the antithesis, but was afterwards ashamed of my momentary petulance. Yet no one, that I find, ever spares me.

Some persons seek out and obtrude themselves on public characters, in order, as it might seem, to pick out their failings, and afterwards betray them. Appearances are for it, but truth and a better knowledge of nature are against this interpretation of the matter. Sycophants and flatterers are undesignedly treacherous and fickle. They are prone to admire inordinately at first, and not finding a constant supply of food for this kind of sickly appetite, take a distaste to the object of their idolatry. To be even with themselves for their credulity, they sharpen their wits to spy out faults, and are delighted to find that this answers better than their first employment. It is a course of study, 'lively, audible, and full of vent'.[13] They have the organ of wonder and the organ of fear in a prominent degree. The first requires new objects of admiration to satisfy its uneasy cravings: the second makes them crouch to power wherever its shifting standard appears, and willing to curry favour with all parties, and ready to betray any out of sheer weakness and servility. I do not think they mean any harm. At least, I can look at this obliquity with indifference in my own particular case. I have been more disposed to resent it as I have seen it practised upon others, where I have been better able to judge of the extent of the mischief, and the heartlessness and idiot folly it discovered.

I do not think great intellectual attainments are any recommendation to the women. They puzzle them, and are a diversion to the main question. If scholars talk to ladies of what they understand, their hearers are none the wiser: if they talk of other things, they only prove themselves fools. The conversation between Angelica and Foresight, in *Love for Love*, is a receipt in full for all such overstrained nonsense: while he is wandering among the signs of the zodiac, she is standing a tip-toe on the earth.[14] It has been remarked that poets do not choose mistresses very wisely. I believe it is not choice, but necessity. If they could throw the handkerchief like the Grand Turk, I imagine we should see scarce mortals, but rather goddesses, surrounding their steps, and each exclaiming, with Lord Byron's own Ionian maid –

So shalt thou find me ever at thy side,
Here and hereafter, if the last may be![15]

Ah! no, these are bespoke, carried off by men of mortal, not ethereal mould, and thenceforth the poet, from whose mind the ideas of love and beauty are inseparable as dreams from sleep, goes on the forlorn hope of the passion, and dresses up the first Dulcinea[16] that will take compassion on him, in all the colours of fancy. What boots it to complain if the delusion lasts for life, and the rainbow still paints its form in the cloud?

There is one mistake I would wish, if possible, to correct. Men of letters, artists, and others, not succeeding with women in a certain rank of life, think the objection is to their want of fortune, and that they shall stand a better chance by descending lower, where only their good qualities or talents will be thought of. Oh! worse and worse. The objection is to themselves, not to their fortune – to their abstraction, to their absence of mind, to their unintelligible and romantic notions. Women of education may have a glimpse of their meaning, may get a clue to their character, but to all others they are thick darkness. If the mistress smiles at their ideal advances, the maid will laugh outright; she will throw water over you, get her little sister to listen, send her sweetheart to ask you what you mean, will set the village or the house upon your back;[17] it will be a farce, a comedy, a standing jest for a year, and then the murder will out. Scholars should be sworn at Highgate.[18] They are no match for chamber maids, or wenches at lodging-houses. They had better try their hands on heiresses or ladies of quality. These last have high notions of themselves that may fit some of your epithets! They are above mortality, so are your thoughts! But with low life, trick, ignorance, and cunning, you have nothing in common. Whoever you are, that think you can make a compromise or a conquest there by good nature, or good sense, be warned by a friendly voice, and retreat in time from the unequal contest.

If, as I have said above, scholars are no match for chambermaids, on the other hand, gentlemen are no match for blackguards. The former are on their honour, act on the square; the latter take all advantages, and have no idea of any other principle. It is astonishing how soon a fellow without education will learn to cheat. He is impervious to any ray of liberal knowledge; his understanding is

Not pierceable by power of any star –[19]

but it is porous to all sorts of tricks, chicanery, stratagems, and knavery, by which any thing is to be got. Mrs Peachum, indeed, says, that 'to succeed at the gaming-table, the candidate should have the education of a nobleman.[20] I do not know how far this example contradicts my theory. I think it is a rule that men in business should not be taught other things. Any one will be almost sure to make money who has no other idea in his head. A college education, or intense study of abstract truth, will not enable a man to drive a bargain, to over-reach another, or even to guard himself from being over-reached. As Shakespeare says, that 'to have a good face is the effect of study, but reading and writing come by nature':[21] so it might be argued, that to be a knave is the gift of fortune, but to play the fool to advantage it is necessary to be a learned man. The best politicians are not those who are deeply grounded in mathematical or in ethical science. Rules stand in the way of expediency. Many a man has been hindered from pushing his fortune in the world by an early cultivation of his moral sense, and has repented of it at leisure during the rest of his life. A shrewd man said of my father, that he would not send a son of his to school to him on any account, for that by teaching him to speak the truth, he would disqualify him from getting his living in the world!

It is hardly necessary to add any illustration to prove that the most original and profound thinkers are not always the most successful or popular writers. This is not merely a temporary disadvantage; but many great philosophers have not only been scouted while they were living, but forgotten as soon as they were dead. The name of Hobbes is perhaps sufficient to explain this assertion. But I do not wish to go farther into this part of the subject, which is obvious in itself. I have said, I believe, enough to take off the air of paradox which hangs over the title of this essay.

On the Knowledge of Character

Hazlitt wrote this in Scotland in February 1822 while waiting for his divorce. It was first published in the second volume of *Table-Talk* (1824).

How should one respond to the controversial elements in *Liber Amoris* and its related writings? One strategy, popular with Hazlitt enthusiasts, is to dismiss them as atypical, the products of a temporary personal crisis, in no way characteristic of their hero. Another is to consider them less of an aberration than a watershed, marking the moment at which a life-long Jacobin finally realised that the Revolution had failed. This is one way of reading the bitter attacks on women and servants in 'On the Knowledge of Character' – as reluctant, belated avowals of the stubborn obstacles of sex and class. Nor does it detract from the piquancy of these passages to detect a note of self-conscious exaggeration in them, as if Hazlitt the disappointed idealist were deliberately seeking to redress a previous imbalance.

Designedly irascible in places, 'On the Knowledge of Character' is also remarkably resigned in others, offering some new perspectives on the experiences described in *Liber Amoris*. The delightful meditation on the mystery of one's own character is one example of this, the little passage on *love at first sight* another: 'We generally make up our minds beforehand to the sort of person we should like, grave or gay, black, brown or fair; with golden tresses or with raven locks;– and when we meet with a complete example of the qualities we admire, the bargain is soon struck [...] it has been present to our waking thoughts, it has haunted us in our dreams, like some fairy vision.'

It is astonishing, with all our opportunities and practice, how little we know of this subject. For myself, I feel that the more I learn, the less I understand it.

I remember, several years ago, a conversation in the *Diligence*[1] coming from Paris, in which, on its being mentioned that a man had married his wife after thirteen years' courtship, a fellow-countryman of mine observed, that 'then, at least, he would be acquainted with her character'; when a Monsieur P——, inventor and proprietor of the *Invisible Girl*,[2] made answer, 'No, not at all; for that the very next day she might turn out the very reverse of the character that she had appeared in during all the preceding time.'* I could not help admiring the superior sagacity of the French juggler, and it struck me then that we could never be sure when we had got at the bottom of this riddle.

There are various ways of getting at a knowledge of character – by looks, words, actions. The first of these, which seems the most superficial, is perhaps the safest, and least liable to deceive: nay, it is that which mankind, in spite of their pretending to the contrary, are generally governed by. Professions pass for nothing, and actions may be counterfeited: but a man cannot help his looks. 'Speech', said a celebrated wit, 'was given to man to conceal his thoughts.' Yet I do not know that the greatest hypocrites are the least silent. The mouth of Cromwell is pursed up in the portraits of him, as if he was afraid to trust himself with words. Lord Chesterfield advises us, if we wish to know the real sentiments of the person we are conversing with, to look in his face, for he can more easily command his words than his features.[3] A man's whole life may be a lie to himself and others: and yet a picture painted of him by a great artist would probably stamp his true character on the canvas, and betray the secret to posterity. Men's opinions were divided, in their life-times, about such prominent personages as Charles V and Ignatius Loyola, partly, no doubt, from passion and interest, but partly from contradictory evidence in their ostensible conduct: the spectator, who has ever seen their pictures by Titian, judges of them at once, and truly. I had rather leave a good portrait of myself behind me than have a fine epitaph. The face, for the most part, tells what we have thought and felt – the rest is nothing. I have a higher idea of Donne from a rude, half-effaced outline of him prefixed to his poems than from any thing he ever wrote. Caesar's *Commentaries* would not have redeemed him in my opinion, if the bust of him had resembled the Duke of W[ellington]. My old friend, Fawcett[4] used to say, that if Sir Isaac Newton himself had lisped, he could not have thought any thing of him. So I cannot

* 'It is not a year or two shows us a man.' – Aemilia, in *Othello*.

persuade myself that any one is a great man, who looks like a blockhead. In this I may be wrong.

First impressions are often the truest, as we find (not unfrequently) to our cost, when we have been wheedled out of them by plausible professions or studied actions. A man's look is the work of years, it is stamped on his countenance by the events of his whole life, nay, more, by the hand of nature, and it is not to be got rid of easily. There is, as it has been remarked repeatedly, something in a person's appearance at first sight which we do not like, and that gives us an odd twinge, but which is overlooked in a multiplicity of other circumstances, till the mask is taken off, and we see this lurking character verified in the plainest manner in the sequel. We are struck at first, and by chance, with what is peculiar and characteristic; also with permanent *traits* and general effect; these afterwards go off in a set of unmeaning, commonplace details. This sort of *prima facie* evidence, then, shows what a man is, better than what he says or does; for it shows us the habit of his mind, which is the same under all circumstances and disguises. You will say, on the other hand, that there is no judging by appearances, as a general rule. No one, for instance, would take such a person for a very clever man, without knowing who he was. Then, ten to one, he is not; he may have got the reputation, but it is a mistake. You say, there is Mr ——,[5] undoubtedly a person of great genius: yet, except when excited by something extraordinary, he seems half dead. He has wit at will, yet wants life and spirit. He is capable of the most generous acts, yet meanness seems to cling to every motion. He looks like a poor creature – and in truth he is one! The first impression he gives you of him answers nearly to the feeling he has of his personal identity; and this image of himself, rising from his thoughts, and shrouding his faculties, is that which sits with him in the house, walks out with him into the street, and haunts his bedside. The best part of his existence is dull, cloudy, leaden: the flashes of light that proceed from it, or streak it here and there, may dazzle others, but do not deceive himself. Modesty is the lowest of the virtues, and is a real confession of the deficiency it indicates. He who undervalues himself is justly undervalued by others. Whatever good properties he may possess are, in fact, neutralised by a 'cold rheum' running through his veins, and taking away the zest of his pretensions, the pith and marrow of his performances. What is it to me that I can write these *Table-talks*? It is true I can, by a reluctant effort, rake up a parcel of half-forgotten observations, but they do not float on the surface of my mind, nor stir it with any sense of pleasure, nor even of pride. Others have more property in them than I have: *they* may reap the benefit, *I* have only had the pain. Otherwise, they are to me as if they had never existed: nor should I know that I had ever thought at all, but that I am reminded of it by the strangeness of my appearance, and my unfitness for every thing else. Look in C[oleridge]'s face while he is talking. His words are such as might 'create a soul under the ribs of death'.[6] His face is a blank. Which are we to consider as the true index of his mind? Pain, languor, shadowy remembrances are the uneasy inmates there: his lips move mechanically!

There are people whom we do not like, though we may have known them long, and have no fault to find with them, except that 'their appearance is so much against them'. That is not all, if we could find it out. There is, generally, a reason for this prejudice; for nature is true to itself. They may be very good sort of people, too, in their way, but still something is the matter. There is a coldness, a selfishness, a levity, an insincerity, which we cannot fix upon any particular phrase or action, but we see it in their whole persons and deportment. One reason that we do not see it in any other way may be, that they are all the time trying to conceal this defect by every means in their power. There is, luckily, a sort of *second sight* in morals: we discern the lurking indications of temper and habit a long while before their palpable effects appear. I once used to meet with a person at an ordinary,[7] a very civil, good-looking man in other respects, but with an odd look about his eyes, which I could not explain, as if he saw you under their fringed lids, and you could not see him again: this man was a common sharper. The greatest hypocrite I ever knew was a little, demure, pretty, modest-looking girl,[8] with eyes timidly cast upon the ground, and an air soft as enchantment; the only circumstance that could lead to a suspicion of her true character was a cold, sullen, watery, glazed look about the eyes, which she bent on vacancy, as if determined to avoid all explanation with yours. I might have spied in their glittering, motionless surface, the rocks and quicksands that awaited me below! We do not feel quite at ease in the company or friendship of those who have any natural obliquity or imperfection of person. The reason is, they are not on the best terms with themselves, and are sometimes apt to play off on others the tricks that nature has played them. This, however, is a remark that, perhaps, ought not to have been made. I know a person to whom it has been objected as a disqualification for friendship, that he never shakes you cordially by the hand.[9] I own this is a damper to sanguine and florid temperaments, who abound in these practical demonstrations and 'compliments extern'. The same person, who testifies the least pleasure at meeting you, is the last to quit his seat in your company, grapples with a subject in conversation right earnestly, and is, I take it, backward to give up a cause or a friend. Cold and distant in appearance, he piques himself on being the king of *good haters,* and a no less zealous partisan. The most phlegmatic constitutions often contain the most inflammable spirits – as fire is struck from the hardest flints.

And this is another reason that makes it difficult to judge of character. Extremes meet; and qualities display themselves by the most contradictory appearances. Any inclination, in consequence of being generally suppressed, vents itself the more violently when an opportunity presents itself: the greatest grossness sometimes accompanies the greatest refinement, as a natural relief, one to the other and we find the most reserved and indifferent tempers at the beginning of an entertainment, or an acquaintance, turn out the most communicative and cordial at the end of it. Some spirits exhaust themselves at first: others gain strength by progression. Some minds have a greater facility of throwing off impressions, and are, as it were, more transparent or porous than others. Thus the French present a marked contrast to the English in this respect. A Frenchman addresses you at once with a sort of lively indifference; an Englishman is more on his guard, feels his way, and is either exceedingly silent, or lets you into his whole confidence, which he cannot so well impart to an entire stranger. Again, a Frenchman is naturally humane: an Englishman is, I should say, only friendly by habit. His virtues and his vices cost him more than they do his more gay and volatile neighbours. An Englishman is said to speak his mind more plainly than others: – yes, if it will give you pain to hear it. He does not care whom he offends by his discourse: a foreigner generally strives to oblige in what he says. The French are accused of promising more than they perform. That may be, and yet they may perform as many good-natured acts as the English, if the latter are as averse to perform as they are to promise. Even the professions of the French may be sincere at the time, or arise out of the impulse of the moment; though their desire to serve you may be neither very violent nor very lasting. I cannot think, notwithstanding, that the French are not a serious people;

nay, that they are not a more reflecting people than the common run of the English. Let those who think them merely light and mercurial, explain that enigma, their everlasting prosing tragedy. The English are considered as comparatively a slow, plodding people. If the French are quicker, they are also more plodding. See, for example, how highly finished and elaborate their works of art are! How systematic and correct they aim at being in all their productions of a graver cast! 'If the French have a fault', as Yorick said, 'it is that they are too grave.'[10] With wit, sense, cheerfulness, patience, good-nature and refinement of manners, all they want is imagination and sturdiness of moral principle! Such are some of the contradictions in the character of the two nations, and so little does the character of either appear to have been understood! Nothing can be more ridiculous indeed than the way in which we exaggerate each other's vices and extenuate our own. The whole is an affair of prejudice on one side of the question, and of partiality on the other. Travellers who set out to carry back a true report of the case appear to lose not only the use of their understandings, but of their senses, the instant they set foot in a foreign land. The commonest facts and appearances are distorted, and discoloured. They go abroad with certain preconceived notions on the subject, and they make everything answer, in reason's spite, to their favourite theory. In addition to the difficulty of explaining customs and manners foreign to our own, there are all the obstacles of willful prepossession thrown in the way. It is not, therefore, much to be wondered at that nations have arrived at so little knowledge of one another's characters; and that, where the object has been to widen the breach between them, any slight differences that occur are easily blown into a blaze of fury by repeated misrepresentations, and all the exaggerations that malice or folly can invent!

This ignorance of character is not confined to foreign nations: we are ignorant of that of our own countrymen in a class a little below or above ourselves. We can hardly pretend to pronounce magisterially on the good or bad qualities of strangers; and, at the same time, we are ignorant of those of our friends, of our kindred, and of our own. We are in all these cases either too near or too far off the object to judge of it properly.

Persons, for instance, in a higher or middle rank of life know little or nothing of the characters of those below them, as servants, country people, etc. I would lay it down in the first place as a general rule on this subject, that all uneducated people are hypocrites.[11] Their sole business is to deceive. They conceive themselves in a state of hostility with others, and stratagems are fair in war. The inmates of the kitchen and the parlour are always (as far as respects their feeling and intentions towards each other) in Hobbes's 'state of nature'. Servants and others in that line of life have nothing to exercise their spare talents for invention upon but those about them. Their superfluous electrical particles of wit and fancy are not carried off by those established and fashionable conductors, novels and romances. Their faculties are not buried in books, but all alive and stirring, erect and bristling like a cat's back. Their coarse conversation sparkles with 'wild wit, invention ever new'. Their betters try all they can to set themselves up above them, and they try all they can to pull them down to their own level. They do this by getting up a little comic interlude, a daily, domestic, homely drama out of the odds and ends of the family failings, of which there is in general a pretty plentiful supply, or make up the deficiency of materials out of their own heads. They turn the qualities of their masters and mistresses inside out, and any real kindness or condescension only sets them the more against you. They are not to be taken in in that way – they will not be baulked in the spite they have to you. They only set to work with redoubled alacrity, to lessen the favour or to blacken your character. They feel themselves like a degraded *caste,* and cannot understand how the obligations can be all on one side, and the advantages all on the other. You cannot come to equal terms with them – they reject all such overtures as insidious and hollow – nor can you ever calculate upon their gratitude or goodwill, any more than if they were so many strolling Gipsies or wild Indians. They have no fellow-feeling, they keep no faith with the more privileged classes. They are in your power, and they endeavour to be even with you by trick and cunning, by lying and chicanery. In this they have nothing to restrain them. Their whole life is a succession of shifts, excuses, and expedients. The love of truth is a principle with those only who have made it their study, who have applied themselves to the pursuit of some art or science, where the intellect is severely tasked, and learns by habit to take a pride in, and to set a just value on, the correctness of its conclusions. To have a disinterested regard for truth, the mind must have contemplated it in abstract and remote questions; whereas the ignorant and vulgar are only conversant with those things in which their own interest is concerned. All their notions are local, personal, and consequently gross and selfish. They say whatever comes uppermost – turn whatever happens to their own account – and invent any story, or give any answer that suits their purposes. Instead of being bigoted to general principles, they trump up any lie for the occasion, and the more of a *thumper* it is, the better they like it; the more unlooked-for it is, why, so much the more of a *Godsend*! They have no conscience about the matter; and if you find them out in any of their manoeuvres, are not ashamed of themselves, but angry with you. If you remonstrate with them, they laugh in your face. The only hold you have of them is their interest – you can but dismiss them from your employment; and *service is no inheritance*. If they affect any thing like decent remorse, and hope you will pass it over, all the while they are probably trying to recover the wind of you. Persons of liberal knowledge or sentiments have no kind of chance in this sort of mixed intercourse with these barbarians in civilised life. You cannot tell, by any signs or principles, what is passing in their minds. There is no common point of view between you. You have not the same topics to refer to, the same language to express yourself. Your interests, your feelings are quite distinct. You take certain things for granted as rules of action: they take nothing for granted but their own ends, pick up all their knowledge out of their own occasions, are on the watch only for what they can catch – are

Subtle as the fox for prey:
Like warlike as the wolf, for what they eat.[12]

They have indeed a regard to their character, as this last may affect their livelihood or advancement, none as it is connected with a sense of propriety; and this sets their mother-wit and native talents at work upon a double file of expedients, to bilk their consciences, and salve their reputation. In short, you never know where to have them, any more than if they were of a different species of animals; and in trusting to them, you are sure to be betrayed and over-reached. You have other things to mind, they are thinking only of you, and how to turn you to advantage. Give and take is no maxim here. You can build nothing on your own moderation or on their false delicacy. After a familiar conversation with a waiter at a tavern, you overhear him calling you by some provoking nick-name. If you make a present to the daughter of the house where you lodge, the mother is sure to recollect some addition to her bill. It is a running fight. In fact, there is a principle in human nature not willingly to endure the idea of a superior, a sour jacobinical disposition to wipe out the score of obligation, or efface the tinsel of external advantages – and where others have the opportunity of coming in contact with us, they generally find the means to establish a sufficiently marked degree of degrading equality. No man is a hero to his valet-de-chambre, is an old maxim. A new illustration of this principle occurred the other day. While Mrs Siddons was giving her readings of Shakespeare to a brilliant and admiring drawing-room, one of the servants in the hall below was saying, 'What, I find the old lady is making as much noise as ever!' So little is there in common between the different classes of society, and so impossible is it ever to unite the diversities of custom and knowledge which separate them.

Women, according to Mrs Peachum, are 'bitter bad judges' of the characters of men;[13] and men are not much better of theirs, if we can form any guess from their choice in marriage. Love is proverbially blind. The whole is an affair of whim and fancy. Certain it is, that the greatest favourites with the other sex are not those who are most liked or respected among their own. I never knew but one clever man who was what is called a *lady's man*; and he (unfortunately for the argument) happened to be a considerable coxcomb. It was by this irresistible quality, and not by the force of his genius, that he vanquished. Women seem to doubt their own judgments in love, and to take the opinion which a man entertains of his own prowess and accomplishments for granted. The wives of poets are (for the most part) mere pieces of furniture in the room.[14] If you speak to them of their husbands' talents or reputation in the world, it is as if you made mention of some office that they held. It can hardly be otherwise, when the instant any subject is started or conversation arises, in which men are interested, or try one another's strength, the women leave the room, or attend to something else. The qualities then in which men are ambitious to excel, and which ensure the applause of the world, eloquence, genius, learning, integrity, are not those which gain the favour of the fair. I must not deny, however, that wit and courage have this effect. Neither is youth or beauty the sole passport to their affections.

> The way of woman's will is hard to find,
> Harder to hit.[15]

Yet there is some clue to this mystery, some determining cause; for we find that the same men are universal favourites with women, as others are uniformly disliked by them. Is not the lodestone that attracts so powerfully, and in all circumstances, a strong and undisguised bias towards them, a marked attention, a conscious preference of them to every other passing object or topic? I am not sure, but I incline to think so. The successful lover is the *cavalier servente* of all nations. The man of gallantry behaves as if he had made an assignation with every woman he addresses. An argument immediately draws off the scholar's attention from the prettiest woman in the room. He accordingly succeeds better in argument than in love! – I do not think that what is called *Love at first sight* is so great an absurdity as it is sometimes imagined to be. We generally make up our minds beforehand to the sort of person we should like, grave or gay, black, brown, or fair; with golden tresses or with raven locks; – and when we meet with a complete example of the qualities we admire, the bargain is soon struck. We have never seen any thing to come up to our newly discovered goddess before, but she is what we have been all our lives looking for. The idol we fall down and worship is an image familiar to our minds. It has been present to our waking thoughts, it has haunted us in our dreams, like some fairy vision. Oh! thou,[16] who, the first time I ever beheld thee, didst draw my soul into the circle of thy heavenly looks, and wave enchantment round me, do not think thy conquest less complete because it was instantaneous; for in that gentle form (as if another Imogen had entered) I saw all that I had ever loved of female grace, modesty, and sweetness!

I cannot say much of friendship as giving an insight into character, because it is often founded on mutual infirmities and prejudices. Friendships are frequently taken up on some sudden sympathy, and we see only as much as we please of one another's characters afterwards. Intimate friends are not fair witnesses to character, anymore than professed enemies. They cool, indeed, in time – part, and retain only a rankling grudge at past errors and oversights. Their testimony in the latter case is not quite free from suspicion.

One would think that near relations, who live constantly together, and always have done so, must be pretty well acquainted with one another's character. They are nearly in the dark about it. Familiarity confounds all traits of distinction: interest and prejudice take away the power of judging. We have no opinion on the subject, any more than of one another's faces. The Penates, the household-gods, are veiled. We do not see the features of those we love, nor do we clearly distinguish their virtues or their vices. We take them as they are found in the lump: by weight, and not by measure. We know all about the individuals, their sentiments, history, manners, words, actions, everything: but we know all these too much as facts, as inveterate, habitual impressions, as clothed with too many associations, as sanctified with too many affections, as woven too much into the web of our hearts, to be able to pick out the different threads, to cast up the items of the debtor and creditor account, or to refer them to any general standard of right and wrong. Our impressions with respect to them are too strong, too real, too much *sui generis*, to be capable of a comparison with any thing but themselves. We hardly inquire whether those for whom we are thus interested, and to whom we are thus knit, are *better* or *worse* than others – the question is a kind of profanation – all we know is they are *more* to us than any one else can be. Our sentiments of this kind are rooted and grow in us, and we cannot eradicate them by voluntary means. Besides, our judgments are bespoke, our interests take part with our blood. If any doubt arises, if the veil of our implicit confidence is drawn aside by any accident for a moment, the shock is too great, like that of a dislocated limb, and we recoil on our habitual impressions again. Let not that veil ever be rent entirely asunder, so that those images may be left bare of reverential awe, and lose their religion: for nothing can ever support the desolation of the heart afterwards!

The greatest misfortune that can happen among relations is a different way of bringing up, so as to set one another's opinions and characters in an entirely new point of view. This often lets in an unwelcome daylight on the subject, and breeds schisms, coldness, and incurable heart-burnings in families. I have sometimes thought whether the progress of society and march of knowledge does not do more harm in this respect, by loosening the ties of domestic attachment, and preventing those who are most interested in, and anxious to think well of one another, from feeling a cordial sympathy and approbation of each other's sentiments, manners, views, etc. than it does good by any real advantage to the community at large. The son, for instance, is brought up to the church, and nothing can exceed the pride and pleasure the father takes in him, while all goes on well in this favourite direction. His notions change, and he imbibes a taste for the Fine Arts. From this moment there is an end of any thing like the same unreserved communication between them.[17] The young man may talk with enthusiasm of his 'Rembrandts, Correggios, and stuff': it is all

Hebrew to the elder; and whatever satisfaction he may feel in the hearing of his son's progress, or good wishes for his success, he is never reconciled to the new pursuit, he still hankers after the first object that he had set his mind upon. Again, the grandfather is a Calvinist, who never gets the better of his disappointment at his son's going over to the Unitarian side of the question. The matter rests here, till the grandson, some years after, in the fashion of the day and 'infinite agitation of men's wit', comes to doubt certain points in the creed in which he has been brought up, and the affair is all abroad again. Here are three generations made uncomfortable and in a manner set at variance, by a veering point of theology, and the officious meddling biblical critics! Nothing, on the other hand, can be more wretched or common than that upstart pride and insolent good fortune which is ashamed of its origin; nor are there many things more awkward than the situation of rich and poor relations. Happy, much happier, are those tribes and people who are confined to the same caste and way of life from sire to son, where prejudices are transmitted like instincts, and where the same unvarying standard of opinion and refinement blends countless generations in its improgressive, everlasting mould!

Not only is there a wilful and habitual blindness in near kindred to each other's defects, but an incapacity to judge from the quantity of materials, from the contradictoriness of the evidence. The chain of particulars is too long and massy for us to lift it or put it into the most approved ethical scales. The concrete result does not answer to any abstract theory, to any logical definition. There is black, and white, and grey, square and round – there are too many anomalies, too many redeeming points in poor human nature, such as it actually is, for us to arrive at a smart, summary decision on it. We know too much to come to any hasty or partial conclusion. We do not pronounce upon the present act, because a hundred others rise up to contradict it. We suspend our judgments altogether, because in effect one thing unconsciously balances another; and perhaps this obstinate, pertinacious indecision would be the truest philosophy in other cases, where we dispose of the question of character easily, because we have only the smallest part of the evidence to decide upon. Real character is not one thing, but a thousand things; actual qualities do not conform to any factitious standard in the mind, but rest upon their own truth and nature. The dull stupor under which we labour in respect of those whom we have the greatest opportunities of inspecting nearly, we should do well to imitate, before we give extreme and uncharitable verdicts against those whom we only see in passing, or at a distance. If we knew them better, we should be disposed to say less about them.

In the truth of things, there are none utterly worthless, none without some drawback on their pretensions, or some alloy of imperfection. It has been observed that a familiarity with the worst characters lessens our abhorrence of them; and a wonder is often expressed that the greatest criminals look like other men. The reason is that *they are like other men in many respects*. If a particular individual was merely the wretch we read of, or conceive in the abstract, that is, if he was the mere personified idea of the criminal brought to the bar, he would not disappoint the spectator, but would look like what he would be – a monster! But he has other qualities, ideas, feelings, nay, probably virtues, mixed up with the most profligate habits or desperate acts. This need not lessen our abhorrence of the crime, though it does of the criminal; for it has the latter effect only by showing him to us in different points of view, in which he appears a common mortal, and not the caricature of vice we took him for, nor spotted all over with infamy. I do not at the same time think this a lax or dangerous, though it is a charitable view of the subject. In my opinion, no man ever answered in his own mind (except in the agonies of conscience or of repentance, in which latter case he throws the imputation from himself in another way) to the abstract idea of a *murderer*. He may have killed a man in self-defence, or 'in the trade of war', or to save himself from starving, or in revenge for an injury, but always 'so as with a difference', or from mixed and questionable motives. The individual, in reckoning with himself, always takes into the account the considerations of time, place, and circumstance, and never makes out a case of unmitigated, unprovoked villainy, of 'pure defecated evil' against himself. There are degrees in real crimes: we reason and moralise only by names and in classes. I should be loth, indeed, to say, that 'whatever is, is right': but almost every actual choice inclines to it, with some sort of imperfect, unconscious bias. This is the reason, besides the ends of secrecy, of the invention of *slang* terms for different acts of profligacy committed by thieves, pickpockets, etc. The common names suggest associations of disgust in the minds of others, which those who live by them do not willingly recognise, and which they wish to sink in a technical phraseology. So there is a story of a fellow who, as he was writing down his confession of a murder, stopped to ask how the word *murder* was spelt; this, if true, was partly because his imagination was staggered by the recollection of the thing, and partly because he shrunk from the verbal admission of it. '*Amen* stuck in his throat!' The defence made by Eugene Aram[18] of himself against a charge of murder, some years before, shows that he in imagination completely flung from himself the *nominal* crime imputed to him: he might, indeed, have staggered an old man with a blow, and buried his body in a cave, and lived ever since upon the money he found upon him, but there was 'no malice in the case, none at all', as Peachum says. The very coolness, subtlety, and circumspection of his defence (as masterly a legal document as there is upon record) prove that he was guilty of the act, as much as they prove that he was unconscious of the *crime*.* In the same spirit, and I conceive with great metaphysical truth, Mr Coleridge, in his tragedy of *Remorse,* makes Ordonio (his chief character) waive the acknowledgment of his meditated guilt to his own mind, by putting into his mouth that striking soliloquy:

> Say, I had lay'd a body in the sun!
> Well! in a month there swarm forth from the corse
> A thousand, nay, ten thousand sentient beings
> In place of that one man. Say I had *kill'd* him!
> Yet who shall tell me, that each one and all
> Of these ten thousand lives is not as happy
> As that one life, which being push'd aside,
> Made room for these unnumber'd. – Act II. Sc. II.

I am not sure, indeed, that I have not got this whole train of speculation from him; but I should not think the worse of it on that account. That gentleman, I recollect, once asked me whether I thought that the different members of a family really liked one another so well, or had so much attachment as was generally supposed: and I said that I conceived the regard they had towards each other was expressed by the word *interest*, rather than by any other; which he said was the true answer. I do not know that I could mend it now. Natural affection is not pleasure in one

* The bones of the murdered man were dug up in an old hermitage. On this, as one instance of the acuteness which he displayed all through the occasion, Aram remarks, 'Where would you expect to find the bones of a man sooner than in a hermit's cell, except you were to look for them in a cemetery?' See *Newgate Calendar* for the year 1758 or 9.

another's company, nor admiration of one another's qualities; but it is an intimate and deep knowledge of the things that affect those, to whom we are bound by the nearest ties, with pleasure or pain; it is an anxious, uneasy, fellow-feeling with them, a jealous watchfulness over their good name, a tender and unconquerable yearning for their good. The love, in short, we bear them, is the nearest to that we bear ourselves. *Home*, according to the old saying, is *home, be it never so homely*. We love ourselves, not according to our deserts, but our cravings after good: so we love our immediate relations in the next degree (if not even sometimes in a higher one) because we know best what they have suffered and what sits nearest to their hearts. We are implicated, in fact, in their welfare, by habit and sympathy, as we are in our own.

If our devotion to our own interests is much the same as to theirs, we are ignorant of our own characters for the same reason. We are parties too much concerned to return a fair verdict, and are too much in the secret of our own motives or situation not to be able to give a favourable return to our actions. We exercise a liberal criticism upon ourselves, and put off the final decision to a late day. The field is large and open. Hamlet exclaims, with a noble magnanimity, 'I count myself indifferent honest, and yet I could accuse me of such things!'[19] If you could prove to a man that he is a knave, it would not make much difference in his opinion; his self-love is stronger than his love of virtue. Hypocrisy is generally used as a mask to deceive the world, not to impose on ourselves: for once detect the delinquent in his knavery, and he laughs in your face or glories in his iniquity. This at least happens except where there is a contradiction in the character, and our vices are involuntary, and at variance with our convictions. One great difficulty is to distinguish ostensible motives, or such as we acknowledge to ourselves, from tacit or secret springs of action. A man changes his opinion readily, he thinks it candour: it is levity of mind. For the most part, we are stunned and stupid in judging of ourselves. We are callous by custom to our defects or excellencies, unless where vanity steps in to exaggerate or extenuate them. I cannot conceive how it is that people are in love with their own persons, or astonished at their own performances, which are but a nine days' wonder to every one else. In general it may be laid down that we are liable to this twofold mistake in judging of our own talents: we, in the first place, nurse the rickety bantling, we think much of that which has cost us much pains and labour, and which goes against the grain;

and we also set little store by what we do with most ease to ourselves, and therefore best. The works of the greatest genius are produced almost unconsciously, with an ignorance on the part of the persons themselves that they have done any thing extraordinary. Nature has done it for them. How little Shakespeare seems to have thought of himself or of his fame! Yet, if 'to know another well, were to know one's self', he must have been acquainted with his own pretensions and character, 'who knew all qualities with a learned spirit'.[20] His eye seems never to have been bent upon himself, but outwards upon nature. A man, who thinks highly of himself, may almost set it down that it is without reason. Milton, notwithstanding, appears to have had a high opinion of himself, and to have made it good. He was conscious of his powers, and great by design. Perhaps his tenaciousness, on the score of his own merit, might arise from an early habit of polemical writing, in which his pretensions were continually called to the bar of prejudice and party-spirit, and he had to plead not guilty to the indictment. Some men have died unconscious of immortality, as others have almost exhausted the sense of it in their life-times. Correggio might be mentioned as an instance of the one, Voltaire of the other.

There is nothing that helps a man in his conduct through life more than a knowledge of his own characteristic weaknesses (which, guarded against, become his strength), as there is nothing that tends more to the success of a man's talents than his knowing the limits of his faculties, which are thus concentrated on some practicable object. One man can do but one thing. Universal pretensions end in nothing. Or, as Butler has it, too much wit requires

As much again to govern it.[21]

There are those who have gone, for want of this self-knowledge, strangely out of their way, and others who have never found it. We find many who succeed in certain departments, and are yet melancholy and dissatisfied, because they failed in the one to which they first devoted themselves, like discarded lovers who pine after their scornful mistress. I will conclude with observing, that authors in general overrate the extent and value of posthumous fame: for what (as it has been asked) is the amount even of Shakespeare's fame? That in that very country which boasts his genius and his birth, perhaps scarce one person in ten has ever heard of his name, or read a syllable of his writings!

On the Fear of Death

Hazlitt wrote this in Scotland in February 1822 while waiting for his divorce. It was first published in the second volume of *Table-Talk* (1824).

There is a sceptical equanimity about this essay that marks it out from its neighbours. Hazlitt argues that our attachment to life is not abstract but habitual, which means that our greatest fear is not death but disappointment. It gives us no concern that there was once a time when we were not, he suggests, or that we shall not be around a hundred years hence, because it is essentially *our* life that we are wedded to, not life in general. 'If I had lived *indeed,*' Hazlitt says, 'I should not care to die. But I do not like a contract of pleasure broken off unfulfilled, a marriage with joy unconsummated, a promise of happiness rescinded. My public and private hopes have been left a ruin, or remain only to mock me. I would wish them to be re-edified.' It is not surprising that he was brooding upon life's brevity at this time: his hero Napoleon Bonaparte, his editor John Scott and his friend the poet John Keats had all met untimely deaths in the previous year, and his own father had passed away only eighteen months before. Significantly, it was almost exactly one month after William senior's demise that Hazlitt got his first glimpse of Sarah Walker, as she brought up his breakfast tray at No. 9 Southampton Buildings on that fateful 16 August 1820.

And our little life is rounded with a sleep.[1]

Perhaps the best cure for the fear of death is to reflect that life has a beginning as well as an end. There was a time when we were not: this gives us no concern – why then should it trouble us that a time will come when we shall cease to be? I have no wish to have been alive a hundred years ago, or in the reign of Queen Anne: why should I regret and lay it so much to heart that I shall not be alive a hundred years hence, in the reign of I cannot tell whom?

When Bickerstaff wrote his Essays,[2] I knew nothing of the

subjects of them: nay, much later, and but the other day, as it were, in the beginning of the reign of George III, when Goldsmith, Johnson, Burke used to meet at the Globe, when Garrick was in his glory, and Reynolds was over head and ears with his portraits, and Sterne brought out the volumes of *Tristram Shandy* year by year,[3] it was without consulting me: I had not the slightest intimation of what was going on: the debates in the Houses of Commons on the American war, or the firing at Bunker's Hill,[4] disturbed not me: yet I thought this no evil – I neither ate, drank, nor was merry, yet I did not complain: I had not then looked out into this breathing world, yet I was well; and the world did quite as well without me as I did without it! Why then should I make all this outcry about parting with it, and being no worse off than I was before? There is nothing in the recollection that at a certain time we were not come into the world, that 'the gorge rises at'[5] – why should we revolt at the idea that we must one day go out of it? To die is only to be as we were before we were born; yet no one feels any remorse, or regret, or repugnance, in contemplating this last idea. It is rather a relief and disburthening of the mind: it seems to have been holiday-time with us then: we were not called to appear upon the stage of life, to wear robes or tatters, to laugh or cry, be hooted or applauded; we had lain *perdu* all this while, snug, out of harm's way; and had slept out our thousands of centuries without wanting to be waked up; at peace and free from care, in a long nonage, in a sleep deeper and calmer than that of infancy, wrapped in the softest and finest dust. And the worst that we dread is, after a short, fretful, feverish being, after vain hopes, and idle fears, to sink to final repose again, and forget the troubled dream of life! ... Ye armed men, knights templars, that sleep in the stone aisles of that old Temple Church, where all is silent above, and where a deeper silence reigns below (not broken by the pealing organ), are ye not contented where ye lie? Or would you come out of your long homes to go to the Holy War? Or do ye complain that pain no longer visits you, that sickness has done its worst, that you have paid the last debt to nature, that you hear no more of the thickening phalanx of the foe, or your lady's waning love; and that while this ball of earth rolls its eternal round, no sound shall ever pierce through to disturb your lasting repose, fixed as the marble over your tombs, breathless as the grave that holds you! And thou, oh! thou, to whom my heart turns, and will turn while it has feeling left, who didst love in vain, and whose first was thy last sigh, wilt not thou too rest in peace (or wilt thou cry to me complaining from thy clay-cold bed) when that sad heart is no longer sad, and that sorrow is dead which thou wert only called into the world to feel![6]

It is certain that there is nothing in the idea of a pre-existent state that excites our longing like the prospect of a posthumous existence. We are satisfied to have begun life when we did; we have no ambition to have set out on our journey sooner; and feel that we have had quite enough to do to battle our way through since. We cannot say,

> The wars we well remember of King Nine,
> Of old Assaracus and Inachus divine:[7]

neither have we any wish: we are contented to read of them in story, and to stand and gaze at the vast sea of time that separates us from them. It was early days then: the world was not *well-aired* enough for us: we have no inclination to have been up and stirring. We do not consider the six thousand years of the world before we were born[8] as so much time lost to us: we are perfectly indifferent about the matter. We do not grieve and lament that we did not happen to be in time to see the grand mask and pageant of human life going on in all that period; though we are mortified at being obliged to quit our station before the rest of the procession passes.

It may be suggested in explanation of this difference, that we know from various records and traditions what happened in the time of Queen Anne, or even in the reigns of the Assyrian monarchs: but that we have no means of ascertaining what is to happen hereafter but by awaiting the event, and that our eagerness and curiosity are sharpened in proportion as we are in the dark about it. This is not at all the case; for at that rate we should be constantly wishing to make a voyage of discovery to Greenland or to the Moon, neither of which we have, in general, the least desire to do. Neither, in truth, have we any particular solicitude to pry into the secrets of futurity, but as a pretext for prolonging our own existence. It is not so much that we care to be alive a hundred or a thousand years hence, any more than to have been alive a hundred or a thousand years ago: but the thing lies here, that we would all of us wish the present moment to last for ever. We would be as we are, and would have the world remain just as it is, to please us.

> The present eye catches the present object –[9]

to have and to hold while it may; and we abhor, on any terms, to have it torn from us, and nothing left in its room. It is the pang of parting, the unloosing our grasp, the breaking asunder some strong tie, the leaving some cherished purpose unfulfilled, that creates the repugnance to go, and 'makes calamity of so long life', as it often is.

– Oh thou strong heart!
There's such a covenant 'twixt the world and thee.
Ye're loth to break![10]

The love of life, then, is an habitual attachment, not an abstract principle. Simply *to be* does not 'content man's natural desire': we long to be in a certain time, place, and circumstance. We would much rather be now, 'on this bank and shoal of time', than have our choice of any future period, than take a slice of fifty or sixty years out of the Millennium, for instance. This shows that our attachment is not confined either to *being* or to *well-being*; but that we have an inveterate prejudice in favour of our immediate existence, such as it is. The mountaineer will not leave his rock, nor the savage his hut; neither are we willing to give up our present mode of life, with all its advantages and disadvantages, for any other that could be substituted for it. No man would, I think, exchange his existence with any other man, however fortunate. We had as lief *not be*, as *not be ourselves*. There are some persons of that reach of soul that they would like to live two hundred and fifty years hence, to see to what height of empire America will have grown up in that period, or whether the English constitution will last so long. These are points beyond me. But I confess I should like to live to see the downfall of Legitimacy. That is a vital question with me; and I shall like it the better, the sooner it happens!

No young man ever thinks he shall die. He may believe that others will, or assent to the doctrine that 'all men are mortal' as an abstract proposition, but he is far enough from bringing it home to himself individually.* Youth, buoyant activity, and animal spirits, hold absolute antipathy with old age as well as with death; nor have we, in the heyday of life, any more than in the thoughtlessness of childhood, the remotest conception how

* 'All men think all men mortal but themselves.' – Young.[11]

This sensible warm motion can become
A kneaded clod –[12]

nor how sanguine, florid health and vigour, shall 'turn to withered, weak, and grey'. Or if in a moment of idle speculation we indulge in this notion of the close of life as a theory, it is amazing at what a distance it seems; what a long, leisurely interval there is between; what a contrast its slow and solemn approach affords to our present gay dreams of existence! We eye the farthest verge of the horizon, and think what a way we shall have to look back upon, ere we arrive at our journey's end; and without our in the least suspecting it, the mists are at our feet, and the shadows of age encompass us. The two divisions of our lives have melted into each other: the extreme points close and meet with none of that romantic interval stretching out between them, that we had reckoned upon; and for the rich, melancholy, solemn hues of age, 'the sear, the yellow leaf', the deepening shadows of an autumnal evening, we only feel a dank, cold mist encircling all objects, after the spirit of youth is fled. There is no inducement to look forward; and what is worse, little interest in looking back to what has become so trite and common. The pleasures of our existence have worn themselves out, are 'gone into the wastes of time', or have turned their indifferent side to us: the pains by their repeated blows have worn us out, and have left us neither spirit nor inclination to encounter them again in retrospect. We do not want to rip up old grievances, nor to renew our youth like the phoenix, nor to live our lives twice over. Once is enough. As the tree falls, so let it lie. We shut up the book and close the account once and for all!

It has been thought by some that life is like the exploring of a passage that grows narrower and darker the farther we advance, without a possibility of ever turning back, and where we are stifled for want of breath at last. For myself, I do not complain of the greater thickness of the atmosphere as I approach the *narrow house*. I felt it more formerly,* when the idea alone seemed to suppress a thousand rising hopes, and weighed upon the pulses of the blood. At present I rather feel a thinness and want of support, I stretch out my hand to some object and find none, I am too much in a world of abstraction; the naked map of life is spread out before me, and

* I remember once, in particular, having this feeling in reading Schiller's *Don Carlos*, where there is a description of death, in a degree that almost choked me.

in the emptiness and desolation I see Death coming to meet me. In my youth I could not behold him for the crowd of objects and feelings, and Hope stood always between us, saying – 'Never mind that old fellow!' If I had lived *indeed*, I should not care to die. But I do not like a contract of pleasure broken off unfulfilled, a marriage with joy unconsummated, a promise of happiness rescinded. My public and private hopes have been left a ruin, or remain only to mock me. I would wish them to be re-edified. I should like to see some prospect of good to mankind, such as my life began with. I should like to leave some sterling work behind me. I should like to have some friendly hand to consign me to the grave. On these conditions I am ready, if not willing, to depart. I could then write on my tomb – GRATEFUL AND CONTENTED! But I have thought and suffered too much to be willing to have thought and suffered in vain. In looking back, it sometimes appears to me as if I had in a manner slept out my life in a dream or trance on the side of the hill of knowledge, where I have fed on books, on thoughts, on pictures, and only heard in half-murmurs the trampling of busy feet, or the noises of the throng below. Waked out of this dim, twilight existence, and startled with the passing scene, I have felt a wish to descend to the world of realities, and join in the chase. But I fear too late, and that I had better return to my bookish chimeras and indolence once more! *Zanetto, lascia le donne, et studia la matematica.*[13]

It is not wonderful that the contemplation and fear of death become more familiar to us as we approach nearer to it: that life seems to ebb with the decay of blood and youthful spirits; and that as we find every thing about us subject to chance and change, as our strength and beauty die, as our hopes and passions, our friends and our affections leave us, we begin by degrees to feel ourselves mortal!

I have never seen death but once, and that was in an infant. It is years ago. The look was calm and placid, and the face was fair and firm. It was as if a waxen image had been laid out in the coffin, and strewed with innocent flowers. It was not like death, but more like an image of life! No breath moved the lips, no pulse stirred, no sight or sound would enter those eyes or ears more. While I looked at it, I saw no pain was there; it seemed to smile at the short pang of life which was over: but I could not bear the coffin-lid to be closed – it almost stifled me; and still as the nettles wave in a corner of the churchyard over his little grave, the welcome breeze helps to refresh me and ease the tightness at my breast![14]

An ivory or marble image, like Chantry's monument of the two children, is contemplated with pure delight.[15] Why do we not grieve and fret that the marble is not alive, or fancy that it has a shortness of breath? It never was alive; and it is the difficulty of making the transition from life to death, the struggle between the two in our imagination, that confounds their properties painfully together, and makes us conceive that the infant that is but just dead, still wants to breathe, to enjoy, and look about it, and is prevented by the icy hand of death, locking up its faculties and benumbing its senses; so that, if it could, it would complain of its own hard state. Perhaps religious considerations reconcile the mind to this change sooner than any others, by representing the spirit as fled to another sphere, and leaving the body behind it. But in reflecting on death generally, we mix up the idea of life with it, and thus make it the ghastly monster it is. We think how we should feel, not how the dead feel.

Still from the tomb the voice of nature cries;
Even in our ashes live their wonted fires![16]

There is an admirable passage on this subject in Tucker's *Light of Nature Pursued,* which I shall transcribe, as by much the best illustration I can offer of it.[17]

'The melancholy appearance of a lifeless body, the mansion provided for it to inhabit, dark, cold, close and solitary, are shocking to the imagination; but it is to the imagination only, not the understanding; for whoever consults this faculty will see at first glance, that there is nothing dismal in all these circumstances: if the corpse were kept wrapped up in a warm bed, with a roasting fire in the chamber, it would feel no comfortable warmth therefrom; were the store of tapers lighted up as soon as day shuts in, it would see no objects to divert it; were it left at large it would have no liberty, nor if surrounded with company would be cheered thereby; neither are the distorted features expressions of pain, uneasiness, or distress. This everyone knows, and will readily allow upon being suggested, yet still cannot behold, nor even cast a thought upon those objects without shuddering; for knowing that a living person must suffer grievously under such appearances, they become habitually formidable to the mind, and strike a mechanical horror, which is increased by the customs of the world around us.'

There is usually one pang added voluntarily and unnecessarily to the fear of death, by our affecting to compassionate the loss which others will have in us. If that were all, we might reasonably set our minds at rest. The pathetic exhortation on country tombstones, 'Grieve not for me, my wife and children dear', etc. is for the most part speedily followed to the letter. We do not leave so great a void in society as we are inclined to imagine, partly to magnify our own importance, and partly to console ourselves by sympathy. Even in the same family the gap is not so great; the wound closes up sooner than we should expect. Nay, our room is not unfrequently thought better than our company. People walk along the streets the day after our deaths just as they did before, and the crowd is not diminished. While we were living, the world seemed in a manner to exist only for us, for our delight and amusement, because it contributed to them. But our hearts cease to beat, and it goes on as usual, and thinks no more about us than it did in our lifetime. The million are devoid of sentiment, and care as little for you or me as if we belonged to the moon. We live the week over in the Sunday's newspaper, or are decently interred in some obituary at the month's end. It is not surprising that we are forgotten so soon after we quit this mortal stage: we are scarcely noticed, while we are on it. It is not merely that our names are not known in China – they have hardly been heard of in the next street. We are hand and glove with the universe, and think the obligation is mutual. This is an evident fallacy. If this, however, does not trouble us now, it will not hereafter. A handful of dust can have no quarrel to pick with its neighbours, or complaint to make against Providence, and might well exclaim, if it had but an understanding and a tongue, 'Go thy ways, old world, swing round in blue ether, voluble to every age, you and I shall no more jostle!'

It is amazing how soon the rich and titled, and even some of those who have wielded great political power, are forgotten:

A little rule, a little sway,
Is all the great and mighty have
Betwixt the cradle and the grave! –[18]

and, after its short date, they hardly leave a name behind them. 'A great man's memory may, at the common rate, survive him half a year.' His heirs and successors take his titles, his power, and his wealth – all that made him considerable or courted by others; and he has left nothing else behind him either to flatter or benefit the world. Posterity are not by any means so disinterested as they are supposed to be. They give their gratitude and admiration only in return for benefits conferred. They cherish the memory of those to whom they are indebted for instruction and delight; and they cherish it just in proportion to the instruction and delight they are conscious of receiving. The sentiment of admiration springs immediately from this ground; and cannot be otherwise than well founded.*

The effeminate clinging to life as such, as a general or abstract idea, is the effect of a highly civilised and artificial state of society. Men formerly plunged into all the vicissitudes and dangers of war, or staked their all upon a single die, or some one passion, which if they could not have gratified, life became a burthen to them – now our strongest passion is to think, our chief amusement is to read new plays, new poems, new novels, and this we may do at our leisure, in perfect security, *ad infinitum*. If we look into the old histories and romances, before the *belles-lettres* neutralised human affairs and reduced passion to a state of mental equivocation, we find the heroes and heroines not setting their lives 'at a pin's fee', but rather courting opportunities of throwing them away in very wantonness of spirit. They raise their fondness for some favourite pursuit to its height, to a pitch of madness, and think no price too dear to pay for its full gratification. Every thing else is dross. They go to death as to a bridal bed, and sacrifice themselves or others without remorse at the shrine of love, of honour, of religion, or any other prevailing feeling. Romeo runs his 'sea-sick, weary bark upon the rocks' of death, the instant he finds himself deprived of his Juliet; and she clasps his neck in their last agonies, and follows him to the same fatal shore. One strong idea takes possession of the mind and overrules every other; and even life itself, joyless without that, becomes an object of indifference or loathing. There is at least more of imagination in such a state of things, more vigour of feeling and promptitude to act than in our lingering, languid, protracted attachment to life for its own poor sake. It is, perhaps,

* It has been usual to raise a very unjust clamour against the enormous salaries of public singers, actors, and so on. This matter seems, reducible to a *moral equation*. They are paid out of money raised by voluntary contribution, in the strictest sense; and if they did not bring certain sum, into the treasury, the managers would not engage them. These sums are exactly in proportion to the number of individuals to whom their performance gives an extraordinary degree of pleasure. The talents of a singer, actor, etc. are therefore worth just as much as they will fetch.

also better, as well as more heroical, to strike at some daring or darling object, and if we fail in that, to take the consequences manfully, than to renew the lease of a tedious, spiritless, charmless existence, merely (as Pierre says) 'to lose it afterwards in some vile brawl' for some worthless object.[19] Was there not a spirit of martyrdom as well as a spice of the reckless energy of barbarism in this bold defiance of death? Had not religion something to do with it; the implicit belief in another state of being, which rendered this of less value, and embodied something beyond it to the imagination; so that the rough soldier, the infatuated lover, the valorous knight, etc. could afford to throw away the present venture, and take a leap into the arms of futurity, which the modern sceptic shrinks back from, with all his boasted reason and vain philosophy, weaker than a woman! I cannot help thinking so myself; but I have endeavoured to explain this point before, and will not enlarge farther on it here.

A life of action and danger moderates the dread of death. It not only gives us fortitude to bear pain, but teaches us at every step the precarious tenure on which we hold our present being. Sedentary and studious men are the most apprehensive on this score. Dr Johnson was an instance in point. A few years seemed to him soon over, compared with those sweeping contemplations on time and infinity with which he had been used to pose himself. In the *still-life* of a man of letters, there was no obvious reason for a change. He might sit in an armchair and pour out cups of tea to all eternity. Would it had been possible for him to do so! The most rational cure after all for the inordinate fear of death is to set a just value on life. If we merely wish to continue on the scene to indulge our headstrong humours and tormenting passions, we had better begone at once: and if we only cherish a fondness for existence according to the benefits we reap from it, the pang we feel at parting with it will not be very severe![20]

from Characteristics *in the Manner of Rochefoucault's Maxims*

The collection of maxims from which the following extracts have been taken was first published anonymously on 5 July 1823, two months after the first appearance of *Liber Amoris*.

If memoirs are always tending to the subjective, the sentimental and the effusive, maxims are, by their very nature, abstract, rational and restrained. The maxim, as a form, invariably strives to distil from the remains of experience a concentrated and edifying liquor. Unconsciously at war with all that is chaotic and corporeal, personal and particular, it is the rationalist form *par excellence*. How fascinating, then, to see Hazlitt embarking upon a book of axioms so soon after completing his book of confessions, with the former following hard upon the latter like a hastily-sought antidote. How intriguing, also, to see him swapping romantic Rousseau, the inspiration behind *Liber Amoris*, for dryasdust de Rochefoucauld, with his tart Louis Quatorze style. Controversial but concise, the aphorism does not need to explain itself; it glories in its own irresponsibility; it is one of the most aristocratic of forms. It is for this reason, perhaps, that maxim-crunching did not come naturally to Hazlitt. The spirit of dialogue was too powerful within him; his tendency was always to illustrate, elaborate and *essay* his ideas. For all that, however, the *Characteristics* does constitute a satisfyingly cynical revisiting of many of the central themes of *Liber Amoris*, and a fine example of what form can do to content.

Preface

The following work was suggested by a perusal of Rochefoucault's *Maxims and Moral Reflections*. I was so struck with the force and beauty of the style and matter, that I felt an earnest ambition to embody some occasional thoughts of my own in the same form.

This was much easier than to retain an equal degree of spirit. Having, however, succeeded indifferently in a few, the work grew under my hands; and both the novelty and agreeableness of the task impelled me forward. There is a peculiar stimulus, and at the same time a freedom from all anxiety, in this mode of writing. A thought must tell at once, or not at all. There is no opportunity for considering how we shall make out an opinion by labour and prolixity. An observation must be self-evident; or a reason or illustration (if we give one) must be pithy and concise. Each maxim should contain the essence or groundwork of a separate essay, but so developed as of itself to suggest a whole train of reflections to the reader; and it is equally necessary to avoid paradox or commonplace. The style also must be sententious and epigrammatic, with a certain pointedness and involution of expression, so as to keep the thoughts distinct, and to prevent them from running endlessly into one another. Such are the conditions to which it seemed to me necessary to conform, in order to insure anything like success to a work of this kind, or to render the pleasure of the perusal equal to the difficulty of the execution. There is only one point in which I dare even allude to a comparison with Rochefoucault – *I have had no theory to maintain*; and have endeavoured to set down each thought as it occurred to me, without bias or prejudice of any sort.

I. Of all virtues, magnanimity is the rarest. There are a hundred persons of merit for one who willingly acknowledges it in another.

II. It is often harder to praise a friend than an enemy. By the last we may acquire a reputation for candour; by the first we only seem to discharge a debt, and are liable to a suspicion of partiality. Besides, though familiarity may not breed contempt, it takes off the edge of admiration; and the shining points of character are not those we chiefly wish to dwell upon. Our habitual impression of anyone is very different from the light in which he would choose to appear before the public. We think of him *as a friend*: we must forget that he is one, before we can extol him to others.

XV. The silence of a friend commonly amounts to treachery. His not daring to say anything in our behalf implies a tacit censure.[1]

XVI. It is hard to praise those who are dispraised by others. He is little short of a hero, who perseveres in thinking well of a friend who has become a butt for slander, and a byeword.

XVII. However we may flatter ourselves to the contrary, our friends think no higher of us than the world do. They see us with the jaundiced or distrustful eyes of others. They may know better, but their feelings are governed by popular prejudice. Nay, they are more shy of us (when under a cloud) than even strangers; for we involve them in a common disgrace, or compel them to embroil themselves in continual quarrels and disputes in our defence.[2]

XIX. Envy, among other ingredients, has a mixture of the love of justice in it. We are more angry at undeserved than at deserved good-fortune.

XXI. The assumption of merit is easier, less embarrassing, and more effectual than the positive attainment of it.

XXII. Envy is the most universal passion. We only pride ourselves on the qualities we possess or think we possess; but we envy the pretensions we have, and those which we have not, and do not even wish for. We envy the greatest qualities and every trifling advantage. We envy the most ridiculous appearance or affectation of superiority. We envy folly and conceit: nay, we go so far as to envy whatever confers distinction or notoriety, even vice and infamy.

XXIII. Envy is a littleness of soul, which cannot see beyond a certain point, and if it does not occupy the whole space, feels itself excluded.

XXV. The secret of our self-love is just the same as that of our liberality and candour. We prefer ourselves to others, only because we have a more intimate consciousness and confirmed opinion of our own claims and merits than of any other person's.

XXVI. It argues a poor opinion of ourselves, when we cannot admit any other class of merit besides our own, or any rival in that class.

XXVII. Those who are the most distrustful of themselves, are the most envious of others; as the most weak and cowardly are the most revengeful.

XXX. Persons of slender intellectual *stamina* dread competition, as dwarfs are afraid of being run over in the street. Yet vanity often prompts them to hazard the experiment, as women through foolhardiness rush into a crowd.

XXXIII. A distinction has been made between acuteness and subtlety of understanding. This might be illustrated by saying, that acuteness consists in taking up the points or solid atoms, subtlety in feeling the *air* of truth.

XXXIV. Hope is the best possession. None are completely wretched but those who are without hope; and few are reduced so low as that.

XXXV. Death is the greatest evil; because it cuts off hope.

XXXVI. While we desire, we do not enjoy; and with enjoyment desire ceases, which should lend its strongest zest to it. This, however, does not apply to the gratification of sense, but to the passions in which distance and difficulty have a principal share.

XXXVII. To deserve any blessing is to set a just value on it. The pains we take in its pursuit are only a consequence of this.

XLII. Self-sufficiency is more provoking than rudeness or the most unqualified or violent opposition, inasmuch as the latter may be retorted, and implies that we are worth notice; whereas the former strikes at the root of our self-importance, and reminds us that even our good opinion is not worth having. Nothing precludes sympathy so much as a perfect indifference to it.

XLIII. The confession of our failings is a thankless office. It savours less of sincerity or modesty than of ostentation. It seems as if we thought our weaknesses as good as other people's virtues.

XLV. Nothing is more successful with women than that sort of condescending patronage of the sex, which goes by the general name of gallantry. It has the double advantage of imposing on their weakness and flattering their pride. By being indiscriminate, it tantalises and keeps them in suspense; and by making a profession of an extreme deference for the sex in general, naturally suggests the reflection, what a delightful thing it must be to gain the exclusive regard of a man who has so high an opinion of what is due to the female character. It is possible for a man, by talking of what is *feminine* or *unfeminine, vulgar* or *genteel,* by saying *how shocking such an article of dress is,* or that *no lady ought to touch a particular kind of food,* fairly to starve or strip a whole circle of simpletons half-naked, by mere dint of impertinence, and an air of commonplace assurance. How interesting to be acquainted with a man whose every thought turns upon the sex! How charming to make a conquest of one who sets up for a consummate judge of female perfections!

XLVI. We like characters and actions which we do not approve. There are amiable vices and obnoxious virtues, on the mere principle that our sympathy with a person who yields to obvious temptations and agreeable impulses (however prejudicial) is itself agreeable, while to sympathise with exercises of self-denial or fortitude, is a painful effort. Virtue costs the spectator, as well as the performer, something. We are touched by the immediate motives of actions, we judge of them by the consequences. We like a convivial character better than an abstemious one, because the idea of conviviality in the first instance is pleasanter than that of sobriety. For the same reason, we prefer generosity to justice, because the imagination lends itself more easily to an ebullition of feeling, than to the suppression of it on remote and abstract principles; and we like a good-natured fool, or even knave better than the severe professors of wisdom and morality. Cato, Brutus, etc. are characters to admire and applaud, rather than to love or imitate.

XLVII. Personal pretensions alone ensure female regard. It is not the eye that sees whatever is sublime or beautiful in nature that the fair delight to see gazing in silent rapture on themselves, but that which is itself a pleasing object to the sense. I may look at a Claude or a Raphael by turns, but this does not alter my own appearance; and it is that which women attend to.

LV. If a man is disliked by one woman, he will succeed with none. The sex (one and all) have the same secret, or *freemasonry,* in judging of men.

LVI. Any woman may act the part of a coquet successfully, who has the reputation without the scruples of modesty. If a woman passes the bounds of propriety for our sakes, and throws herself unblushingly at our heads, we conclude it is either from a sudden and violent liking, or from extraordinary merit on our parts, either of which is enough to turn any man's head, who has a single spark or gallantry or vanity in his composition.

LVII. The surest way to make ourselves agreeable to others is by seeming to think them so. If we appear fully sensible of their good qualities, they will not complain of the want of them in us.

LVIII. We often choose a friend as we do a mistress, for no particular excellence in themselves, but merely from some circumstance that flatters our self-love.

LIX. Silence is one great art of conversation. He is not a fool who knows when to hold his tongue; and a person may gain credit for sense, eloquence, wit, who merely says nothing to lessen the opinion which others have of these qualities in themselves.

LX. There are few things in which we deceive ourselves more than in the esteem we profess to entertain for our friends. It is little better than a piece of quackery. The truth is, we think of them as we please – that is, as *they* please or displease us. As long as we are in good humour with them, we see nothing but their good qualities; but no sooner do they offend us than we rip up all their bad ones (which we before made a secret of, even to ourselves) with double malice. He who but now was little less than an angel of light shall be painted in the blackest colours for a slip of the tongue, 'some trick not worth an egg',[3] for the slightest suspicion of offence given or received. We often bestow the most opprobrious epithets on our best friends, and retract them twenty times in the course of a day, while the man himself remains the same. In love, which is all rhapsody and passion, this is excusable; but in the ordinary intercourse of life, it is preposterous.

LXIV. We do not like our friends the worse because they sometimes give us an opportunity to rail at them heartily. Their faults reconcile us to their virtues. Indeed, we never have much esteem or regard, except for those that we can afford to speak our minds of freely; whose follies vex us in proportion to our anxiety for their welfare, and who have plenty of redeeming points about them to balance their defects. When we 'spy abuses' of this kind, it is a wiser and more generous proceeding to give vent to our impatience and ill-humour, than to brood over it, and let it, by sinking into our minds, poison the very sources of our goodwill.

LXVI. It is well that there is no one without a fault; for he would not have a friend in the world. He would seem to belong to a different species.

LXIX. The study of metaphysics has this advantage, at least – it promotes a certain integrity and uprightness of understanding, which is a cure for the spirit of lying. He who has devoted himself to the discovery of truth feels neither pride nor pleasure in the invention of falsehood, and cannot condescend to any such paltry expedient. If you find a person given to vulgar shifts and rhodomontade, and who at the same time tells you he is a metaphysician, do not believe him.

LXXII. Satirists gain the applause of others through fear, not through love.

LXXIV. Parodists, like mimics, seize only on defects, or turn beauties into blemishes. They make bad writers and indifferent actors.

LXXXI. There is a natural principle of *antithesis* in the human mind. We seldom grant one excellence but we hasten to make up for it by a contrary defect, to keep the balance of criticism even. Thus we say, *Titian was a great colourist, but did not know how to draw.* The first is true: the last is a mere presumption from the first, like alternate rhyme and reason; or a compromise with the weakness of human nature, which soon tires of praise.

LXXXIV. It was ridiculous to set up Mr Kean as a rival to Mr Kemble.[4] Whatever merits the first might have, they were of a totally different class, and could not possibly interfere with, much less injure those of his great predecessor. Mr Kemble stood on his own ground, and he stood high on it. Yet there certainly was a *reaction* in this case. Many persons saw no defect in Mr Kemble till Mr Kean came, and then finding themselves mistaken in the abstract idea of perfection they had indulged in, were ready to give up their opinion altogether. When a man is a great favourite with the public, they incline by a natural spirit of exaggeration and love of the marvellous, to heap all sorts of perfections upon him, and when they find by another's excelling him in some one thing that this is not the case, they are disposed to strip their former idol, and leave him 'bare to weather'. Nothing is more unjust or capricious than public opinion.

LXXXV. The public have neither shame nor gratitude.

XCVI. Livery-servants (I confess it) are the only people I do not like to sit in company with. They offend not only by their own meanness, but by the ostentatious display of the pride of their masters.

XCVII. It has been observed, that the proudest people are not nice in love. In fact, they think they raise the object of their choice above everyone else.

XCVIII. A proud man is satisfied with his own good opinion, and does not seek to make converts to it. Pride erects a little kingdom of its own, and acts as sovereign in it. Hence we see why some men are so proud they cannot be affronted, like kings who have no peer or equal.

XCIX. The proudest people are as soon repulsed as the most humble. The last are discouraged by the slightest objection or hint of their conscious incapacity, while the first disdain to enter into any competition, and resent whatever implies a doubt of their self-evident superiority to others.

C. What passes in the world for talent or dexterity or enterprise, is often only a want of moral principle. We may succeed where others fail, not from a greater share of invention, but from not being nice in the choice of expedients.

CI. Cunning is the art of concealing our own defects, and discovering other people's weaknesses. Or it is taking advantages of others which they do not suspect, because they are contrary to propriety and the settled practice. We feel no inferiority to a fellow who picks our pockets; though we feel mortified at being overreached by trick and cunning. Yet there is no more reason for it in the one case than in the other. Anyone may win at cards by cheating – *till he is found out.* We have been playing against odds. So anyone may deceive us by lying, or take an unfair advantage of us, who is not withheld by a sense of shame or honesty from doing so.

CII. The completest hypocrites are so by nature. That is, they are without sympathy with others to distract their attention – or any of that nervous weakness, which might revolt or hesitate at the baseness of the means necessary to carry on their system of deception. You can no more tell what is passing in the minds of such people than if they were of a different species. They, in fact, are so as to all moral intents and purposes; and this is the advantage they have over you. You fancy there is a common link between you, while in reality there is none.[5]

CIII. The greatest hypocrites are the greatest dupes. This is either because they think only of deceiving others and are off their guard, or because they really know little about the feelings or characters of others from their want of sympathy, and of consequent sagacity. Perhaps the resorting to trick and artifice in the first instance implies not only a callousness of feeling, but an obtuseness of intellect, which cannot get on by fair means. Thus a girl who is ignorant and stupid may yet have cunning enough to resort to silence as the only chance of conveying an opinion of her capacity.

CIV. The greatest talents do not generally attain to the highest stations. For though high, the ascent to them is narrow, beaten, and crooked. The path of genius is free, and its own. Whatever requires the concurrence and co-operation of others, must depend chiefly on routine and an attention to rules and *minutiae.* Success in business is therefore seldom owing to uncommon talents or original power, which is untractable and self-willed, but to the greatest degree of commonplace capacity.

CV. The error in the reasonings of Mandeville, Rochefoucault, and others, is this: they first find out that there is something mixed in the motives of all our actions, and they then proceed to argue, that they must all arise from one motive, *viz.* self-love. They make the exception the rule. It would be easy to reverse the argument, and prove that our most selfish actions are disinterested. There is honour among thieves. Robbers, murderers, etc. do not commit those actions, from a pleasure in pure villainy, or for their own benefit only, but from a mistaken regard to the welfare or good opinion of those with whom they are immediately connected.[6]

CVI. It is ridiculous to say, that compassion, friendship, etc. are at bottom only selfishness in disguise, because it is *we* who feel pleasure or pain in the good or evil of others; for the meaning of self-love is not that it is I who love, but that I love myself. The motive is no more selfish because it is I who feel it, than the action is selfish because it is I who perform it. To prove a man selfish, it is not surely enough to say, that it is *he who feels* (this is a mere quibble) but to show that he does not feel *for another*; that is, that the idea of the suffering or welfare of others does not excite any feeling whatever of pleasure or pain in his mind, except from some reference to or reflection on himself. Self-love or the love of self means, that I have an immediate interest in the contemplation of my own good, and that this is a motive to action; and benevolence or the love of others means in like manner, that I have an immediate interest in the idea of the good or evil that may befall them, and a disposition to assist them, in consequence. Self-love, in a word, is sympathy with myself, that is, it is I who feel it, and I who am the object of it: in benevolence or compassion, it is I who still feel sympathy, but another (not myself) is the object of it. If I feel sympathy with others at all, it must be disinterested. The pleasure it may give me is the consequence, not the cause, of my feeling it. To insist that sympathy is self-love because we cannot feel for others, without being ourselves affected pleasurably or painfully, is to make nonsense of the question; for it is to insist that in order to feel for others properly and truly, we must in the first place feel nothing. *C'est une mauvaise plaisanterie*. That the feeling exists in the individual must be granted, and never admitted of a question: the only question is, how that feeling is caused, and what is its object – and it is to express the two opinions that may be entertained on this subject, that the terms *self-love* and *benevolence* have been appropriated. Any other interpretation of them is an evident abuse of language, and a subterfuge in argument, which, driven from the fair field of fact and observation, takes shelter in verbal sophistry.[7]

CVII. Humility and pride are not easily distinguished from each other. A proud man, who fortifies himself in his own good opinion, may be supposed not to put forward his pretensions through shyness or deference to others: a modest man, who is really reserved and afraid of committing himself, is thought distant and haughty: and the vainest coxcomb, who makes a display of himself and his most plausible qualifications, often does so to hide his deficiencies and to prop up his tottering opinion of himself by the applause of others. Vanity does not refer to the opinion a man entertains of himself, but to that which he wishes others to entertain of him. Pride is indifferent to the approbation of others; as modesty shrinks from it, either through bashfulness, or from an unwillingness to take any undue advantage of it. I have known several very forward, loquacious, and even overbearing persons, whose confidential communications were oppressive from the sense they entertained of their own demerits. In company they talked on in mere bravado, and for fear of betraying their weak side, as children make a noise in the dark.

CXV. We do not hate those who injure us, if they do not at the same time wound our self-love. We can forgive any one sooner than those who lower us in our own opinion. It is no wonder, therefore, that we as often dislike others for their virtues as for their vices. We naturally hate whatever makes us despise ourselves.

CXVI. When you find out a man's ruling passion, beware of crossing him in it.

CXXIII. As we scorn them who scorn us, so the contempt of the world (not seldom) makes men proud.

CXXVI. The affected modesty of most women is a decoy for the generous, the delicate, and unsuspecting; while the artful, the bold, and unfeeling either see or break through its slender disguises.

CXXXI. The fear of punishment may be necessary to the suppression of vice; but it also suspends the finer motives to virtue.

CXXXII. No wise man can have a contempt for the prejudices of others; and he should even stand in a certain awe of his own, as if they were aged parents and monitors. They may in the end prove wiser than he.

CXXXIII. We are only justified in rejecting prejudices, when we can explain the grounds of them; or when they are at war with nature, which is the strongest prejudice of all.

CXXXIV. Vulgar prejudices are those which arise out of accident, ignorance, or authority. Natural prejudices are those which arise out of the constitution of the human mind itself.

CXXXV. Nature is stronger than reason: for nature is, after all, the text, reason but the comment. He is indeed a poor creature who does not *feel* the truth of more than he *knows* or can explain satisfactorily to others.

CXXXVI. The mind revolts against certain opinions, as the stomach rejects certain foods.

CXXXVII. The drawing a certain positive line in morals, beyond which a single false step is irretrievable, makes virtue formal, and vice desperate.

CXXXVIII. Most codes of morality proceed on a supposition of *Original Sin*; as if the only object was to coerce the headstrong propensities to vice, and there were no natural disposition to good in the mind, which it was possible to improve, refine, and cultivate.

CXXXIX. This *negative* system of virtue leads to a very low style of moral sentiment. It is as if the highest excellence in a picture was to avoid gross defects in drawing; or in writing, instances of bad grammar. It ought surely to be our aim in virtue, as well as in other things, 'to snatch a grace beyond the reach of art'.[8]

CXL. We find many things to which the prohibition of them constitutes the only temptation.

CXLI. There is neither so much vice nor so much virtue in the world, as it might appear at first sight that there is. Many people commit actions that they hate, as they affect virtues that they laugh at, merely because others do so.

CXLII. When the imagination is continually led to the brink of vice by a system of terror and denunciations, people fling themselves over the precipice from the mere dread of falling.

CXLIII. The maxim – *Video meliora proboque, deteriora sequor*[9] – has not been fully explained. In general, it is taken for granted, that those things that our reason disapproves, we give way to from passion. Nothing like it. The course that persons in the situation of Medea pursue has often as little to do with inclination as with judgement: but they are led astray by some object of a disturbed imagination, that shocks their feelings and staggers their belief; and they grasp the phantom to put an end to this state of tormenting suspense, and to see whether it is human or not.

CXLIV. Vice, like disease, floats in the atmosphere.

CXLV. Honesty is one part of eloquence. We persuade others by being in earnest ourselves.

CXLVI. A mere sanguine temperament often passes for genius and patriotism.

CLIV. If we do not aspire to admiration, we shall fall into contempt. To expect sheer, evenhanded justice from mankind, is folly. They take the gross inventory of our pretensions; and not to have them overlooked entirely, we must place them in a conspicuous point of view, as men write their trades or fix a sign over the doors of their houses. Not to conform to the established practice in either respect, is false delicacy in the commerce of the world.

CLVIII. Man is an intellectual animal, and therefore an everlasting contradiction to himself. His senses centre in himself, his ideas reach to the ends of the universe; so that he is torn in pieces between the two, without a possibility of its ever being otherwise. A mere physical being, or a pure spirit, can alone be satisfied with itself.

CLXIII. We are never so much disposed to quarrel with others as when we are dissatisfied with ourselves.

CLXIV. We are never so thoroughly tired of the company of any one else as we sometimes are of our own.

CLXV. People outlive the interest, which, at different periods of their lives, they take in themselves. When we forget old friends, it is a sign we have forgotten ourselves; or despise our former ways and notions, as much as we do their present ones.

CLXVI. We fancy ourselves superior to others, because we find that we have improved; and at no time did we think ourselves inferior to them.

CLXVII. The notice of others is as necessary to us as the air we breathe. If we cannot gain their good opinion, we change our battery, and strive to provoke their hatred and contempt.

CLXVIII. Some malefactors, at the point of death, confess crimes of which they have never been guilty, thus to raise our wonder and indignation in the same proportion; or to show their superiority to vulgar prejudice, and brave that public opinion, of which they are the victims.

CLXIX. Others make an ostentatious display of their penitence and remorse, only to invite sympathy, and create a diversion in their own minds from the subject of their impending punishment. So that we excite a strong emotion in the breasts of others, we care little of what kind it is, or by what means we produce it. We have equally the feeling of power. The sense of insignificance or of being an object of perfect indifference to others, is the only one that the mind never covets nor willingly submits to.

CLXXII. We talk little, if we do not talk about ourselves.

CLXXVI. We compliment ourselves on our national reserve and taciturnity by abusing the loquacity and frivolity of the French.

CLXXX. The best kind of conversation is that which may be called *thinking aloud*. I like very well to speak my mind on any subject (or to hear another do so) and to go into the question according to the degree of interest it naturally inspires, but not to have to get up a thesis upon every topic. There are those, on the other hand, who seem always to be practising on their audience, as if they mistook them for a DEBATING-SOCIETY, or to hold a general retainer, by which they are bound to explain every difficulty, and answer every objection that can be started. This, in private society and among friends, is not desirable. You thus lose the two great ends of conversation, which are to learn the sentiments of others, and see what they think of yours. One of the best talkers I ever knew had this defect – that he evidently seemed to be considering less what he felt on any point than what might be said upon it, and that he listened to you, not to weigh what you said, but to reply to it, like counsel on the other side. This habit gave a brilliant smoothness and polish to his general discourse, but, at the same time, took from its solidity and prominence: it reduced it to a tissue of lively, fluent, ingenious *commonplaces*, (for original genuine, observations are like 'minute drops from off the eaves',[10] and not an incessant shower) and, though his talent in this way was carried to the very extreme of cleverness, yet I think it seldom, if ever, went beyond it.

CLXXXV. In an Englishman, a diversity of profession and pursuit (as the having been a soldier, a valet, a player, etc.) implies a dissipation and dissoluteness of character, and a fitness for nothing. In a Frenchman, it only shows a natural vivacity of disposition, and a fitness for everything.

CLXXXVII. Half the miseries of human life proceed from our not perceiving the incompatibility of different attainments, and consequently aiming at too much. We make ourselves wretched in vainly aspiring after advantages we are deprived of; and do not consider that if we had these advantages, it would be quite impossible for us to retain those which we actually do possess, and which, after all, if it were put to the question, we would not consent to part with for the sake of any others.

CXC. People in general consult their prevailing humour or ruling passion (whatever it may be) much more than their interest.

CXCII. When we speak ill of people behind their backs, and are civil to them to their faces, we may be accused of insincerity. But the contradiction is less owing to insincerity than to the change of circumstances. We think well of them while we are with them; and in their absence recollect the ill we durst not hint at or acknowledge to ourselves in their presence.

CXCIII. Our opinions are not our own, but in the power of sympathy. If a person tells us a palpable falsehood, we not only dare not contradict him, but we dare hardly disbelieve him *to his face*. A lie boldly uttered has the effect of truth for the instant.

CXCIV. A man's reputation is not in his own keeping, but lies at the mercy of the profligacy of others. Calumny requires no proof. The throwing out malicious imputations against any character leaves a stain, which no after-reputation can wipe out. To create an unfavourable impression, it is not necessary that certain things should be *true*, but that they *have been said*. The imagination is of so delicate a texture, that even words wound it.

CXCV. A nickname is a mode of insinuating a prejudice against another under some general designation, which, as it offers no proof, admits of no reply.

CXCVII. Want of principle is power. Truth and honesty set a limit to our efforts, which impudence and hypocrisy easily overleap.

CXCIX. Nothing gives such a blow to friendship as the detecting another in an untruth: it strikes at the root of our confidence ever after.

CC. In estimating the value of an acquaintance or even friend, we give a preference to intellectual or convivial over moral qualities. The truth is, that in our habitual intercourse with others, we much oftener require to be amused than assisted. We consider less, therefore, what a person with whom we are intimate is ready to do for us in critical emergencies, than what he has to say on ordinary occasions. We dispense with his services, if he only saves us from *ennui*. In civilised society, words are of as much importance as things.

CCXX. Cunning is natural to mankind. It is the sense of our weakness, and an attempt to effect by concealment what we cannot do openly and by force.

CCXXI. In love we never think of moral qualities, and scarcely of intellectual ones. Temperament and manner alone (with beauty) excite love.

CCXXX. In the course of a long acquaintance we have repeated all but good things, and discussed all our favourite topics several times over, so that our conversation becomes a mockery of social intercourse. We might as well talk to ourselves. The soil of friendship is worn out with constant use. Habit may still attach us to each other, but we feel ourselves fettered by it. Old friends might be compared to old married people without the tie of children.

CCXXXII. If we are long absent from our friends, we forget them: if we are constantly with them, we despise them.

CCXXXIII. There are no rules for friendship. It must be left to itself; we cannot force it any more than love.

CCXXXIV. The most violent friendships soonest wear themselves out.

CCXXXV. To be capable of steady friendship or lasting love, are the two greatest proofs, not only of goodness of heart, but of strength of mind.

CCXXXVI. It makes us proud when our love of a mistress is returned: it ought to make us prouder that we can love her for herself alone, without the aid of any such selfish reflection. This is the religion of love.

CCXLII. We may hate and love the same person, nay even at the same moment.

CCXLIII. We never hate those whom we have once loved, merely because they have injured us. 'We may kill those of whom we are jealous,' says Fielding, 'but we do not hate them.' We are enraged at their conduct and at ourselves as the objects of it, but this does not alter our passion for them. The reason is, we loved them without their loving us; we do not hate them because they hate us. Love may turn to indifference with possession, but is irritated by disappointment.

CCXLIV. Revenge against the object of our love is madness. No one would kill the woman he loves, but that he thinks he can bring her to life afterwards. Her death seems to him as momentary as his own rash act. See *Othello*. – 'My wife! I have no wife', etc.[11] He stabbed not at her life, but at her falsehood; he thought to kill the wanton, and preserve the wife.

CCXLV. We revenge in haste and passion: we repent at leisure and from reflection.

CCXLVI. By retaliating our sufferings on the heads of those we love, we get rid of a present uneasiness, and incur lasting remorse. With the accomplishment of our revenge our fondness returns; so that we feel the injury we have done them, even more than they do.

CCXLVII. I think men formerly were more jealous of their rivals in love – they are now more jealous of their mistresses, and lay the blame on them. That is, we formerly thought more of the mere possession of the person, which the removal of a favoured lover prevented, and we now think more of a woman's affections, which may still follow him to the tomb. To kill a rival is to kill a fool; but the Goddess of our idolatry may be a sacrifice worthy of the Gods. Hackman did not think of shooting Lord Sandwich, but Miss Ray.[12]

CCXLVIII. Many people in reasoning on the passions make a continual appeal to common sense. But passion is without common sense, and we must frequently discard the one in speaking of the other.

CCXLIX. It is provoking to hear people at their ease talking reason to others in a state of violent suffering. If you can remove their suffering by speaking a word, do so; and then they will be in a state to hear calm reason.

CCLI. People try to reconcile you to a disappointment in love, by asking why you should cherish a passion for an object that has proved itself worthless. Had you known this before, you would not have encouraged the passion; but that having been once formed, knowledge does not destroy it. If we have drank poison, finding it out does not prevent its being in our veins: so passion leaves its poison in the mind! It is the nature of all passion and of all habitual affection; we throw ourselves upon it at a venture, but we cannot return by choice. If it is a wife that has proved unworthy, men compassionate the loss, because there is a tie, they say, which we cannot get rid of. But has the heart no ties? Or if it is a child, they understand it. But is not true love a child? Or when another has become a part of ourselves, 'where we must live or have no life at all',[13] can we tear them from us in an instant? No: these bargains are for life; and that for which our souls have sighed for years, cannot be forgotten with a breath, and without a pang.

CCLII. Besides, it is uncertainty and suspense that chiefly irritate jealousy to madness. When we know our fate, we become gradually reconciled to it, and try to forget a useless sorrow.

CCLIV. The contempt of a wanton for a man who is determined to think her virtuous, is perhaps the strongest of all others. He officiously reminds her of what she ought to be; and she avenges the galling sense of lost character on the fool who still believes in it.

CCLV. To find that a woman whom we loved has forfeited her character, is the same thing as to learn that she is dead.

CCLVI. The only vice that cannot be forgiven is hypocrisy. The repentance of a hypocrite is itself hypocrisy.

CCLXIX. The best kind of conversation is that which is made up of observations, reflections, and anecdotes. A string of stories without application is as tiresome as a long-winded argument.

CCLXXI. More remarks are made upon any one's dress, looks, etc. in walking twenty yards along the streets of Edinburgh, or other provincial towns, than in passing from one end of London to the other.

CCLXXII. There is less impertinence and more independence in London than in any other place in the kingdom.

CCLXXIII. A man who meets thousands of people in a day who never saw or heard of him before, if he thinks at all, soon learns to think little of himself. London is the place where a man of sense is soonest cured of his coxcombry, or where a fool may indulge his vanity with impunity, by giving himself what airs he pleases. A valet and a lord are there nearly on a level. Among a million of men, we do not count the units, for we have not time.

CCLXXIV. There is some virtue in almost every vice, except hypocrisy; and even that, while it is a mockery of virtue, is at the same time a compliment to it.

CCLXXV. It does not follow that a man is a hypocrite, because his actions give the lie to his words. If he at one time seems a saint, and at other times a sinner, he possibly is both in reality, as well as in appearance. A person may be fond of vice and of virtue too; and practise one or the other, according to the temptation of the moment. A priest may be pious, and a sot or bigot. A woman may be modest, and a rake at heart. A poet may admire the beauties of nature, and be envious of those of other writers. A moralist may act contrary to his own precepts, and yet be sincere in recommending them to others. These are indeed contradictions, but they arise out of the contradictory qualities in our nature. A man is a hypocrite only when he affects to take a delight in what he does not feel, not because he takes a perverse delight in opposite things.

CCLXXVI. The greatest offence against virtue is to speak ill of it. To recommend certain things is worse than to practise them. There may be an excuse for the last in the frailty of passion; but the former can arise from nothing but an utter depravity of disposition. Anyone may yield to temptation, and yet feel a sincere love and aspiration after virtue; but he who maintains vice in theory, has not even the idea or capacity for virtue in his mind. Men err: fiends only make a mock at goodness.

CCLXXVII. The passions make antitheses and subtle distinctions, finer than any pen.

CCLXXXI. To marry an actress for the admiration she excites on the stage, is to imitate the man who bought Punch.

CCLXXXVII. Good and ill seem as necessary to human life as light and shade are to a picture. We grow weary of uniform success, and pleasure soon surfeits. Pain makes ease delightful; hunger relishes the homeliest food, fatigue turns the hardest bed to down; and the difficulty and uncertainty of pursuit in all cases enhance the value of possession. The wretched are in this respect fortunate, that they have the strongest yearnings after happiness; and to desire is in some sense to enjoy. If the schemes of Utopians could be realised, the tone of society would be changed from what it is, into a sort of insipid high life. There could be no fine tragedies written; nor would there be any pleasure in seeing them. We tend to this conclusion already with the progress of civilisation.

CCLXXXIX. The question respecting dramatic illusion has not been fairly stated. There are different degrees and kinds of belief. The point is not whether we do or do not believe what we see to be a positive reality, but how far and in what manner we believe in it. We do not say every moment to ourselves, 'This is real': but neither do we say every moment, 'This is not real.' The involuntary impression steals upon us till we recollect ourselves. The appearance of reality, in fact, is the reality, so long and in as far as we are not conscious of the contradictory circumstances that disprove it. The belief in a well-acted tragedy never amounts to what the witnessing the actual scene would prove, and never sinks into a mere phantasmagoria. Its power of affecting us is not, however, taken away, even if we abstract the feeling of identity; for it still suggests a stronger idea of what the reality *would be*, just as a picture reminds us more powerfully of the person for whom it is intended, though we are conscious it is not the same.

CCXCI. It is remarkable how virtuous and generously disposed every one is at a play. We uniformly applaud what is right and condemn what is wrong, when it costs us nothing but the sentiment.

CCXCIX. We are egotists in morals as well as in other things. Every man is determined to judge for himself as to his conduct in life, and finds out what he ought to have done, when it is too late to do it. For this reason, the world has to begin again with each successive generation.

CCCI. The best lesson we can learn from witnessing the folly of mankind is not to irritate ourselves against it.

CCCV. Every man, in his own opinion, forms an exception to the ordinary rules of morality.

CCCVI No man ever owned to the title of a *murderer*, a *tyrant*, etc. because, however notorious the facts might be, the epithet is accompanied with a reference to motives and marks of opprobrium in common language and in the feelings of others, which he does not acknowledge in his own mind.

CCCVII. There are some things, the *idea* of which alone is a clear gain to the human mind. Let people rail at virtue, at genius and friendship as long as they will – the very *names* of these disputed qualities are better than anything else that could be substituted for them, and embalm even the most angry abuse of them.

CCCVIII. If goodness were only a theory, it were a pity it should be lost to the world.

CCCX. Women, when left to themselves, talk chiefly about their dress: they think more about their lovers than they talk about them.

CCCXI. With women, the great business of life is love; and they generally make a mistake in it. They consult neither the heart nor the head, but are led away by mere humour and fancy. If instead of a companion for life, they had to choose a partner in a country-dance or to trifle away an hour with, their mode of calculation would be right. They tie their true-lover's knots with idle, thoughtless haste, while the institutions of society render it indissoluble.

CCCXII. When we hear complaints of the wretchedness or vanity of human life, the proper answer to them would be that there is hardly any one who at some time or other *has not been in love.* If we consider the high abstraction of this feeling, its depth, its purity, its voluptuous refinement, even in the meanest breast, how sacred and how sweet it is, this alone may reconcile us to the lot of humanity. That drop of balm turns the bitter cup to a delicious nectar –

> And vindicates the ways of God to man.[14]

CCCXIII. It is impossible to love entirely, without being loved again. Otherwise, the fable of Pygmalion would have no meaning. Let any one be ever so much enamoured of a woman who does not requite his passion, and let him consider what he feels when he finds her scorn or indifference turning to mutual regard, the thrill, the glow of rapture, the melting of two hearts into one, the creation of another self in her – and he will own that he was before only half in love!

CCCXIV. Women never reason, and therefore they are (comparatively) seldom wrong. They judge instinctively of what falls under their immediate observation or experience, and do not trouble themselves about remote or doubtful consequences. If they make no profound discoveries, they do not involve themselves in gross absurdities. It is only by the help of reason and logical inference, according to Hobbes, that 'man becomes excellently wise, or excellently foolish'.*

CCCXV. Women are less cramped by circumstances or education than men. They are more the creatures of nature and impulse, and less cast in the mould of habit or prejudice. If a young man and woman in common life are seen walking out together on a holiday, the girl has the advantage in point of air and dress. She has a greater aptitude in catching external accomplishments and the manners of her superiors, and is less depressed by a painful consciousness of her situation in life. A Quaker girl is often as sensible and conversable as any other woman: while a Quaker man is a bundle of quaint opinions and conceit. Women are not spoiled by education and an affectation of superior wisdom. They take their chance for wit and shrewdness, and pick up their advantages, according to their opportunities and turn of mind. Their faculties (such as they are) shoot out freely and gracefully, like the slender trees in a forest; and are not clipped and cut down, as the understandings of men are, into uncouth shapes and distorted fancies, like yew-trees in an old-fashioned garden. Women in short resemble self-taught men, with more pliancy and delicacy of feeling.

CCCXVI. Women have as little imagination as they have reason. They are pure egotists. They cannot go out of themselves. There is no instance of a woman having done anything great in poetry or philosophy. They can act tragedy, because this depends very much on the physical expression of the passions – they can sing, for they have flexible throats and nice ears – they can write romances about love – and talk for ever about nothing.

CCCXVII. Women are not philosophers or poets, patriots, moralists or politicians – they are simply women.

CCCXVIII. Women have a quicker sense of the ridiculous than men, because they judge from immediate impressions, and do not wait for the explanation that may be given of them.

* *Leviathan*.[15]

CCCXXV. The Dutch perhaps finished their landscapes so carefully, because there was a want of romantic and striking objects in them, so that they could only be made interesting by the accuracy of the details.

CCCXXXIX. We learn a great deal from coming into contact and collision with individuals of other nations. The contrast of character and feeling – the different points of view from which they see things – is an admirable test of the truth or reasonableness of our opinions. Among ourselves we take a number of things for granted, which, as soon as we find ourselves among strangers, we are called upon to account for. With those who think and feel differently from our habitual tone, we must have a reason for the faith that is in us, or we shall not come off very triumphantly. By this comparing of notes, by being questioned and cross-examined, we discover how far we have taken up certain notions on good grounds, or barely on trust. We also learn how much of our best knowledge is built on a sort of acquired instinct, and how little we can analyse those things that seem to most of us self-evident. He is no mean philosopher who can give a reason for one half of what he thinks. It by no means follows that our tastes or judgments are wrong, because we may be at fault in an argument. A Scotchman and a Frenchman would differ equally from an Englishman, but would run into contrary extremes. He might not be able to make good his ground against the levity of the one or the pertinacity of the other, and yet he might be right, for they cannot both be so. By visiting different countries and conversing with their inhabitants, we strike a balance between opposite prejudices, and have an average of truth and nature left.

CCCXLI. We learn little from mere captious controversy, or the collision of opinions, unless where there is this collision of character to account for the difference, and remind one, by implication, where one's own weakness lies. In the latter case, it is a shrewd presumption that inasmuch as others are wrong, so are we: for the widest breach in argument is made by mutual prejudice.

CCCXLV. There is a double aristocracy of rank and letters, which is hardly to be endured – *monstrum ingens, biforme.*[16] A lord, who is a poet as well, regards the House of Peers with contempt, as a set of dull fellows; and he considers his brother authors as a Grub

Street crew. A king is hardly good enough for him to touch: a mere man of genius is no better than a worm. He alone is all-accomplished. Such people should be *sent to Coventry*; and they generally are so, through their insufferable pride and self-sufficiency.

CCCXLVI. The great are fond of patronising men of genius, when they are remarkable for personal insignificance, so that they can dandle them like parroquets or lapdogs, or when they are distinguished by some awkwardness which they can laugh at, or some meanness which they can despise. They do not wish to encourage or show their respect for wisdom or virtue, but to witness the defects or ridiculous circumstances accompanying these, that they may have an excuse for treating all sterling pretensions with supercilious indifference. They seek at best to be amused, not to be instructed. Truth is the greatest impertinence a man can be guilty of in polite company; and players and buffoons are the *beau idéal* of men of wit and talents.

CCCXLVII. We do not see nature merely from looking at it. We fancy that we see the whole of any object that is before us, because we know no more of it than what we see. The rest escapes us, as a matter of course; and we easily conclude that the idea in our minds and the image in nature are one and the same. But in fact we only see a very small part of nature, and make an imperfect abstraction of the infinite number of particulars, which are always to be found in it as well as we can. Some do this with more or less accuracy than others, according to habit or natural genius. A painter, for instance, who has been working on a face for several days, still finds out something new in it which he did not notice before, and which he endeavours to give in order to make his copy more perfect, which shows how little an ordinary and unpractised eye can be supposed to comprehend the whole at a single glance. A young artist, when he first begins to study from nature, soon makes an end of his sketch, because he sees only a general outline and certain gross distinctions and masses. As he proceeds, a new field opens to him; differences crowd upon differences; and as his perceptions grow more refined, he could employ whole days in working upon a single part, without satisfying himself at last. No painter, after a life devoted to the art and the greatest care and length of time given to a single study of a head or other object, ever succeeded in it to his wish, or did not leave something still to be done. The greatest artists that have ever appeared are those who have been able to employ some one view or aspect of nature, and no more. Thus Titian was famous for colouring; Raphael for drawing; Correggio for the gradations, Rembrandt for the extremes of light and shade. The combined genius and powers of observation of all the great artists in the world would not be sufficient to convey the whole of what is contained in any one object in nature; and yet the most vulgar spectator thinks he sees the whole of what is before him, at once and without any trouble at all.

CCCL. We are not weaned from a misplaced attachment by (at last) discovering the unworthiness of the object. The character of a woman is one thing; her graces and attractions another; and these last acquire even an additional charm and piquancy from the disappointment we feel in other respects. The truth is, a man in love prefers his passion to every other consideration, and is fonder of his mistress than he is of virtue. Should she prove vicious, she makes vice lovely in his eyes.

CCCLI. An accomplished coquet excites the passions of others, in proportion as she feels none herself. Her forwardness allures, her indifference irritates desire. She fans the flame that does not scorch her own bosom; plays with men's feelings, and studies the effect of her several arts at leisure and unmoved.

CCCLII. Grace in women is the secret charm that draws the soul into its circle, and binds a spell round it for ever. The reason of which is, that habitual grace implies a continual sense of delight, of ease and propriety, which nothing can interrupt, ever varying, and adapting itself to all circumstances alike.

CCCLIII. Even among the most abandoned of the sex, there is generally found to exist one strong and individual attachment, which remains unshaken through all circumstances. Virtue steals like a guilty thing into the secret haunts of vice and infamy, clings to their devoted victim, and will not be driven quite away. Nothing can destroy the human heart.

CCCLV. We judge of character too much from names and classes and modes of life. It alters very little with circumstances. The theological doctrines of *Original Sin*, of *Grace*, and *Election*, admit of a moral and natural solution. Outward acts or events hardly reach the inward disposition or fitness for good or evil. Humanity is to be met with in a den of robbers, nay, modesty in a brothel. Nature prevails, and vindicates its rights to the last.

CCCLVI. Women do not become abandoned with the mere loss of character. They only discover the vicious propensities which they before were bound to conceal. They do not (all at once) part with their virtue, but throw aside the veil of affectation and prudery.

CCCLXXVIII. It is not easy to write essays like Montaigne, nor Maxims in the manner of the Duke de la Rochefoucault.

CCCLXXIX. The most perfect style of writing may be that which treats strictly and methodically of a given subject; the most amusing (if not the most instructive) is that, which mixes up the personal character of the author with general reflections.

CCCLXXX. The seat of knowledge is in the head; of wisdom, in the heart. We are sure to judge wrong, if we do not feel right.

CCCLXXXIV. Mental cowards are afraid of expressing a strong opinion, or of striking hard, lest the blow should be retaliated. They throw themselves on the forbearance of their antagonists, and hope for impunity in their insignificance.

CCCLXXXV. No one ever gained a good word from friend or foe, man or woman, by want of spirit. The public know how to distinguish between a contempt for themselves and the fear of an adversary.

CCCLXXXVI. Never be afraid of attacking a bully.

CCCLXXXVII. An honest man speaks truth, *though* it may give offence; a vain man, *in order that* it may.

CCCLXXXVIII. Those only deserve a monument who do not need one; that is, who have raised themselves a monument in the minds and memories of men.

CCCLXXXIX. Fame is the inheritance not of the dead, but of the living. It is we who look back with lofty pride to the great names of antiquity, who drink of that flood of glory as of a river, and refresh our wings in it for future flight.

CCCXC. The inhabitant of a metropolis is apt to think this circumstance alone gives him a decided superiority over every one else, and does not improve that natural advantage so much as he ought.

CCCXCI. A true-bred *cockney* fancies his having been born in London is a receipt in full for every other species of merit. He belongs, in his own opinion, to a *privileged class.*

CCCXCII. The number of objects we see from living in a large city amuses the mind like a perpetual raree-show, without supplying it with any ideas. The understanding thus becomes habitually mechanical and superficial.

CCCXCIII. In proportion to the number of persons we see, we forget that we know less of mankind.

CCCXCIV. Pertness and conceit are the characteristics of a true *cockney*. He feels little respect for the greatest things, from the opportunity of seeing them often and without trouble; and at the same time he entertains a high opinion of himself from his familiarity with them. He who has seen all the great actors, the great public characters, the chief public buildings, and the other wonders of the metropolis, thinks less of them from this circumstance; but conceives a prodigious contempt for all those who have not seen what he has.

CCCXCV. The confined air of a metropolis is hurtful to the minds and bodies of those who have never lived out of it. It is impure, stagnant – without breathing-space to allow a larger view of ourselves or others – and gives birth to a puny, sickly, unwholesome, and degenerate race of beings.

CCXCVIII. A hypocrite despises those whom he deceives, but has no respect for himself. He would make a dupe of himself too, if he could.

CCCCI. He will never have true friends who is afraid of making enemies.

CCCCII. The way to procure insults is to submit to them. A man meets with no more respect than he exacts.

CCCCXVI. Men of genius do not excel in any profession because they labour in it, but they labour in it, because they excel.

CCCCXVII. Vice is man's nature: virtue is a habit – or a mask.

CCCCXVIII. The foregoing maxim shews the difference between truth and sarcasm.

CCCCXXI. We can bear to be deprived of everything but our self-conceit.

CCCCXXIII. The reputation of science which ought to be the most lasting, as synonymous with truth, is often the least so. One discovery supersedes another; and the progress of light throws the past into obscurity. What has become of the Blacks, the Lavoisiers, the Priestleys, in chemistry? In political economy, Adam Smith is laid on the shelf, and Davenant and De Witt have given place to the Says, the Ricardos, the Malthuses, and the Macullochs. These persons are happy in one respect – they have a sovereign contempt for all who have gone before them, and never dream of those who are to come after them and usurp their place. When any set of men think theirs the only science worth studying, and themselves the only infallible persons in it, it is a sign how frail the traces are of past excellence in it, and how little connection it has with the general affairs of human life. In proportion to the profundity of any inquiry, is its futility. The most important and lasting truths are the most obvious ones. Nature cheats us with her mysteries, one after another, like a juggler with his tricks; but shows us her plain honest face, without our paying for it. The understanding only blunders more or less in trying to find out what things are in themselves: the heart judges at once of its own feelings and impressions; and these are true and the same.

CCCCXXIX. To be remembered after we are dead, is but a poor recompense for being treated with contempt while we are living.

CCCCXXX. Mankind are so ready to bestow their admiration on the dead because the latter do not hear it, or because it gives no pleasure to the objects of it. Even fame is the offspring of envy.

CCCCXXXI Truth is not one, but many; and an observation may be true in itself that contradicts another equally true, according to the point of view from which we contemplate the subject.[17]

Notes

On the Past and Future

1. From Lothario's dying speech in Nicholas Rowe's *The Fair Penitent* (1703), IV, i.
2. A reminiscence of Adam's heroic speech to Eve in Milton's *Paradise Lost* where he volunteers to fall with her: 'yet loss of thee / Would never from my heart' (IX, 912–13).
3. A quotation from one of Hazlitt's touchstone poems, Wordsworth's ode *Intimations of Immortality* (1807), 178–81.
4. Wordsworth, *Lines Written Near Richmond* (1798), 5–6.
5. From Promenade No. 10 of Rousseau's *Rêveries d'un promeneur solitaire* (1782).
6. A paean, in the Rousseauvian style, to the woods of Tuderley, near Winterslow, where the Hazlitts had a country cottage. In the spring of 1810 Hazlitt had fallen in love with a local girl called Sally Shepherd, and it is this affair that is being recollected in this passage.
7. 'Perhaps at some time it will please us to remember these things', Aeneas says to his men after the enormous hardships suffered in the journey from Troy (Virgil, *Aeneid*, I, 203).
8. Wordsworth, *Laodamia* (1815), 72.
9. Wordsworth, Sonnet 'The world is too much with us', 12.
10. This is a reference to a painting by Nicholas Poussin depicting idealised shepherds from classical antiquity clustering around an austere tomb with the *memento mori* inscription 'Et in arcadio ego' on its base. There is one copy of this painting in the Louvre and one at Chatsworth, Derbyshire.
11. A tag quoted in Shakespeare's *Comedy of Errors* (IV. iv. 44) meaning 'look to the end'.
12. *3 Henry VI*, II. v. 21–40.
13. Gray, 'Ode on a Distant Prospect of Eton College' (1747), 43–4.
14. Joseph Spence's *Observations* (1820), II, 569 (Oxford, 1966).
15. Sir Joshua Reynolds (1723–92), the seminal painter and writer on art.

Liber Amoris

1. In fact, the dramatis personae were so far from being adequately disguised that within a week or so of publication the *Literary Register* had successfully identified almost everybody in the book, including Hazlitt and Sarah Walker.

Part I

The Picture

2. The portrait on the original title page of *Liber Amoris* was Hazlitt's own copy of an old master thought to resemble Sarah Walker. Of Sarah's

appearance, Hazlitt's friend Bryan Waller Proctor (alias Barry Cornwall, the author of *Mirandola*) later wrote: 'Her face was round and small, and her eyes were motionless, glassy, and without any speculation (apparently) in them ... she went onwards in a sort of wavy, sinuous manner, like the movement of a snake. She was silent, or uttered monosyllables only, and was very demure. Her steady unmoving gaze upon the person whom she was addressing was exceedingly unpleasant' (*An Autobiographical Fragment*, 1870, pp. 181–2).

3. Milton, *Il Penseroso* (1633), 39.

The Invitation

4. Hazlitt's essays are full of comparisons of the French and the English; see, for example, 'On the Knowledge of Character' in this volume.
5. In December 1821 we know that Hazlitt was contemplating an Italian tour at the suggestion of his publisher Henry Colbourn.
6. Hazlitt could not marry Sarah Walker because he was already married to another Sarah, Sarah Stoddart Hazlitt, from whom he had informally separated in 1820. Hence his trip to Scotland in the spring of 1822 to arrange a divorce; hence his terrible frustration as the proceedings became ever more difficult and drawn-out; hence the extended correspondence with his friend in London P.G. Patmore, which provides the emotional core of *Liber Amoris*.
7. In the MS: '... you mould me as you please'.
8. From the song by Robert Burns, 'My love is like a red, red rose' (1794), 15–16.

The Message

9. Mrs E——: Mrs Follett, one of the other lodgers at No. 9 Southampton Buildings. During the period in which the action of *Liber Amoris* takes place, a married couple called the Folletts were occupying the rooms on the first floor, while Hazlitt had the two back rooms on the second, both of which looked west over a garden to the lawyers' offices in Chancery Lane. In October 1821 a young lawyers' clerk called John Tomkins took the front-facing rooms on the first floor, while a Welsh pharmacist called Griffiths was paying ten shillings for the garret. The rent for Hazlitt's room was fourteen shillings; it was fifteen for Tomkins's.
10. Infelice (Unhappy, Unfortunate) is a character in Thomas Dekker's play *The Honest Whore* (1604–5). A young woman apparently dead and buried at the beginning of the play, she is promised eternal constancy by her young lover Hippolito: 'I will be true,/Even to her dust and ashes: could her tomb/Stand whilst I lived, so long that it might rot,/That should fall down, but she be ne'er forgot.' In Part II Hippolito and Infelice are married and Act III scene i sees a dramatic confrontation between them in which Infelice punishes her husband's supposed adultery with a former prostitute by pretending to have been unfaithful herself, with their Irish footman. Hippolito's indignation is intense: 'Could I not feed your appetite? O women/You were created angels, pure and fair;/But since the first fell, tempting devils

that you are,/You should be men's bliss, but you prove their rods:/Were there no women, men might live like gods'. Infelice responds by accusing him in return, and soon afterwards Hippolito does find himself very close to committing adultery with Bellafront, the 'Honest Whore' of the title. Fortunately, Bellafront has learnt the lesson Hippolito had taught her in Part I, and resists his advances, thus enabling Dekker to present her as the ideal type of the reformed fallen woman. Hazlitt's reference is probably to the Infelice of Part I, but the confrontation in Part II does also carry hidden parallels with *Liber Amoris*, not only because of Hazlitt's suspicions about Sarah and the other men in their household, but also because he himself seems to have both used and befriended prostitutes (see note 21 below). There are further references on pp. 70 and 144 to 'Infelice'.

11. Milton, *Il Penseroso* (1633), 31.

The Confession

12. Internal evidence relating to Sarah's former beau suggests that this section originally came earlier in the text.

The Quarrel

13. A decoy is one who entices, allures or inveigles another into some trap, deception or evil situation (*OED*). For Hazlitt the term 'lodging-house decoy' is clearly an understood term for a servant girl who blackmails male lodgers either for money or into marriage.
14. A convenience is a particular appliance or utensil (*OED*). This is a class-laden term in this context, particularly when placed alongside 'lips as common as the stairs'. Intriguingly, the latter phrase has its origin in a slur by Iachimo upon Posthumus in Act I scene vii, lines 104–6 of Shakespeare's *Cymbeline*: 'Should I/Slaver with lips as common as the stairs/That mount the Capitol'.
15. Betsey Walker, who was then about ten years old.
16. Robert Roscoe, fourth son of the celebrated Liverpool banker William Roscoe, married Martha, eldest daughter of Micaiah Walker, at St. Andrew's, Holborn, on 1 May 1819. For lower middle-class parents such as the Walkers this was a highly advantageous match, and it raised hopes that Sarah, their second daughter, might make a similar. Apart from Sarah, there were three other children in the Walker household: a daughter, Betsey, who has already been mentioned, and two sons, sixteen-year-old Cajah and two-year-old John.
17. Sarah first brought Hazlitt his breakfast on 16 August 1820.
18. In the MS Hazlitt appended a note to these words, which was later deleted: 'upwards of £30 worth – a trifle. Among others, is my hair in a golden heart, which I see set down in the jeweler's bill, a gold chased heart. A chased heart indeed, but not given for a chaste heart!'
19. In the MS Hazlitt wrote: 'Indeed you once owned that, if I had been a 'gay young man' you should not have let me proceed so far with you – as if I was out of the question, & you could trifle with me with impunity.'
20. In the MS, but subsequently deleted, is this paragraph: 'Once, as I was

kissing her and she was struggling from me, she exclaimed – "However I might agree to my own ruin, I never will consent to bring disgrace upon my family!" So that the disgrace to the family was the motive that held her back. This was pretty well for one who now tells me she never had any regard for me. No wonder I went off, after I did not take this hint! How could I take advantage of her when I worshipped her, and in spite of evidence, believed her to be all I could fancy or wish a woman to be?'

21. In her journal for 1822 his estranged wife Sarah Stoddart Hazlitt records a conversation in which she criticised Hazlitt for dragging their son William along 'when he went picking up the girls on the town' arguing that it 'it was likely to corrupt and vitiate him, and bring him up to like such ruinous practices'. Hazlitt conceded that she might have a point, while adding that 'he did not know that it was any good to bring up children in ignorance of the world'. Sarah Hazlitt's journal is also the source of an anecdote suggesting that prostitutes used to visit Hazlitt's rooms at Southampton Buildings, and that Sarah Walker sometimes showed them up. On 17 July 1822, that is, on the very day his divorce came through, Hazlitt embarked on a violent (and astonishingly hypocritical) diatribe against the Walker family, saying that 'the mother was the most disgusting, vulgar old wretch that could be, and corrupted her children's minds by her bawdy indecent conversation, though he had never heard an improper or indelicate word from the girl; yet it had often struck him, that they had never objected to the girls of the town coming up to him continually, and that Sarah would often send them up when her mother had said he was not at home, for which they praised her and said she was a nice girl'. Sarah Stoddart concluded, 'I told him it showed what the house and the people were well enough. He said he was determined to ascertain what the real state of things was, and was going to the house to watch her narrowly, and perhaps he might kill her and himself too, when he got there' (*Journals*, pp. 196, 247).
22. In the MS Hazlitt related a lewd-sounding but ultimately rather obscure exchange between Sarah, her sister Betsey, her brother Micaiah (Cajah) and their mother Martha, before adding his own comment: 'It is not surprising I have been mad ever since I heard this conversation.' The exchange in question was first discussed in a letter to P.G. Patmore sent from Scotland on 10 June 1822. This letter, which is one of the few *not* to make it into the published version of *Liber Amoris*, leaves us in no doubt as to the profoundly sexual nature of Hazlitt's obsession. See Letter X, note 42 for a transcript of the conversation itself.
23. This must refer to another occasion when Hazlitt deemed Sarah's behaviour to have been loose or flirtatious in some way.
24. In the MS: 'pull up your petticoats … pulls up mine'.
25. The servant's bell, here acting as a kind of emergency cord.
26. John Tomkins, a young lawyer's clerk, who first moved into No. 9 Southampton Buildings in October 1821.
27. Significantly, an allusion to what Adam says to Eve after her fall in

Milton's *Paradise Lost* (IX, 911–13): 'Should God create another Eve, and I/Another rib afford, yet loss of thee/Would never from my heart'. See also 'On the Past and the Future', note 2.

28. The weed image, to which Hazlitt returns on the last page of *Liber Amoris*, is an extremely interesting one in this context, simultaneously evoking deception, fragility, pity and waste. One possible source is Othello's swipe at Desdemona in Act IV scene ii, lines 68–70 of Shakespeare's play: 'Oh thou weed: /Who art so lovely fair, and smells't so sweet, /That the sense aches at thee, /Would thou hadst never been born.'

The Reconciliation

29. Sarah Walker's father Micaiah was a tailor by trade, and at forty-eight only four years Hazlitt's senior. His wife Martha was forty-five. They made use of Southampton Buildings' position at the very heart of legal London, letting rooms to young lawyers and lawyers' clerks, who stayed there two or three years, for the term of their articles. Possessing only one maid, Mrs Walker had no qualms about enlisting her daughters' help to look after the lodgers. Hence Sarah's ambiguous status in the house as a servant in all but name.
30. Hazlitt's inordinate admiration for the French emperor was to culminate in the vast, three-volume *Life of Napoleon Bonaparte*, which was published shortly before his death in 1830.
31. In Chaucer's *Knight's Tale* Arcite beats his bitter rival Palamon to the hand of the fair Emily in a ceremonial joust before Theseus, Duke of Athens, only to be unexpectedly and fatally thrown from his horse while taking his lap of honour. These famous words are from Arcite's dying speech to Palamon and Emily some hundred lines later. See *Canterbury Tales* (c. 1390), 2765–97.

Letters to the Same

32. These letters were posted from Renton Inn in Berwickshire in February 1822, where Hazlitt was fulfilling the forty-day residence requirement for a Scottish divorce and writing volume II of *Table-Talk*. See note 33 below.
33. In a letter of early March to his friend P.G. Patmore Hazlitt rattled off a list of eight new essays composed during his first month in Scotland, including 'On the Knowledge of Character', 'On the Fear of Death' and 'On the Disadvantages of Intellectual Superiority', all of which are reprinted in this volume (*Letters*, p. 237).
34. A smack is a single-masted vessel, usually employed as a coaster, or for fishing.
35. These lines are spoken at the sickbed of Sardanapalus the King of Ninevah by his devoted mistress Myrrha, a Greek slave, in Act IV scene I of Byron's tragedy *Sardanapalus* (published in the previous year, 1821). See also Part II, Letter III, note 10.
36. This mirrors the pattern of disappointment mingled with gratitude in Hazlitt's essay on Wordsworth and Coleridge, 'My First Acquaintance with Poets', first published in *The Liberal* in 1823.

37. Thomas Noon Talfourd (1794–1854), a minor critic and friend of Lamb and Hazlitt.
38. Peter George Patmore (1786–1855), a journalist and friend of Lamb and Hazlitt. He is 'Pigott' in Hazlitt's essay 'The Fight'. Patmore's other great claim to fame, apart from his involvement in the *Liber Amoris* affair, is that he was John Scott's inept second in the fatal duel between Scott, the editor of the *London Magazine*, and Jonathon Henry Christie of *Blackwood's*, which took place at Chalk Farm, near Hampstead in January 1821 as a result of the prolonged 'Cockney School' controversy (see Patrick O'Leary, *Regency Editor: Life of John Scott*, Aberdeen: Aberdeen University Press, 1983).
39. At this point in the MS Patmore entered Sarah's answer of 26 February 1822 which Hazlitt later incorporated into *Liber Amoris* Part Two, Letter II.
40. The original of this letter, postmarked 9 March 1822 from Dunbar in Scotland, is a little longer than the published version, and carries the following little anecdote: 'The house-maid, in the absence of the waiter (you can't think what an ugly fellow the waiter is) has been up to know what I will have for supper, for the cook wishes to get her things done out of the way. "Why, what's the matter?" "Oh, nothing, only it's our cook's court-night." "Court-night! what's that?" "Why her sweet-heart's coming to see her." "And is he not come yet then?" "No; nor won't go away till morning light." "And when are they to be married?" "Oh, as soon as they can get money, to buy some bedding." And away she goes laughing ready to split her sides, that I should not know what court-night means in Scotch. The wind raves like ten demons at the window, has broken a pane on one of them, blown out the candles, and I think will blow the cook's lover away if he does not make haste' (*Letters*, p. 242). Excruciatingly for Hazlitt, the *John Bull*, an ebullient Tory rag of the period, somehow managed to get hold of this letter not long after the first appearance of *Liber Amoris* in May 1823, and in the last of three violent attacks on the book (dated 8 June, 15 June and 22 June 1823 respectively) the editor took great delight in parading it before his readers as a typical example of 'Cockney' mawkishness.
41. William Macready played Romeo at Covent Garden on 24 January 1822. Hazlitt left for Scotland on 27 January.
42. The author of *Endymion* (1818), John Keats, was a friend and admirer of Hazlitt's, before his untimely death in 1821 at the age of twenty-six. The plot is not dissimilar to that of the Pygmalion myth, and concentrates on the relationship between ideal and earthly love.
43. These lines are spoken by Troilus to Cressida in Act III scene ii, lines 154–66 of Shakespeare's play. The reference is decidedly ominous given Cressida's later infidelity.

Part II

Letter I

1. Written between 19–25 February 1822. This was Hazlitt's first letter to Patmore after arriving in Scotland a fortnight earlier, i.e. 4 February.
2. Bees-Inn, Renton, was forty miles east of Edinburgh on the mail coach

road approximately halfway between Berwick and Dunbar. Hazlitt had checked in on 10 February 1822. In order to obtain a divorce in Scotland, one had to have been in residence at least forty days, hence Hazlitt's lengthy stay at Renton, which he spent writing essays for the second volume of *Table-Talk*.

Letter II

3. A frank: a superscribed signature from a person such as a Member of Parliament who was entitled to send letters post free.
4. *The Red-Book* was the popular name for *The Royal Kalendar*, an alphabetical list of the nobility and gentry.
5. Calypso, one of the daughters of Atlas, offered Ulysses immortality if he would stay with her (Homer, *Odyssey*, Book I). Hence 'New Calypso' is in keeping with Hazlitt's subtitle for *Liber Amoris*, the 'New Pygmalion', since in both cases 'new' means 'in reverse'.
6. Extreme caution, indecisiveness and a habit of avoiding major clashes was the successful practice of Quintus Fabius Maximus in his war against Hannibal.
7. 'And in the height of this bath, when I was more than half stewed in grease, like a Dutch dish, to be thrown into the Thames, and cooled, glowing hot, in that surge, like a horse-shoe; think of that, hissing hot, think of that, Master Brook!': Falstaff complaining of the humiliations he has suffered while in pursuit of another man's wife in *The Merry Wives of Windsor*, III. v. 106–14.

Letter III

8. In the original letter itself, which dates from 30 March 1822, the following lines filled the gap: 'O I feel like one of the damned. To be hated, loathed as I have been all my life, & to feel the utter impossibility of its ever being otherwise while I live – take what pains I may!'
9. Mrs Sarah Hazlitt, Hazlitt's first wife, whose presence was required in Scotland to effect the divorce. In the journal that she kept during this period there is a detailed account of her dealings with her husband and of his highly distracted state of mind. (See *Further Reading*.)
10. Myrrha, a Greek slave, is the faithful but forthright mistress of the liberal king Sardanapalus in Byron's play of that name (1821). The piece was on Hazlitt's mind because he had completed an article on it shortly after arriving in Scotland. However, the review as eventually published in the *Edinburgh Review* was largely the work of the magazine's editor, Francis Jeffrey.

Letter IV

11. A reversal of the Shakespearean original, since in the course of duping Othello into believing that his wife has committed adultery, Iago's actual words are: 'O, 'tis the spite of hell, the Fiend's Arch-Mock, / To lip a wanton in a secure Couch, / And to suppose her chaste' (*Othello*, IV. i. 70–2).
12. A key word in *Othello*, where it means both 'true' and 'chaste'.
13. *Macbeth*, III. i. 137.

14. Hazlitt's forty-day residence had ended by 16 March, but Sarah Stoddart Hazlitt, who stayed behind to look after their son over the Easter holidays, did not arrive on Scottish soil until 21 April, the day this letter was written. Hazlitt was right to describe the business of getting a divorce as unpleasant. Sarah Hazlitt's first duty on arrival was to swear an oath that she was not colluding with her husband, and the more she thought about it, the more uneasy she became, increasingly fearful of being charged with perjury. It was only after repeated efforts on the part of the barrister and Hazlitt's friend William Ritchie, the editor of *The Scotsman*, that she was re-persuaded. The next stage of the process involved Hazlitt being formally identified as an adulterer by arranging to be discovered *in flagrante delicto* with a local prostitute, whose name (ironically enough) was Mary Walker. Then Sarah Stoddart made a legal declaration that she wanted to be divorced from Hazlitt on the grounds of repeated adulteries in both England and Scotland, but especially on account of his relations with the said Mary Walker. Thereafter there was nothing for them to do but wait a further two months for the divorce to be granted – hence Hazlitt's lecturing-cum-walking tour in early May 1822 and his brief trip to London afterwards.
15. Rousseau was a man of forty-five, that is, roughly the same age as the Hazlitt of *Liber Amoris*, when he fell deeply and, as it turned out, unrequitedly, in love with the thirty-year-old *comtesse* Sophie d'Houdetot, who was the mistress of a friend of his. The story of this catastrophic mid-life crisis is told with excruciating candour in Book IX of the *Confessions* (1788), one of Hazlitt's favourite books and one of the leading models behind *Liber Amoris*. In the section Hazlitt is alluding to, Rousseau gives an eloquent account of the sentimental evenings he and Mme d'Houdetot spent together in his cottage on the Montmorency estate, she talking of her lover, he talking of her: 'Tender confidants, our feelings were so closely connected, that it was impossible that they should not unite in something; and yet, amidst this dangerous intoxication, she never forgot herself for a moment; as for myself, I protest, I swear that if, sometimes carried away by my senses, I attempted to make her unfaithful, I never truly desired it. The vehemence of my passion of itself kept it within bounds. The duty of self-denial had exalted my soul. The splendour of all the virtues adorned in my eyes the idol of my heart; to have soiled its divine image would have been its annihilation' (*Confessions*, ed. P.N. Furbank, p. 476). This overheated, open style is the implicit model behind *Liber Amoris*, but whereas Rousseau's words were addressed to an elegant young aristocrat and framed by a beautiful pastoral landscape, Hazlitt's were 'cribb'd, cabin'd and confin'd' by their Cockney setting.

Letter V

16. The original upon which this letter is based was written before Letter IV, on 7 April 1822, but Hazlitt clearly thought it would improve the narrative rhythm of *Liber Amoris* if he placed it afterwards (see *Letters*, p. 249).

17. *Macbeth*, III. ii. 24.
18. The corresponding passage in the original letter is even more passionate and jealous:

 Do you know I like to think of her best in her morning gown, in her dirt and her mob-cap; it is so she has oftenest sat [on my knee with her arms round my neck – Damn her, I could devour her, it is *herself* that I love]. [*Two lines obliterated*] When I but touch her hand, I enjoy perfect happiness and contentment of soul. Yet I think I am in the wrong box. What security can I have that she does not flirt or worse with everyone that comes in her way when I recollect how she took my first advances: how can I think she has any regard for me when she knows the tortures she puts me to by her silence? And what can I think of a girl who grants a man she has no particle of regard for the freedoms she has done to me? My idea is that in refusing to marry she has made up her mind to a sporting-life (keeping safe as well as she can) between disappointment and wantonness and a love of intrigue. I think she would sooner come and live with me than marry me. So that I have her in my arms and for life, I care not how; I never could tire of her sweetness, I feel as if I could grow to her, body and soul! (*Letters*, pp. 249–50)

Letter VI

19. Between 16 and 28 May 1822 Hazlitt broke away from divorce proceedings in Scotland and returned briefly to London. The sole aim of this journey had been to see Sarah Walker and, if possible, to establish a permanent understanding with her. This letter was written on 30 May on the boat back to Scotland. All we are told at this point is that the trip has been a disaster; it is not until much later in *Liber Amoris* that we find out what had actually taken place. At first sight, this might look like moral self-censorship on Hazlitt's part, given the sexually obsessive nature of the material. But it is in fact an act of dramatic reshaping, since much of what is suppressed here resurfaces in even more explosive fashion in Part III, where it helps provide the book with a suitable climax.
20. Duncan Wu points out that this passage derives not from the letter of 30 May but from a cancelled draft of 'The Fight' (see note 11, p. 239).
21. The relief did not last long, for the next day Hazlitt posted another letter, one of the few that did not make it into *Liber Amoris*, urging Patmore to 'try' Sarah. Once again this letter contains sentiments that are expressed more fully in Part III:

 31 May 1822

 My dear friend, I wrote yesterday by Scarborough to say that the iron had entered my soul – forever. I have since thought more profoundly about it than ever before, and am convinced beyond a doubt that she is a regular lodging-house decoy, who leads a sporting life with everyone who comes in succession, and goes different lengths according as she is urged or inclined. This is why she will not marry, because she hankers after this sort of thing. She has an itch for being slabbered and felt, and this she is determined to gratify upon system, and has a pride in making fools of the different men she indulges herself with and at the same time can stop short from the habit of running the gauntlet with so many. The impudent whore to taunt me, that 'she had always had no affection for me,' as a salve for her new lewdness – and how did she tell me this, sitting in my lap, twining herself round me, [a line inked out, but rewritten in another hand: 'letting me enjoy her through her petticoats'] looking as if she would faint with tenderness and modesty, admitting all sorts of indecent liberties and declaring 'however she might agree to her own ruin, she would never consent to bring disgrace upon her family', as if this last circumstance only prevented her, and all this without any affection – is it not to write whore, hardened, impudent, heartless whore after her name? Her look is exactly this. It is that of suppressed lewdness and conscious and refined hypocrisy, instead of innocence or timidity, or real feeling. She never looks at you, nor has a single involuntary emotion. For anyone to suffer what she has done from me, without feeling it, is unnatural and monstrous. A common whore would take a liking to a man who had shown the same love of her and to whom she had granted the same incessant intimate favours. But her heart is seared, as her eyes gloat, with habitual hypocrisy and *lech* for the mere act of physical contact with the other sex. 'Do you let anyone else do so' I said to her when I was kissing her. 'No, not now,' was her answer, that is, because there was nobody in the house to do it with her. While the coast was clear, I had it all my own way: but the instant Tomkins came, she made a dead set at him, ran breathless upstairs before him, blushed when his foot was heard, watched for him in the passage, and he going away either tired of her or without taking the hint,* she has taken up in my absence with this quack-doctor, a tall, stiff-backed able bodied half blackguard that she can make use of and get rid of when she pleases.** The bitch wants a stallion, and hates a lover, that is, any one who talks of affection and is prevented by fondness or regard for her from going or attempting to go all lengths. I at present think she liked me to a certain extent as a friend but still I was not good enough for her. She wanted to be courted not as a bride, but as a common wench. 'Why, could we not go on as we were, and never mind about the word, forever?' She would not agree to 'a tie,' because she would leave herself open to any new pretender that answered her purpose better, and bitch me without ceremony or mercy, and then say – 'She had always told me she had no regard for me' – as a rea[son] for transferring her obscenities (for such they were without doubt), from me to her next favourite. Her addicting herself to Tomkins was endurable, because he was a gentlemanly sort of man, but her putting up with this prick of a fellow, merely for bore and measurement and gross manners, sets me low indeed. The monster of lust and duplicity! I that have spared her so often because I hoped better things of her and to make her my future wife, and to be refused in order that she may be the trull of an itinerant apothecary, a fellow that she made a jest of and despised, till she had nobody else in the way to pamper her body and supply her morning's meal of studied wantonness. 'That way madness lies.' I do not feel as I can ever get the better of it. I have sucked the poison of her seeming modesty and tenderness too long. I thought she was dreaming of her only love and worshipped her equivocal face, when she wanted only a codpiece and I ought to have pulled up her petticoats and felt her. But I could not insult the adored of my heart, and find out her real character; and you see what has become of me. I was wrong at first in fancy[ing] a wench at a lodging house to be a Vestal, merely for her demure looks. The only chance I had was the first day: after that my hands were tied and I became the fool of love. Do you know the only thing that soothes or melts me is the idea of taking my little boy*** whom I can no longer support and wandering through the country as beggars, not through the wide world, for I cannot leave the country where she is. Oh God! Oh God! The slimy, varnished marble fiend to bring me to this when three kind words would have saved me! Yet if I only knew she was a whore, *flagrante delicto*, it would wean me from her, and burst my chain. Could you ascertain this fact for me, by any means or through any person (E. for example) who might try her as a lodger?**** I should not like her to be seduced by elaborate means, but if she gave up as a matter of course, I should then be no longer the wretch I am or the God I might have been, but what I was before. – plain W.H.' (*Letters*, pp. 263–5)

* Tomkins left Southampton Buildings early in 1822. ** Griffiths, the pharmacist from Penman-Mawr in North Wales, who was increasingly becoming the leading object of Hazlitt's jealousy (see Hazlitt's letter of 10 June, reproduced in note 42 to Part II, Letter X). *** Hazlitt's eleven-year-old son William, who is actually mentioned in the next letter of *Liber Amoris*. **** Hazlitt makes a number of references to 'E.' as someone appropriate to 'try' Sarah, but when the attempt was eventually made in March 1823, the man involved was dubbed 'F.', possibly indicating William Farren, an actor friend of his (see the 'Journal of F.').

Letter VII

22. Hazlitt has brought this letter forward in the sequence, since the original dates from 17 June. To that end, the following sentence has been omitted from the original: 'Mrs H. took the oath on Friday (they say manfully) – and nothing remains but to wait a week or two longer for the sentence of divorce' (*Letters*, p. 274).
23. This is the first mention in *Liber Amoris* of William Hazlitt junior, who was then eleven years old, and constitutes yet another giveaway personal detail that Hazlitt neglected to omit for publication. To the naïve reader, who takes the information supplied in the Advertisement at face value, this reference to suicide is, of course, darkly suggestive.

24. *As You Like It*, III. ii. 9–10.
25. Omitted from the original letter are the following lines: 'Do you know I think G[riffiths] (the fellow in the back parlour] is the very man her mother was commending to her daughter's lecherous thoughts that night o[f] the seven inch conversation for I recollect he tumbled over me one night half drunk which was one of the circumstances related as proof of his huge prowess' (*Letters*, p. 275). The seven inch conversation is first referred to in Part I, 'The Quarrel', note 22; and a transcript is given in Letter X, note 42.
26. That Hazlitt was by now almost at the end of his tether can be seen from the following unpublished letter (written *c.* 19 June) enlisting Patmore to get a friend to 'try' Sarah:

    Ascertain if that wretched rival is there still.* I am almost satisfied she is a wretched creature myself, but my only hope of happiness rests on the alternative. Ours was the sweetest friendship –oh! might the delusion be renewed that I might die in it! If there is any insolence – TRY HER through (anyone) someone, E. for example, who will satisfy my soul I have lost only a lovely frail one that I was not like to gain by true love. Oh! that I was once back to London. I am going to see Knowles to get him to go with me to the Highlands, and talk about her. I shall be back Thursday week, to appear in court *pro forma* the next day, and then for Heaven or for Hell. Send me a line about my little boy. WH. 10 George Street, Edinburgh. (*Letters*, pp. 257–8)

    * This is probably a reference to Tomkins, although as recent letters to Patmore indicate, Hazlitt was beginning to be jealous of Griffiths the other lodger as well.

Letter VIII

27. This letter was written en route to the Renton Inn, and was posted on 9 June.
28. In Goethe's *Sorrows of Young Werther* (1774), perhaps the most celebrated novel of unrequited love in the eighteenth century, and one, like *Liber Amoris*, presented mostly in letters, the despairing protagonist complains that: 'my heart's immense and ardent feeling for living Nature, which overwhelmed me with so great a joy and made the world about me a very paradise, has now become an unbearable torment, a demon that goes with me everywhere, torturing me'. And again, a couple of letters later Werther declares that 'my feeling for Nature has gone' (trans. Michael Hulse, pp. 65, 67).
29. Hazlitt was addicted to tea and drank large quantities every day.

To Edinburgh

30. See Ezekiel, XI. 19.
31. cf. Wordsworth, Sonnet 'Upon Westminster Bridge', 14.
32. Francis Jeffrey, editor of the *Edinburgh Review*, whose first meeting with Hazlitt had been at his home in Craigcrook in the last week of March 1822.
33. In Sir Walter Scott's novel *Kenilworth* (1821).

34. North Berwick Law is a 187-metre-high lump of volcanic rock located just to the south of the town.

A Thought

35. This passage derives from a section cancelled from 'The Fight' (see p. 239, note 11).

Letter IX

36. This letter is preceded by Letters XI, XII and the original that lurks behind Letter X, and was not posted until 7 July.
37. That of pulling up her petticoats. This is not specified in *Liber Amoris* but see the notes to Part I, 'The Quarrel', for the cancelled lines from the original letter.
38. Burns, 'Lament for James, Earl of Glencairn' (1791), 74.
39. See Part I, 'The Reconciliation', p. 54.
40. This takes place after Tom's proposal of marriage in Henry Fielding's *Tom Jones* (1749).
41. The image may well be inspired by Hazlitt's friend Keats's narrative poem *Lamia* (1820), about a woman who is really a serpent in disguise.

Letter X

42. This fictional epistle, which is full of picturesque landscape description an unconvincing reference to 'law-cases', replaces a much lewder and more obsessive original, which was sent by Hazlitt to Patmore on 10–14 June 1822. In the original letter Hazlitt's jealousy of Griffiths is given full expression, and once again Patmore is urged to 'try her':

> My dear friend, Here I am at Renton amid the hills and groves which I greeted in their barrenness in winter, but which have now put on their full green attire that shews lovely in this northern twilight, but speaks a tale of sadness to this heart widowed of its last, its dearest, its only hope. For a man who writes such nonsense, I write a good hand. Musing over my only subject (Othello's occupation, alas! is gone) seeking for rest and finding none, I have at last hit upon a truth, that if true explains all and satisfies me, I hope forever. This is it. You will by this time probably know something from having called and seen how the land lies that will make you judge how far I am stepped into madness in my conjectures. If you think me right, all engines set at work at once that punish ungrateful woman. Oh! lovely Renton-Inn, here I wrote a volume of Essays, here I wrote my enamoured follies to her, thinking her human and that 'below was not all the fiend's' here I got two answers from the little witch, and here I was cuckolded and I was damned. I am only a fool, would I were mad! By this time you probably know enough to know whether the following solution is *in rerum natura* at No. 9 S[outhampton]B[uildings]. Mark. The conversation that passed in the kitchen that evening that ruined me was this:
>
> Betsey. 'Oh! If those trousers were to come down, what a sight there would be.' (A general loud laugh.)

Mother. 'Yes! He's a proper one: Mr Follett is nothing to him.'

Mr Cajah. (aged seventeen) 'Then I suppose he must be seven inches.'

Mother W. 'He's quite a monster. He nearly tumbled over Mr Hazlitt one night.'

Sarah. (At that once, that still as ever dear name, ah! Why do I grow pale, why do I weep and forgive) said something inaudible, but in connection.

Cajah. (Laughing) 'Sarah says ... '

Sarah. 'I say, Mr Follett wears straps' –*

– [I ask you candidly whether on hearing this I ought not to have walked quietly out of the house and never have thought of it again.]

She also said to me the other evening when I told her (I don't know what) that 'she had heard enough of that sort of conversation'. No wonder, when she had heard for years this kind of kitchen-stuff. Who do you think this hero, this Hercules, this plenipotentiary was? Why, I recollect the person who once tumbled over me half drunk was this very Griffiths who keeps possession of his ten-shillings garrett, in spite of an offer of marriage from me, and a hundred guineas a year for his apartment. Can there be a doubt, when the mother dilates in this way on codpieces and the son replies in measured terms, that the girl runs mad for size? Miss is small, and exaggerates dimensions by contrast. Misjudging fair! Yet it is she whom [I have] spared a hundred times from witnessing the consummation devoutly wished by the whole kitchen in chorus, after she has been rubbing against me, hard at it for an hour together, thinking to myself, 'The girl is a good [girl] etc. and means no harm – it is only [her fondness] for me, not her lech after a man.' [...] You say I accuse her of grossness inconsistent with her character. It is she who accuses herself of it; for did she not tell me 'she never had any affection for me', and do I not know what she has done with me a hundred times? Will she not do so much or more with her fancy-man, in spite of her hypocritical looks and pretty speeches? Did she not say to me once, in the height of our caresses, and struggling from me – 'However I might agree to my own ruin, I never will consent to bring disgrace upon my family!' – This speech she addressed to one she never could like – What will she do with one she does like, and is just as mad after? You seem inclined at present to give up 'her real regard and affection for me', and yet without this, having done what she has, is she not all that I say of her, a whore and a consummate hypocrite, a little monster of lust or avarice or treachery? I don't suppose she goes with everyone, but that she must have a man to wheedle and fondle her, and she took up with me for no other reason. What else can it be by her own repeated declaration? She says she'll never marry and that it was not love, so that it could be nothing but either a hoax or to gratify her soft itch without a particle of affection. I call this unnatural, but not impossible. If it had been friendship or esteem, she would not have treated me as she has. The instant I slackened in my lascivious approaches and wanted to fix her forever, she was off – first flinging herself at Tomkins and he failing, taking up with her present groom, but still 'she has no tie' and would I daresay sacrifice him to a more gentlemanly pretender. As to her looking like a whore, I only say she is a bitch, and I believe her object is to go all lengths but the last, which her changing about and want of natural affections enables her to do. She hates me only because I did not try to 'ruin her'. I believe the whole family to be bad, and you have no proof but her appearance that she is different from the rest, and her looks, I know, are not a clue to her conduct with me. – Do you know that last night I had given up all thoughts of her. I thought the [fury] was over and my burning love turned to indifference and even disgust. Your letter had this effect, I mean the contrast between the picture you drew of her, *viz.* of the creature I loved, and what I felt to be her true character. This morning my fit is on again, but by God, I do not stomach her as a wife in my present humour – you will say, circumstances. Oh no! The very thought that she may have in spite of all appearances, a true and tender regard for me, namely, that she would have me and therefore doesn't hate me, makes my heart gush with its old tenderness and melt in heavenly sweetness towards the little [darling *del.*] cherub. Don't go to Roscoe, nor let me have any more formal refusals, till I am quite free at any rate and then if she gives herself airs, she must be tried. But I think you might go and take away the MSS and if you see her, say 'You think it is a pity we should part otherwise than friends, for that you know I had the truest regard for her, & that I should never think of any other lodging but that I feared she had a dislike to seeing me there' in consequence of my past misconduct. [I have hit it.] Say that I shall want it very little the next year, as I shall be abroad for some months, but that I wish to keep it on to have a place to come to when I am in London and not to seem to have parted in anger, where I feel nothing but friendship and esteem. If you get a civil answer to this, take it for me and send me word. Otherwise get E. or anybody to see what flesh she is made of, and send her to hell if possible … (*Letters*, pp. 269–72)

* To Hazlitt this was clearly very suggestive, but to us it is likely to remain obscure. It could refer to a belt or braces of some kind, or possibly a surgical support.

43. The maddened Lear's picture of women in Act IV scene vi, lines 121–3 of Shakespeare's tragedy: 'Down from the waist they're Centaurs, / Though women all above. / But to the Girdle do the Gods inherit; / Beneath is all the Fiend's.'
44. The word omitted is 'cuckolded' in the original, reprinted above.
45. A premonition of the king's madness in Act II scene iv, lines 54–6 of *King Lear*: 'Oh how this Mother wells up towards my heart! / *Hysterica passio*, down thou climbing sorrow, / Thy elements below.'

Letter XI

46. This letter was written on 27 June, and posted on the 28th. Sarah

Hazlitt had taken the oath of calumny on 11 June, so that he expected the divorce to be granted fourteen days later, on the 28th. However, he was to be disappointed (see Jones, *Hazlitt: A Life*, pp. 330–1).

47. An indication that, deep down, Hazlitt knew that Tomkins's claim upon Sarah's affections was much stronger than his own.
48. This is a proverbial phrase for an intoxicating draught of the kind given by Circe to Odysseus's crew in the Odyssey, which transformed them all into swine (Book X).
49. Compare *Othello*, III. iii. 271–2: 'She's gone. I am abused, and my release / Must be to loathe her'.

Unaltered Love

50. Shakespeare, Sonnet 116, 2–6.

From C.P., Esq.

51. On a first reading of *Liber Amoris* it is not completely clear why the entire family should have been so frightened by H. *at this stage*, but when one considers that in real life this letter of Patmore's was written some time *after* the terrible confrontation described in Part III, Letter I, it is much easier to comprehend. To include this letter at all is evidence of extraordinary candour on Hazlitt's part, and, placed where it is, it does have the virtue of suggesting that from everyone else's point of view the affair had a very different complexion.

Letter XIII

52. Shakespeare, *Richard III*, I. ii. 257.
53. Hazlitt visited Dalkeith Place on Saturday 6 July with Alexander Henderson. While at Dalkeith he bumped into Sarah Hazlitt, who recorded the contents of their conversation in her diary. Hazlitt was so struck by this painting by the Italian Luca Giordano that he returned to Dalkeith the following Monday to view it again. This letter was posted on 8 July.
54. The Houris are nymphs of the Muslim Paradise.

Letter the Last

55. This letter was written on 16 July and posted the following day. Hazlitt's divorce was finally granted on the 17th.
56. Psalms, 121, 1.
57. Patmore married his sweetheart Eliza Robertson in 1822.
58. Rousseau's great epistolary novel *Julie, ou La Nouvelle Héloïse* (1761) was one of the best-sellers of the eighteenth century, and a great favourite of Hazlitt's. It offered an intoxicating picture of passionate, pure (and, by the end of the novel, entirely platonic) love. The reference to Meillerie in Switzerland is interesting in that this landscape forms the backdrop for one of the darkest and most dramatic letters of Part I. Banished from Vevey and his beloved Julie, her former tutor Saint-Preux borrows a telescope from a local priest and climbs the rocks of Meillerie. From there he finds can see all the way across the lake that divides him from his lover, and right into her house and quar-

ters. 'Here it is', he writes to Julie, 'that your unhappy lover is enjoying to the full perhaps the last pleasures he will taste in this world,' before concluding his letter with the words: 'the mountainside is steep, the water deep, and I am in despair' (Part I, Letter 26). With reference to Hazlitt's letter to Patmore it is interesting to note that even this apparently sunny allusion to Rousseau carries within it hidden suggestions of painful exile, illicit voyeurism and the urge to suicide.

59. In Thomas Heywood's domestic tragedy *A Woman Killed with Kindness* (1607) John Frankford is kind to a fault. He is so lavish in his hospitality towards his friend Wendoll that the latter is encouraged to seduce his wife. When their infidelity is discovered, Frankford is so restrained in his response that it his wife's own sense of guilt, rather than any violence on his part, that ultimately drives her to the grave. Knowing this, one can feel a secret sting in the tail of this casual allusion to the play, since in *Liber Amoris* too, as we are about to discover, the final effect of H.'s 'kindness' is to drive S. into the arms of a fellow lodger.
60. Patmore's new wife.
61. John Hunt, editor of the *Examiner* newspaper, and publisher of *Liber Amoris*.

Part III

Addressed to J.S.K——

1. James Sheridan Knowles, the poet and dramatist, at whose invitation Hazlitt had lectured in Glasgow in May 1822. No known originals exist, and it is probable that these letters were composed expressly to complete the narrative of *Liber Amoris*, and never actually sent.
2. Hazlitt and Knowles set out on a walking tour of Loch Lomond on Tuesday 7 May 1822 (see Jones, *Hazlitt: A Life*, pp. 328–9).
3. Quotes from the last two lines of Wordsworth's 'Lucy' poem: 'Three years she grew in sun and shower' (1800).
4. 'To Italy! To Italy!' Virgil, *Aeneid*, III, 522–4.
5. *King Lear*, IV. iii. 26–7.
6. In Act III scene i of Thomas Middleton's *Women Beware Women* (c. 1621) Leantio is a poor but jealous husband on the point of returning home to his wife Bianca, and Middleton shows him exulting in his prospective happiness. Significantly, Hazlitt has chosen to omit the following lines from the middle of Leantio's speech, in which he soliloquizes on the merits of 'honest wedlock':

> Honest wedlock
> Is like a banqueting house built in a garden,
> On which the spring's chaste flowers take delight
> To cast their modest odours; when base lust
> With all her powders, paintings, and best pride,
> Is but a fair house built by a ditch side.
> When I behold a glorious, dangerous strumpet,
> Sparkling in beauty and destruction too,
> Both at a twinkling, I do liken straight
> Her beautified body to a goodly temple

That's built on vaults where carcasses lie rotting;
And so by little and little I shrink back again,
And quench desire by a cool meditation;
And I'm as well methinks.

(III. i. 89–102)

Having enjoined his mother to keep Bianca under lock and key while he is away, Leantio clearly feels he can return to his young marriage with confidence. The irony of the situation, as every member of the audience is aware, is that Bianca has already been unfaithful in his absence, an unwilling victim of the unscrupulous Duke of Florence. Unbeknown to himself, therefore, Leantio *is* returning home to a 'fair house built by a ditch side'. The parallels between this homecoming scene and H.'s own situation are striking enough, but the use of literary quotation here does also point up a broader tendency in *Liber Amoris* for allusion itself to function as a 'goodly temple / That's built on vaults where carcasses lie rotting', since it is by no means the only example in the book of a seemingly romantic reference carrying a hidden irony.

7. The first of several indications that Part III begins by returning to a time *before* H.'s divorce has been finalised. See Part II, Letter VI, note 19.
8. It is likely that Hazlitt found these lines from Tibullus in the section on 'Love Melancholy' in Robert Burton's *Anatomy of Melancholy* (1621). In the middle of a discussion of love sufferings and the vehemence of romantic admiration, Burton translates the lines thus: 'Whate'er she doth, or whither e'er she go, / A sweet and pleasing grace attends forsooth' (Part III, section II. memb. 3).
9. These are lines from the play *Mirandola* (1821) by Hazlitt's friend Barry Cornwall (the pseudonym of Bryan Waller Proctor). The play describes a triangular relationship between a loving couple, Guido and Isadora, and a jealous older man, Guido's father the Duke of Mirandola. At the beginning of the play the Duke succeeds in winning Isadora's hand in marriage, but only because she has been tricked by an scheming monk into believing that Guido has died in battle. On Guido's return to the court of Mirandola the Duke grows mad with jealousy in a manner reminiscent of both Leontes and Othello. In the play's dénouement the Duke brings about the death of his wife and son, only to discover shortly afterwards that they were innocent of adultery. The parallels between the Duke in the play and H. in *Liber Amoris* are manifold: both are middle-aged, passionately in love, and unrequited. What is more, both are troubled by dark suspicions of younger men. The speech quoted above is spoken by the Duke in Act I scene ii of the play, as he watches Isadora depart from the stage, and it is followed by a few more lines equally doting in nature: 'I never saw / My beauty look so well; the summer light / Becomes her, though she shames it, being so fair. / Methinks I've cast full twenty years aside, / And am again a boy.'
10. That Hazlitt was something of an Ancient Mariner during this period,

telling 'the whole story' to anybody who would listen is borne out by many of his friends, most notably Benjamin Haydon and Bryan Waller Proctor. In his diary for 9 August 1822 Haydon noted: 'Hazlitt called last night in a state of absolute insanity about the girl who has jilted him,' before adding that '[his] candour is great and his unaffected frankness is interesting'. Proctor related that 'on one occasion I know he told the story of his attachment to five different persons in the same day, and at each time entered into minute details of his love story. "I am a cursed fool," he said to me. "I just saw J—— going into Will's Coffee-house yesterday morning; he spoke to me, I followed him into the house; and whilst he lunched, I told him the whole story. Then" (said he) "I wandered into Regent's Park, where I met one of M——'s sons. I walked with him some time, and on his using some civil expression, by God! Sir, I told him the whole story. Well, sir, then I went and called on Haydon, but he was out. There was only his man, Salmon, there; but by God! I could not help myself. It all came out; the whole cursed story! Afterwards I went to look at some lodgings in Pimlico. The landlady at one place, after some explanations as to rent, etc., said to me very kindly, "I am afraid you are not well, sir?" – "No, Ma'am," said I, "I am not well"; and on her enquiring further, the devil take me if I did not let out the whole story, from beginning to end!' (*The Literary Recollections of Barry Cornwall*, Boston, MA: Meador Publishing, 1936, pp. 81–2, first published in the *New Monthly Magazine*, November 1830).

11. This prefaces the account Othello gives Desdemona's father Brabantio of the manner in which he wooed the old man's daughter in *Othello* I. iii. 93–5. Hazlitt heightens the Shakespearean parallel by referring to Sarah's father as 'the old man' a few lines earlier, but in real life Micaiah Walker was only forty-eight at the time, a mere four years older than Hazlitt himself.

To the Same (in continuation)

12. Three sentimental novels of the late eighteenth century. Oliver Goldsmith's *Vicar of Wakefield* (1766), and Henry MacKenzie's *Man of Feeling* (1771) had a kind of cult status in the period; Elizabeth Inchbald's *Nature and Art* (1796) was slightly less celebrated.
13. William Wycherley, *The Plain Dealer* (1676), IV. i. 25–6. In the fourth of his *Lectures on the English Comic Writers* (1819) Hazlitt wrote of this play: 'The character of Manly, the Plain Dealer, is violent, repulsive, and uncouth, which is a fault, though one that seems to have been intended for the sake of contrast; for the portrait of consummate, artful hypocrisy in Olivia is, perhaps, rendered more striking by it. The indignation excited against this odious and pernicious quality by the masterly exposure to which it is here subjected, is "a discipline of humanity". No one can read this play attentively without being the better for it as long as he lives. It penetrates to the core; it shows the immorality and hateful effects of duplicity, by showing it fixing its harpy fangs in the heart of an honest and worthy man. It is worth ten volumes of sermons.' Put in these terms, the central relationship is not

dissimilar from that which is offered to the reader in *Liber Amoris.*

14. For references to that conversation, see Part I, 'The Quarrel', note 22 and Part II, Letter X, note 42.
15. John Gay, 'Verses on England's Arch-Poet', 13–14.
16. *Macbeth*, II. ii. 6.
17. Hazlitt returned to Scotland by boat on Wednesday 30 May 1822. See Part II, Letter VI.
18. William Ritchie, editor of *The Scotsman*.
19. Francis Jeffrey, who gave Hazlitt £100 to allow him time to recover.
20. This was after the divorce proceedings were concluded, on 20 or 21 July 1822.
21. *As You Like It*, II. vii. 123.
22. This was on the evening of Monday 29 July, after Hazlitt had made his mind up to propose.
23. Somers Town was then a relatively new suburb of London, situated just north of where the British Library and St Pancras Station now stand. Hazlitt had resided there in the 1790s, as is suggested in an essay of his from 1827 'On the Want of Money'.

To the Same (in conclusion)

24. Spenser, *The Faerie Queene*, III, viii.
25. In 'The Story of Sidi-Nouman' from the *Arabian Nights*, Sidi-Nouman grows suspicious of his young wife Amina because she will eat only a few grains of rice at dinner. Seeing Amina steal out of their house late at night, Sidi-Nouman follows her to a nearby cemetery, where she meets up with another ghoul and feasts on dead bodies. Like Amina, Sarah Walker liked a secret rendezvous, and displayed her true character only when out in the open, although her transgressions did not extend to cannibalism, as far as we know.
26. From Hazlitt's friend Leigh Hunt's 'Cockney' rendering of the Paolo and Francesca story, *The Story of Rimini* (1816), III, 205–12.
27. It is worth comparing this section with the contemporaneous essay 'On the Knowledge of Character' in this volume.
28. To bilk is to cheat, deceive or betray. A bully is a pimp.
29. *Hamlet*, IV. v. 189.
30. Yet for a long time Hazlitt was to remain incapable either of forgiving or forgetting Sarah, as the 'Journal of F.', composed in March 1823, shows only too well, concluding as it does with the words 'I also am her lover and will live and die for her only, since she can be true to anyone.'
31. 'That thou among the wastes of time must go' is line 10 of Shakespeare's Sonnet 12, 'When I do count the clock that tells the time'.

The Journal of F.

1. Hazlitt's first collection of essays (1817), culled from articles that had originally appeared in *The Examiner*.
2. *Othello*, I. iii. 146–7.
3. Emma Roscoe, Sarah's niece.

4. 'The first Methodist on record was David.' This is the first sentence of Hazlitt's essay 'On the Causes of Methodism'.
5. Thomas Moore's last long poem, published in 1823 and very fashionable at the time.
6. *Marcian Colonna*, a poem, 1820; *Mirandola*, a tragedy produced at Covent Garden, 1821.
7. See Part III of *Liber Amoris* where Hazlitt quotes the lines from his friend Barry Cornwall's play *Mirandola* (1821).
8 *Hamlet*, I. i. 148–50.
9. *Faerie Queene*, IV, viii, stanza 11; actually, it's Belphebe and the Dove.
10. i.e. suspect something.

The Fight

1. Adapted from Shakespeare, *Hamlet*, II. ii. 604–5.
2. The Fancy: the sporting fraternity.
3. The Hole in the Wall was a public house on Chancery Lane kept by Jack Randall the pugilist.
4. Blue ruin was low-grade gin.
5. Joseph Parkes (1796–1865), a young disciple of Jeremy Bentham, and one of Hazlitt's sporting and social acquaintances.
6. *alter idem*: another and the same.
7. P.G. Patmore, Hazlitt's correspondent in Part II of *Liber Amoris*. Patmore remembers 'The Fight' in *My Friends and Acquaintances* (1854), III. 41.
8. Spenser, *Muiopotmos* (1591), 209–10.
9. Tom Belcher, younger brother of the better known prize-fighter James Belcher, kept the Castle tavern in Furnival Street, Holborn.
10. Caesar's ghost, to Brutus, in Shakespeare, *Julius Caesar*, IV. iii. 280.
11. At this point in the manuscript Hazlitt continued with a passage concerning Sarah Walker, which he later eliminated: 'Oh! thou dumb heart, lonely, sad, shut up in the prison house of this rude form, that hast never found a fellow but for an hour and in very mockery of thy misery, speak, find bleeding words to express thy thoughts, break thy dungeon-gloom, pronouncing the name of thy [Clarissa] [Infelice] or die & wither of pure scorn! I thought of the time when I was a little happy [thoughtless] [careless] child, of my father's house, of my early lessons, of my brother's picture of me when I was a boy, of all that had since happened & of the waste of years to come – I stopped, faltered, & was going to turn back once more to make a longer truce with wretchedness & patch up a hollow league with love – when suddenly the clattering of a Brentford-stage reminded me where I was.'
12. Dryden, *The Indian Emperor* (1665), IV. iii. 3–5.
13. White Horse Cellars, Piccadilly, later known as Hatchett's White Horse Cellars, was the starting-point for stage-coaches for Oxford and the Western counties.
14. According to Hazlitt's son this was John Thurtell (1794–1824), the trainer and sporting promoter, soon to be notorious as the murderer of one of his cronies William Weare.

15. Hamlet, to Yorick's skull, *Hamlet*, V. i. 190.
16. Bill Richmond (1763–1829), a celebrated black boxing teacher, originally from New York.
17. *Macbeth*, III. iv. 37–8.
18. *Henry V*, IV. i. 272–33.
19. *Othello*, I. iii. 350. There is a passage heavily deleted from the MS here: 'That no one else suffers what I do is the only consolation I can find: no one is like me, and I believe the rest of mankind are comparatively happy. That is a parenthesis (reader, I write this in great pain, amidst powerful distractions, to please thee) but on with the story, as Calantha says with the dance of the BROKEN HEART – isn't it called?' Calantha says 'On to the dance' in the extract from John Ford's play given by Hazlitt in the fourth of his *Lectures on the Dramatic Literature of the Age of Elizabeth* (1817).
20. *John Gilpin*, a comic poem by William Cowper (1782).
21. Charles Mathews (1776–1835) a brilliant comic actor, known particularly for his wide range of imitations.
22. From Chaucer, *General Prologue to the Canterbury Tales*, 167.
23. A cudgel.
24. William Cobbett (1763–1835), the popular radical journalist, was much admired for the rough eloquence of his style.
25. Cribb defeated Jem Belcher twice, in 1807 and 1809. In 1803 Belcher had lost an eye in an accident playing rackets.
26. John Gully (1783–1863) afterwards well known in the racing world, had retired from the ring in 1808 after two victories over Bob Gregson.
27. An allusion to the French revolutionary statesmen Jacques Danton's famous rallying call of 1792: 'De l'audace, de l'audace et encore de l'audace, est la France est sauvée.'
28. The Game Chicken was Henry Pearce (1777–1809). It is also the name of a young boxer in Charles Dickens's *Dombey and Son* (1847–8).
29. Shakespeare, *Julius Caesar*, II. i. 63–5.
30. *Paradise Lost*, II, 306. The shoulders are Satan's.
31. *Ibid.*, II, 846. The ghastly smile is Death's.
32. *Ibid.*, II, 714–16. The battle is between Satan and Death.
33. From *The Ancient Ballad of Chevy-Chase*, 119–22.
34. 'Gentleman' John Jackson (1769–1845) was a well-known pugilist of the period.
35. In Etherege's *Man of Mode* (1676) it is Dorimant who speaks the lines: '"Mais au revoir"', as Sir Fopling says' (III. ii. 305).
36. In the original manuscript there followed another passage about Sarah Walker, later deleted: 'Besides, I had better Spirits now than before: for as the pilgrim feels joy when he turns towards Mecca, so I felt a secret satisfaction that every mile we passed brought me nearer to Brentford & to her who is the Goddess of my idolatry. Pigott is a man cut out by nature & circumstances [education *del.*] for a confidant: – so "in dreadful secrecy impart I did" some part of the depth of my despair & the height of her perfections, – he was curious for more particulars which I withheld then, but we are become inseparable from the interest he takes in the subject. The theme, even in the confined limits

in which I indulge myself, is inexhaustible: I could talk about a lock of her hair forever!' There may have been more to this passage, but three of the four deleted pages have been lost.

37. 'O keep away, unsanctified ones!' Virgil, *Aeneid*, VI, 258. The men in question are Cockneys who think that the fight was a disappointment.
38. In the manuscript a few sentences were included here which Hazlitt later deleted: 'He reproached me for wasting my time on such barbarians & I could only defend myself by owning my invincible propensity to argue with any man that would hold an argument with me. Supper-time approached, the mutton-chops & potatoes were brought in by a neat healthy-looking servant girl, Pigott took a glass of sherry negus cold, & I was fain to mortify on spring-water. Our conversation did not flag till twelve, when we retired to our rooms.'
39. Rousseau's famous sentimental novel *Julie, ou La Nouvelle Héloïse* (1761) is also referred to at a crucial moment in *Liber Amoris*: see Part II, Letter the Last, note 58.
40. The *New Monthly Magazine*, where this essay first appeared, both addressed and enjoyed a large female readership.
41. Jack Broughton's (1704–89) last fight with George Stevenson, 'The Coachman', took place, not in 1770, but in 1741.

On Great and Little Things

1. *The Traveller* (1764), 42.
2. See *The Tatler*, No. 79, by Sir Richard Steele (11 October 1709).
3. *Hamlet*, V. i. 286–8.
4. *I Henry IV*, II. iv. 383. Cambyses was the passionate protagonist of an earlier morality play, Robert Preston's *Cambyses, King of Persia* (1569).
5. Napoleon, who died on St. Helena in British custody on 5 May 1821.
6. On the night of the sacking of Troy, the ghost of Hector appears to Aeneas in a dream and urges him to flee the city as it is about to fall to the Greeks: 'If a strong right hand could have saved Troy,' he says, 'mine would have done it' (Virgil, *Aeneid*, II, 291–2).
7. Necessarianism, or Necessitarianism, is the theory (or doctrine) that action is necessarily determined by anterior causes.
8. Hazlitt's friend Charles Lamb's farce *Mr H——* was put on at Drury Lane on 10 December 1806.
9. An opera by Andrew Cherry (1762–1812), first produced at Drury Lane on 22 January 1806.
10. A game of ball played by two persons who strike the ball alternately and endeavour to keep it rebounding from a wall.
11. *Measure for Measure* III. i. 9.
12. 'So much for this', Cicero, *Letters to Atticus*, V (68–43 BC).
13. 'Pleased with a rattle, tickled with a straw', Pope, *Essay on Man* (1734), II, 276.
14. See *The Spectator*, No. 108, by Joseph Addison (4 July 1711).
15. *The Tempest*, II. ii. 39–40.
16. In Laurence Sterne's *Tristram Shandy* (1759–67).
17. The allusion is to a character from Thomas Dekker's two-part play *The*

Honest Whore (1604–5); the ultimate reference, however, is to Sarah Walker. See *Liber Amoris*, Part I, 'The Message', note 10.

18. Madame Vestris (1797–1856), a famous actress of the day.
19. Abraham Cowley's *The Chronicle, A Ballad* (1656).
20. Thomas Davison of Whitefriars in London was the publisher of the first volume of Hazlitt's *Table-Talk* (1821).
21. See Horace's *Odes* and Montaigne's essay 'On Some Verses of Virgil' (*Essais*, 1595, Book III, chapter v).
22. Both Pamela and Fanny were servant girls, of course, which is telling in relation to Sarah Walker. See also the notes to *Liber Amoris*, Part II, Letter V.
23. Rousseau, *Confessions*, Book I (1782), 'with a pathos fit to cleave boulders' (p. 29).
24. 'He loved, and was abhorred; he adored, and was disdained; he implored a savage; he importuned a statue; he hunted the wind; cried aloud to the desert; he was a slave to the most ungrateful of women; and the fruit of his servitude was death' (Smollett's translation of Cervantes's *Don Quixote*, 1755, I, p. 100).
25. A painting by Lodovico Lana (1597–1646). The original, which Hazlitt copied on a visit to France in 1802, is in the Louvre; Hazlitt's copy is in the Maidstone Museum, Kent.
26. The Battle of Austerlitz (1805) was one of Napoleon's most brilliant victories.
27. Spenser, *The Faerie Queene*, II, Proem, stanza 4.
28. Jules Mazarin (1602–61) was the French cardinal and statesmen who shaped the destiny of France in the early years of Louis IV's reign. Jean-Francois Paul de Gandi, Cardinal de Retz (1613–79), one of the leaders of the aristocratic rebellion known as the Fronde (1648–53), wrote a volume of memoirs that remain a classic of French seventeenth-century literature.
29. This paragraph is taken from a paper in the Round Table series in *The Examiner* (26 February 1815) which Hazlitt did not reprint, entitled 'On the Predominant Principles and Excitements in the Human Mind'.
30. In the British Parliament between 1641 and 1967, proposals for raising taxation originated in the Committee of Ways and Means, where they were initiated by a government minister.
31. Most notably Hazlitt's friend Benjamin Robert Haydon, whose canvas *Christ's Entry into Jerusalem*, measuring 4 by 5 metres, was first exhibited in 1821.
32. Henry Bone (1755–1834), the celebrated painter on enamel, elected RA in 1811. He executed eighty-five 'Portraits of Illustrious Englishmen' copied from pictures in the royal and other collections.

On the Disadvantages of Intellectual Superiority

1. In Sonnet 292 of Petrarch's *Canzoniere*, beginning 'Gli occhi di ch'io parlai si caldamente', which laments the death of Laura.
2. *Hamlet*, II. ii. 178–9.
3. *The Faerie Queene*, Mutabilitie Cantos, VI, stanza 28.

4. The conversation of the newly fallen angels, in *Paradise Lost*, II, 560.
5. The *Quarterly Review*, a virulently Tory magazine, attacked Hazlitt on a number of occasions in the 1810s and 1820s.
6. 'Prince Maurice's Parrot' was published in both *The Examiner* and *The Champion* in 1814 and reprinted in *Political Essays* (1819). The essay 'On the Regal Character' was written for *The Yellow Dwarf* in 1818 and reprinted in *Political Essays* and the Paris edition of *Table-Talk* (1825). John Wilson Croker (1780–1857) was a prominent Tory politician, Secretary of the Admiralty and a regular contributor to the ultra-conservative *Quarterly Review*.
7. The Whig antagonist to the *Quarterly*, edited by Francis Jeffrey, for whom Hazlitt wrote a number of articles.
8. It is likely that this letter was in praise of Hazlitt's *Characters of Shakespeare's Plays*, published in 1817. The links between Stendhal and Hazlitt are very interesting. Both were disappointed Bonapartists and sceptical Romantics. Both wrote brilliant, revealing works on the role of imagination in love (Stendhal's *De l'amour* of 1822 is almost exactly contemporaneous with *Liber Amoris*). And the evidence is that the two men got on famously during the Paris leg of Hazlitt's European tour of 1824–5 (see Jones, *Hazlitt: A Life*, pp. 367–8 and Grayling, *The Quarrel of the Age*, p. 312).
9. Hazlitt's 'Answers to Vetus' on the war with France appeared in 1812.
10. See Hazlitt's *A View of the English Stage* (1818), *Complete Works*, V, 255.
11. A reference to Hazlitt's obituary for Cavanagh the fives player, later reprinted at the end of 'The Indian Jugglers' (1821).
12. Contained in Hazlitt's review of Coleridge's *Biographia Literaria* (*Complete Works*, XVI, 130–4).
13. *Coriolanus*, IV. v. 229–30.
14. William Congreve, *Love for Love* (1695), II. i.
15. Byron, *Sardanapalus*, IV. i.
16. Dulcinea is the fictional heroine to whom Don Quixote devotes himself in the novel by Miguel Cervantes.
17. As happened to Hazlitt himself during a visit to the Lake District in 1803.
18. That is, that they should take part in the oath 'never to kiss the maid when you can kiss the mistress'. The 'Highgate Oath' was administered by the keeper of the Gate House and other Highgate taverns to passengers in stage coaches.
19. *The Faerie Queene*, I, i, stanza 7.
20. Actually Peachum in *The Beggar's Opera* (1728), I. iv.
21. *Much Ado About Nothing*, III. iii. 14–16.

On the Knowledge of Character

1. A *diligence* was a French stage-coach.
2. Étienne-Gaspard Robertson (1763–1837), inventor of the phantasmagoria. The Invisible Woman show was a theatrical magic trick involving a girl who could be heard but not seen. It enjoyed huge popularity throughout Europe between 1800 and 1830 (see Jann

Matlock, 'The Invisible Woman and her Secrets Unveiled', *The Yale Journal of Criticism* 9.2, 1996, pp. 175–221). In the 1824 edition of his anthology *Select British Poets* Hazlitt included a lyric by Tom Moore 'To the Invisible Girl' which is very close in spirit to *Liber Amoris*:

They try to persuade me, my dear little sprite,
That you're *not* a true daughter of ether and light,
Nor have any concern with those fanciful forms
That dance upon rainbows and ride upon storms;
That, in short, you're a woman; your lip and your eye
As mortal as ever drew gods from the sky.
But I *will* not believe them – no, Science, to you
I have long bid a last and a careless adieu;
Still flying from Nature to study her laws,
And dulling delight in exploring its cause,
You forget how superior, for mortals below,
Is the fiction they dream to the truth that they know.

3. See Lord Chesterfield's *Letters to his Son*, Letter XVIII, October 30, 1747: 'Observe the looks and countenances of those who speak, which is often a surer way of discovering the truth than what they say.'
4. Joseph Fawcett (c.1758–1804), Presbyterian minister and poet. Wordsworth liked his sermons but saw him as unstable, later modelling the Solitary in his poem *The Excursion* on him (*DNB*).
5. It is possible that this is a covert self-portrait, serving as a kind of preface to the more explicitly autobiographical passage that begins: 'What is it to me that I can write these *Table-Talks*?'
6. Milton, *Comus* (1634), 560–1.
7. An ordinary was an eating-house or tavern where public meals were provided at a fixed price (*OED* 14b).
8. This passage, which all readers of *Liber Amoris* will recognise as a portrait of Sarah Walker, was added at a relatively late stage in composition, when the essay was in proof.
9. The person in question is Hazlitt himself, with the charge having been made by his friend the poet and essayist Leigh Hunt, in an essay in *The Indicator* for 12 July 1820 'On Shaking Hands': 'We have met with two really kind men, who evinced this soreness of hand. Neither of them perhaps thought himself inferior to anybody about him, and both had good reason to think highly of themselves; but both had been sanguine men disappointed in their early hopes. There was a plot to meet the hand of one of them with a fish-slice, in order to show him the disadvantage to which he put his friends by that flat mode of salutation; but the conspirator had not the courage to do it. Whether he heard of the intention we know not; but shortly afterwards he took very kindly to a shake. The other was the only man of a warm set of politicians who remained true to his first love of mankind. He was impatient at the change of his companions and at the folly and inattention of the rest; but though his manner became cold, his consistency still remained warm; and this gave him a right to be as strange as he pleased.' Hazlitt is recognisable as the second of these two specimens, although only

readers who knew him personally would have been able to pin the tail on the donkey.

10. See 'Character. Versailles' in Sterne's *Sentimental Journey* (1768). The same anecdote is quoted at the beginning of 'On the Past and Future'.
11. The following diatribe on servants is astonishingly cynical given Hazlitt's democratic politics, and clearly fuelled by his treatment at the hands of Sarah Walker and her family.
12. Shakespeare, *Cymbeline*, III. iii. 40–1.
13. John Gay, *The Beggar's Opera*, I. iv.
14. It is probable that Hazlitt is thinking of Mary Wordsworth here, and Marianne Hunt.
15. Milton, *Samson Agonistes* (1671), 1013–14.
16. Another covert reference to Sarah Walker, but this time a heartfelt paean of love that contrasts powerfully with his previous comments.
17. Another piece of veiled autobiography, since this was exactly the situation between Hazlitt and his own recently deceased father William senior, who had been a Unitarian minister.
18. Eugene Aram (*bap*. 1704, *d*. 1759), a philologist whose murder of a young shoemaker, Daniel Clark, in Knaresbrough, North Yorkshire, had gone undetected for years.
19. *Hamlet*, III. i. 122–4.
20. *Hamlet*, V. ii. 141–2; *Othello*, III. iii. 263.
21. This is not Butler but Alexander Pope, *An Essay on Criticism* (1709), 80–1: 'There are whom Heav'n has blest with store of Wit, / Yet want as much again to manage it.'

On the Fear of Death

1. Shakespeare, *The Tempest*, IV. i. 156–7.
2. Isaac Bickerstaff is a character in Addison and Steele's *The Tatler* (1709–11).
3. The nine volumes of *Tristram Shandy* were published between 1759 and 1767.
4. On 17 June 1775.
5. *Hamlet*, V. i. 207.
6. This is obscure, but it could refer to Hazlitt's first-born son, who was only six months old when he died in 1809.
7. Spenser, *The Faerie Queene*, II, ix, stanza 56.
8. The traditional estimate of the age of the earth, based on scriptural tradition.
9. Shakespeare, *Troilus and Cressida*, III. iii. 182.
10. Webster, *The White Devil* (1612), V. iii.
11. Young, *Night Thoughts* (1742), I, 424.
12. Shakespeare, *Measure for Measure*, III. i. 119–20.
13. Having been invited to the Venetian boudoir of a beautiful courtesan named Zulietta, Jean-Jacques, alias 'Zanetto' is perplexed that the competition for her has not been fiercer. She must have some secret defect, he tells himself. Eventually the imperfection is discovered: she only has one nipple, and this fascinates and appals Rousseau in just

about equal measure, hastily extinguishing his desire. Grandly indignant, Zulietta strides around the room fanning herself before delivering the immortal lines: 'Zanetto, give up the ladies, and study mathematics' (Rousseau, *Confessions*, ed. P.N. Furbank, Part II, Book vii, pp. 339–41).

14. Hazlitt and his first wife lost two children, both boys, his first, at the age of six months in Winterslow in 1809; the second at seven months in Westminster during 1817.
15. Francis Chantry's 'Sleeping Children' (1820) in Lichfield Cathedral.
16. Gray, *Elegy Written in a Country Churchyard* (1750), 91–2.
17. This is from Book V chapter VI of Tucker's huge philosophical work, of which Hazlitt himself published an abridged edition in 1807.
18. Dyer's *Grongar Hill* (1726), 89–92.
19. In Thomas Otway's *Venice Preserv'd* (1682), Pierre's words are: 'To lose it, may be, at last in a lewd quarrel / For some new friend' (IV. ii. 223–4).
20. Hazlitt's son, in his edition of *Table-Talk*, printed a concluding paragraph to this essay. His source was, presumably, a manuscript draft which is now lost:

> I will add a remark, which in some sense breaks the abruptness of the transition from life to death, and renders it less shocking to the imagination than it usually appears. Death is commonly represented as a monster that devours the whole man; the grave, as swallowing us entire; not only our future projects, but our past enjoyments as its prey, and all the pleasures of our lives collected together to make a rich banquet for the grim tyrant. But, in truth, Time has already anticipated the work of Death, and left him but half his spoils; for we die every moment of our lives. Death can only rob us of the future, the past he has no power over; our being gradually and silently slides from under us: our momentary pleasures follow each other as bubbles rise and disappear on the water, or the snow that melts as it falls: our attachments and friendships and desires wear out and are forgotten: the objects of them are dead to us, and we outlive not only them but ourselves. We ourselves have drunk up the cup of life, and have left only the lees. The stroke of death does not level the stately tree with all its blooming honours full upon it, but strikes the bare trunk and crumbling branches, and a few withered leaves. A shadow is all that generally remains of what we were, and we drag about a mockery of existence long after all the life of life is flown. It is the sense of self alone that makes death formidable, and that hinders us from perceiving that our fleeting existence is long ago lost in itself.

Characteristics

1. A covert reference to the lukewarm public support Hazlitt felt he received from his closest literary friends, Leigh Hunt and Charles Lamb.
2. Many of the *Characteristics* are clearly the work of a mind soured by public obloquy.

3. *Coriolanus*, IV. iv. 21.
4. John Philip Kemble (1757–1823) and Edmund Kean (1787–1833), both actors. Kemble made his reputation in the late eighteenth century, taking part in some notable performances of Shakespeare with his sister, Sarah Siddons. Kean burst upon the scene in 1814, excelling in roles such as Shylock, Macbeth and Othello. In Hazlitt's day the public never tired of comparing Kemble's rather classical approach with the coarser, more naturalistic style of Kean.
5. This and the following maxim are very close to the sentiments expressed in the last part of *Liber Amoris*.
6. Both this and the following are shots in Hazlitt's long-running guerilla war against the self-love philosophy pioneered by Rochefoucauld and Mandeville and carried on in the nineteenth century by the Utilitarian philosophers James Mill and Jeremy Bentham.
7. A succinct summary of the argument of Hazlitt's first published work, the philosophical treatise *On the Principles of Human Action* (1805).
8. Pope, *Essay on Criticism*, 155.
9. 'I see the right way, approve it, and do the opposite'. Against her father's wishes and her own proper judgement, Medea falls in love at first sight with the foreign hero Jason at the beginning of Book VII of Ovid's *Metamorphoses*.
10 Milton, *Il Penseroso*, 130.
11. *Othello*, V. ii. 97.
12. James Hackman (1752–79) shot Martha Ray, mistress of the Earl of Sandwich, on 7 April 1779 as she was leaving Covent Garden theatre. According to his own story he intended to kill neither Miss Ray nor Lord Sandwich but himself.
13. *Othello*, IV. ii. 59.
14. Pope, *Essay on Man*, I, 16.
15. *Leviathan* (1651), chapter iv.
16. Hazlitt is recollecting a line from the *Aeneid* on Polyphemus, referring to him as 'a monster frightful, formless, immense with sight removed' (III, 658).
17. This is perhaps the most characteristic statement of the *Characteristics*.

Two millennia of essential classics
The extensive Fyfield*Books* list includes

Djuna Barnes ***The Book of Repulsive Women and other poems***
edited by Rebecca Loncraine

Elizabeth Barrett Browning ***Selected Poems*** edited by Malcolm Hicks

Charles Baudelaire ***Complete Poems***
in French and English
translated by Walter Martin

The Brontë Sisters ***Selected Poems***
edited by Stevie Davies

Lewis Carroll ***Selected Poems***
edited by Keith Silver

Thomas Chatterton ***Selected Poems***
edited by Grevel Lindop

John Clare ***By Himself***
edited by Eric Robinson and David Powell

Samuel Taylor Coleridge ***Selected Poetry*** edited by William Empson and David Pirie

John Donne ***Selected Letters***
edited by P.M. Oliver

Oliver Goldsmith ***Selected Writings***
edited by John Lucas

Victor Hugo ***Selected Poetry***
in French and English
translated by Steven Monte

Wyndham Lewis ***Collected Poems and Plays*** edited by Alan Munton

Charles Lamb ***Selected Writings***
edited by J.E. Morpurgo

Ben Jonson ***Epigrams and The Forest***
edited by Richard Dutton

Giacomo Leopardi ***The Canti***
with a selection of his prose
translated by J.G. Nichols

Andrew Marvell ***Selected Poems***
edited by Bill Hutchings

Charlotte Mew ***Collected Poems and Selected Prose***
edited by Val Warner

Michelangelo ***Sonnets***
translated by Elizabeth Jennings, introduction by Michael Ayrton

William Morris ***Selected Poems***
edited by Peter Faulkner

Ovid ***Amores***
translated by Tom Bishop

Edgar Allan Poe ***Poems and Essays on Poetry***
edited by C.H. Sisson

Restoration Bawdy
edited by John Adlard

Rainer Maria Rilke ***Sonnets to Orpheus and Letters to a Young Poet***
translated by Stephen Cohn

Christina Rossetti ***Selected Poems***
edited by C.H. Sisson

Sir Walter Scott ***Selected Poems***
edited by James Reed

Sir Philip Sidney ***Selected Writings***
edited by Richard Dutton

Henry Howard, Earl of Surrey ***Selected Poems***
edited by Dennis Keene

Algernon Charles Swinburne ***Selected Poems***
edited by L.M. Findlay

Oscar Wilde ***Selected Poems***
edited by Malcolm Hicks

Sir Thomas Wyatt ***Selected Poems***
edited by Hardiman Scott

For more information, including a full list of Fyfield*Books* and a contents list for each title, and details of how to order the books, visit the Carcanet website at www.carcanet.co.uk or email info@carcanet.co.uk